Ego and
Self Psychology

Ego and Self Psychology
Group Interventions with Children, Adolescents, and Parents

ESTER SCHALER BUCHHOLZ, PH.D.
JUDITH MARKS MISHNE, D.S.W.
EDITORS

JASON ARONSON, INC.
New York   London

Copyright © 1983 by Jason Aronson, Inc.

10 9 8 7 6 5 4 3 2 1

All rights reserved. Printed in the United States of America. No part of this book may be used or reproduced in any manner whatsoever without written permission from *Jason Aronson, Inc.* except in the case of brief quotations in reviews for inclusion in a magazine, newspaper or broadcast.

Library of Congress Cataloging in Publication Data
Main entry under title:
Ego and self psychology: group interventions with children, adolescents, and parents.
  Includes index.
    1. Child psychotherapy.   2. Adolescent psychotherapy.
  3. Family psychotherapy.   4. Ego (Psychology)   5. Self.
  I. Buchholz, Ester Schaler.   II. Mishne, Judith.
  [DNLM: 1. EGO—In infancy and childhood.   2. Psychotherapy, Group.   3. Psychosexual development.   WS 105.5.S3 E31]
  RJ504.E34   616.89'15   81-22806
  ISBN 0-87668-487-8   AACR2

This book is printed on acid-free paper with a life expectancy of 250 years.

Manufactured in the United States of America.

We may ask: in what form does the relation of an individual to his fellow man and to "society" come within the sphere of psychoanalysis?

> *Essays on Ego Psychology: Selected Problems in Psychoanalytic Theory*, Heinz Hartmann

... a firm group self supports the productivity of the group just as a firm individual self supports the productivity of the self.

> *Creativity, Charisma, Group Psychology: Reflections on the Self-analysis of Freud*, Heinz Kohut

Contents

Preface   xi

Acknowledgments   xiii

Contributors   xv

PART I:
AN EGO PSYCHOLOGY AND SELF PSYCHOLOGY PERSPECTIVE   1

Introduction   3

1. Principles of Group Practice / Ester Buchholz, Ph.D., and Judith Mishne, D.S.W.   19
   Group Composition   19
   Setting and Purpose   26
   Level of Intervention—Clinical Techniques   29
   Group Process   32
   Group Dynamics—Resistance, Alliance, Transference, and Countertransference   35

PART 2:
EARLY INTERVENTION   49

Introduction   51

2. The Technique of Psychoanalytically Oriented Parent Education / Lawrence Balter, Ph.D.   57
   Editors' Discussion   63

3. Early Interventive Work with New Mothers / Fay Shutzer, M.A.   65
   Organization   65
   Advantages of the Group Setting   66
   The Leader's Role   66
   Editors' Discussion   77

4. Mother Guidance Groups—An Aid in the Ego Development of Pre-School Children / Eleanor Weisberger, M.S.W.   81
 Editors' Discussion 93

5. Group Work with Single Mothers / Ava L. Siegler, Ph.D.   95
 Cultural Changes: The Single Working Mother 95
 The Function of the Family 96
 Mother-Child Reciprocities in the Absence of the Father 97
 The Special Task of the Mother during Oedipal Development 99
 Clinical Intervention: The Rationale 102
 The Therapeutic Role of the Group Leader 105
 Editors' Discussion 108

PART 3: LATENCY   113
 Introduction   115

6. Learning Disabilities: A Trauma of Latency / Mary Giffin, M.D.   119
 Definition 120
 Asking the Right Questions 122
 The Treatment Spectrum 126
 Influence on Practice 127
 Concluding Remarks 128
 Editors' Discussion 128

7. Activity Groups in a Special Education Setting / Marilyn Wilson, M.A.   131
 Development of the Group 131
 Composition of the Group 132
 Group Membership 133
 Physical Setting 134
 Revision of Goals 135
 Group Process and Dynamics 136
 Editors' Discussion 141

8. Modified Activity Group Therapy with Ego Impoverished Children / Margaret G. Frank, C.S.W.   145
 Activity Group Therapy's Role as Progenitor 146
 Group Formation 148

CONTENTS

Setting Limits: Protection, Not Punishment 149
The Therapist as a Teacher of Ego Capacities 149
Editors' Discussion 152

9. Group Psychotherapy with Primitively Fixated
Children / Eileen Trafimow, Ph.D., and Sandra I.
Pattak, M.A.   157
Theoretical Framework 158
Extrapolation to the Group Setting 160
Clinical Illustrations 162
Translating Theory Into Practice 167
Summary 170
Editors' Discussion 172

PART 4:
ADOLESCENTS AND THEIR PARENTS   175
Introduction   177

10. A Group Approach to Depressed Girls in Foster
Care / Judith A. Lee, D.S.W., and Danielle N. Park,
M.S.   185
Psychodynamics of the Foster Child's Depression 186
Manifestations of Depression in the Ecological Field 187
Group Formation 188
Beginning Phase 189
Work Phase 191
"Making It" and Mutual Aid 197
Endings and Transitions 199
Conclusion 200
Editors' Discussion 203

11. Multiple Family Group Therapy with Adolescent
Drug Addicts and Their Parents / Craig Podell, M.S.W.   207
Review of Theoretical Considerations 208
The Setting 210
Therapists' Roles 212
Conclusion 219
Editors' Discussion 220

12. A Therapeutic Group Experience for Fathers / Richard
R. Raubolt, Ph.D., and Arnold W. Rachman, Ph.D.   223
Forming the Group: Goals and Structure 225
Group Process and Focus 226

The Initial Phase 227
Fathers Reexperience Their Adolescence 229
The Loving Fight: Levels of Dialogue and Acceptance between Fathers and Sons 231
Results and Evaluations 232
Editors' Discussion 234

13. Parent Groups in the Long-Term Treatment of Hospitalized Adolescents / Mady Chalk, A.C.S.W., and Mary Lou Costanzo, A.C.S.W. 237
Historical Background and Development 239
Description of Program 240
Goals of the Parent Group Program 240
Theoretical Foundations 242
Parent and Director Meetings 248
Staff Group 249
Summary 251
Editors' Discussion 253

Epilogue 257

Index 259

Preface

Picture a psychologist on vacation, strolling down an unpopulated beach. She sees a woman sitting alone, reading a book on ego psychology. They begin to talk. The two women, one a clinical psychologist and the other a clinical social worker, discover that they share a psychoanalytic orientation, despite their different professions. Their meeting on a deserted beach marks the beginning of a dialogue between the two women, the result of which is *Ego and Self Psychology: Interventions with Children, Adolescents, and Parents.*

Without the academic practice of midwinter breaks and the compelling beauty of a Puerto Rican seaside resort, this volume would not have been written. We discovered, in addition to our similar interests and orientations, that we shared a background in psychoanalytic ego psychology and that we both had been analyzed in a traditional way. Both of us have taught comparable clinical courses, consulted in public schools, and worked with and supervised analytically oriented groups. We noted the striking compatibility of our students' educational programs: school psychology, clinical psychology, and social work programs at the graduate level all combine didactic course work with intense field practicums.

Unfortunately, the various health and helping professions retain distinct identities by cultivating isolation from one another. Texts customarily cater to one profession. We realized that our collaboration might allay the xenophobia that exists between our professions. Our joint effort might prove fruitful, not only from the exchange born of our similarities, but also from the challenge arising from our differences.

The fact that there is a similar format in the training and practice of clinical social workers and clinical and school psychologists is seldom noted, though on reflection it is hardly surprising. Regardless of their disciplines, students in these fields need assistance integrating clinical theory and clinical work. This task is particularly formidable in the learning of group psychotherapy, given the relative paucity of illustrative case material for teaching group interventions. We decided that trainees involved in analytically oriented work could benefit from a text that would present the practice experiences of both our professions. Thus, the primary focus of this volume—group work—is enhanced by the psychologist's diagnostic acumen and the social worker's environmental perspective. Our theoretical orientation is psychoanalytic and is derived from both ego and self psychology. We hope that this book, with its interdisciplinary approach, will illuminate the problems in clinical practice confronting social workers and psychologists alike.

Acknowledgments

We are deeply indebted to all of our contributors, who responded with enthusiasm to our requests for their work. Their dedication sustained us during the lengthy time needed to write and edit this volume.

The interest and support offered by Dr. Jason Aronson and editor Joan Langs were invaluable. Additionally, we are grateful to editors Paula Sharp, Melinda Wirkus, and Joyce Noulas for their handling of production and their supervision of the progress of the manuscript. Typists Donna Ritter and Jane Freeman were helpful and responsive at all times. A special thank you is owed Melissa Culler for an early reading of the manuscript.

We were continuously encouraged by the patience and consideration of friends and family, who tolerated our periodic preoccupation and unavailability.

Contributors

LAWRENCE BALTER, Ph.D., Professor of Educational Psychology, New York University School of Education, Health, Nursing, and Arts Professions; Training Analyst, National Psychological Association for Psychoanalysis; private practice.

ESTER SCHALER BUCHHOLZ, Ph.D., Associate Professor, School Psychology Program, New York University School of Education, Health, Nursing and Arts Professions; Supervisor, Postgraduate Center for Mental Health, New York City; private practice.

MADY CHALK, A.C.S.W., Director of Social Work and Family Therapy, Yale University School of Medicine, New Haven, Connecticut.

MARY LOU COSTANZO, A.C.S.W., Coordinator, Parent Group Program and Instructor of Social Work in Psychiatry, Yale University School of Medicine, New Haven, Connecticut.

MARGARET G. FRANK, C.S.W., Supervisor, New York School for Psychoanalytic Psychotherapy; seminar leader in Ego Psychology, Northampton, Massachusetts; private practice.

MARY GIFFIN, M.D., Medical Director, Irene Josselyn Clinic, Northfield, Illinois.

JUDITH A. LEE, D.S.W., Associate Professor of Social Work, New York University School of Social Work.

JUDITH MARKS MISHNE, D.S.W., Associate Professor, New York University School of Social Work; summer faculty member, Smith College School for Social Work, Northampton, Massachusetts; private practice.

DANIELLE N. PARK, M.S., Supervisor and Field Instructor, Division of Foster Work Care, Department of Social Services, New York City; Adjunct Assistant Professor, New York University School of Social Work.

SANDRA I. PATTAK, M.A., Clinical Social Worker, Department of Psychiatry, Children's Memorial Hospital, Chicago, Illinois.

CRAIG PODELL, M.S.W., Caseworker, Jewish Board of Family and Children's Services, Midwood Adolescent Project, New York City; private practice.

ARNOLD W. RACHMAN, Ph.D., Senior Supervisor, Postgraduate Center for Mental Health, New York City.

RICHARD R. RAUBOLT, Ph.D., Staff Psychologist, Pine Rest Christian Hospital, Grand Rapids, Michigan.

FAY SHUTZER, M.A., Certified School Psychologist; Fellow, Department of Educational Psychology, New York University.

AVA L. SIEGLER, Ph.D., Director, Child, Adolescent and Family Clinic, Child and Adolescent Analytic Training Program of the Postgraduate Center for Mental Health, New York; Director, Early Intervention Pilot Project, Prescott Day Care Center, New York; Associate Adjunct Professor, Clinical Psychology, Graduate School of Arts and Sciences, New York University; private practice.

EILEEN TRAFIMOW, Ph.D., Chief Psychologist, Pritzker Children's Psychiatric Unit, Michael Reese Hospital and Medical Center, Chicago, Illinois.

ELEANOR WEISBERGER, M.S.W., Assistant Professor of Child Development, Case Western Reserve University School of Medicine, Cleveland, Ohio; private practice (child analyst).

MARILYN WILSON, M.A., Certified School Psychologist; Research Assistant, New York Interface Development Project.

Ego and Self Psychology

PART 1

An Ego Psychology and Self Psychology Perspective

Introduction: Applying Ego and Self Psychology to Group Therapy

Our experiences as practitioners and educators have led us to emphasize the psychoanalytic perspective in our work with intact and disturbed populations. Ego and Self Psychology, though customarily applied to work with individuals, offer a rich repertoire of interventions for use with varied groups. Our examples of group work range from educative parent guidance to psychoanalytic group psychotherapy. Although not all the therapeutic work in this book was initiated with the theories of Ego and Self Psychology in mind, contributions were chosen because they could be—and in our opinion, ought to be—analyzed in light of these newer psychologies. Some groups included children; others were made up of adolescents, parents, or entire families. We present practice principles relevant to critical developmental stages along a continuum of normal to abnormal client populations.

The term "Group psychology" is not easily definable. Freud himself noted that the contrast between individual psychology and group psychology loses its sharpness under close examination (1922, p.1). Eubanks defines a group as "two or more persons in a relationship of psychic interaction, whose relationship with one another may be abstracted and distinguished from their relationships with all others so that they might be thought of as an entity" (1932, p. 163). A therapy group consists of at least three individuals, including a leader, who meet for a fixed duration in a consistent setting, with the aim of improving members' capacity for reality testing, object relationships, self-esteem, and the ability to cope with age-appropriate life tasks. Group therapy creates relationships among members, and between leader and members that facilitate an interchange of verbal and nonverbal expression.

Group psychoanalysis is obviously not a new therapeutic technique. Group work with parents and children dates back to child guidance clinics, and to the imaginative, prescient, and pioneering efforts of Slavson (1958). The history of this intervention is too lengthy to be presented here. However, it should be noted that this modality has the same origin as individual analysis. Its objectives are to understand latent material, to search for unconscious motivation, and to lead the patient from present to past in search of historical antecedents. Group interaction as stated by Wolf and Schwartz (1971) proceeds from the interpersonal to the intrapsychic. Group work or therapy modifies the goals and techniques of group psychoanalysis. Specifically, less regression is encouraged than in analytic treatment, interpersonal process between group members and members and leaders is emphasized, and immediate rather than unresolved early infantile conflicts are the major concerns. The leader assumes a more active ego building stance than the nondirective analyst. The therapy's objective is not to restructure the client's basic personality. Instead therapeutic efforts should enhance ego functioning by increasing capacity for reality testing, strengthening object relations, and improving drive modulation. The methodology offered is mainly interactional: cognitive and educational material is dealt with over and above unconscious fantasy, with the aim of developing self-esteem and competence.

Group treatment is particularly suited to work with parents and children. Children, receptive to learning, can profit from the wide range of interpersonal connections a group experience offers. Parents who come into therapy, typically to handle difficulties concerning their children, gain confidence and support in working together with peers. Peer support between parents often helps diminish guilt and anxiety and mitigates against feelings of low self-esteem. At present there is a broad array of group therapy approaches toward treatment that vary according to their underlying theoretical modes. "Today, every school of personality theory and psychopathy—Freudian, Sullivanian, Horneyan, etc., is represented in group practice" (Kaplan and Sadock 1971, p. 1). However, one model—Developmental Ego Psychology—has remained fundamentally a psychology that emphasizes treatment using the dyadic relationship. Anthony states "... that very little work has been done on the development of the ego's capacity to create and to maintain a group relationship ..."; furthermore, he maintains " . . . that a conceptual model that is also developmental could be very useful in group psychotherapy" (1971, p. 30).

This work endorses a developmental group therapy conceptual mode. Children find aid and effective solutions to conflicts rooted in the infantile phases of psychological growth when free to experience worlds beyond the protective nests of their families. Interpersonal relationships are enriched when a child becomes part of the nonparental social world of peers. Maturational steps depend on successful resolution of earlier phase-specific, normal developmental conflicts (Berkovitz 1972). The assessment of these steps, and in fact, each and every maturational step a child makes, is most clearly delineated by a developmental perspective. Moreover, struggles with dependency and autonomy needs typically constitute the most serious conflicts between children and their families. Psychoanalytic developmental psychology provides an excellent foundation for studying how people handle the opposing wishes for separation from, and identification with, others.

Traditional practice approaches are based on what is frequently referred to as the "old medical model." According to this standard, disease is located in the patient, ascertained via diagnosis, and corrected via treatment. The more recent systems theory accounts for modifications of the environment through, for example, preventative work, and considers the interpersonal and intrapersonal milieu of the family, the significance of diverse ethnic and sociocultural backgrounds of clients, alternative life styles, stress, life transitions, and the impact of the therapy relationship.

In the context of this perspective we begin with a section devoted to preventative work with mothers. We have deliberately presented chapters that deal with varied socioeconomic groups of mothers in order to represent the needs and issues confronting both middle-class married women and single parent minority families. This focus emphasizes the significance of stress and alternative life styles.

Anna Freud, the ego psychologist, has effectively applied many of the principles of systems theory to psychoanalysis. Her use of lines of development provides a framework wherein "the individual is examined for his position on the progressive sequences relevant to drive development, ego and superego development and the age adequate development of internal structuralizations, and the adaption to the environment. Pathology is evaluated in all instances according to its interference with orderly and steady progress in these respects"

(1965, p. 9). Her schema for ongoing assessment of children and adolescents allows for the flux of developmental processes in childhood; the adult assessment does not have the same ongoing focus as it is assumed that, by adulthood, certain developmental milestones have been attained.

An adult's maturity or immaturity is measured in terms of his or her ability to perform age-appropriate life tasks and to function in the realms of sex and work, and his or her capacity for sublimation. Additional areas that are assessed include the pleasure the individual derives from life, as well as the quality of his or her object and community relations. Pathology reveals itself in symptoms that interfere with any of the overall aims, causing suffering for internal reasons, lessening the capacity to relate realistically to the environment, or all of the above. The Developmental Ego Psychology on which this text relies provides a theoretical base for assessing individual members as potential candidates for group interventions; criteria for group composition in addition to group process is emphasized.

A clear definition for, and understanding of ego is needed before a developmental assessment can be undertaken. Ego is best defined as a group of functions. In the structural sense of the word, the ego gradually evolves from the newborn infant's undifferentiated state. This ego-id matrix is based on constitutional factors (the genetically determined growth pattern of the central nervous system, the senses, and the body in general), and experiences with objects in the surrounding world. As the internalized psychic representative of primal instincts, the physiological needs of the body, and the demands of the outer world, the ego mediates between the individual and external reality. It perceives the needs of the self, physical and psychic, and the qualities and attitudes of the environment—evaluating, coordinating, and integrating these perceptions so that internal demands adjust to external requirements. Finally, the ego relieves drive tensions and wishes by either reducing the intensity of the drives (neutralization) or modifying the external situation.

The ego attempts to achieve optimum gratification of instincts and, at the same time, to maintain good relations with the external world and with the superego—the internal representative of behavioral and moral standards. For this task, protective devices must be available to reduce excessively strong stimuli, both internal and external. This is especially important in infancy when other defenses are not adequately developed. (At that time physiological defense mechanisms are referred to collectively as a protective shield or stimulus barrier.)

Physiologically, the sense organs are equipped to select only certain stimuli and to reduce the intensity of others. Psychically, certain defensive functions are developed to protect against conscious awareness of conflicting demands of the id (primitive urges, impulses, and biological needs) or superego (conscience) that could create intolerable anxiety. Defenses, which operate unconsciously, describe the struggles of the ego to protect itself against danger, that is, the possibility that a repressed wish might become conscious—associated with some punishment, real or imagined—and cause anxiety or guilt. Defenses, which occur most often in clusters, include repression, displacement, reaction formation, projection, isolation, undoing, introjection, identification, and denial. Denial is a primitive defense that helps the individual avoid awareness of some painful aspect of reality. Fantasy, for example, can obscure a disagreeable and unwelcome fact. In adults, excessive denial results in severe pathology. A more sophisticated adaptive defense is, e.g., sublimation.

Autonomous ego functions—perception, motor capacity, intention, purpose, planning, intelligence, thinking, speech, and language—generally mature predictably, though under stress these can malfunction. Adaption to reality entails the development in the ego of the capacity for stable relationships with objects. The ability to form close ties to others, with minimum expression of hostile feelings, and to maintain these consistently establishes object constancy. In the developmental view of ego functioning, differentiation of the self from the object world precedes the attainment of object constancy and object love. If the environment is suitably benign, reality is gradually mastered—objective thinking occurs, autonomous activities increase, and a reasonably efficient regulation of drives is achieved. However, specific ego functions continue to develop and mature well into adult life as individuals develop a steadily increasing capacity to love, work, and adapt to the world.

Ego-alien behaviors are those that are not consonant with the ego in relation to drives, affects, ideas, or behavior. In contrast, ego-syntonic behaviors are acceptable to the ego. These differences are diagnostically significant as they correspond to levels of ego and superego development. This perspective on maturation and development is useful not only when considering therapy goals but also in the ongoing process of therapy itself.

In the past psychoanalytic theory moved from an id psychology, based on drive theory, to a perspective based on Ego Psychology; this new theory and its developmental techniques were incorporated by psychotherapists with diverse backgrounds. Most recently, we are seeing another shift in the theoretical stance of some analysts and clinicians, with resultant modifications in treatment goals and techniques. In general, Self Psychologists reconsider internalizations in self and self-object configurations. Their emphasis is less on drive, conflict, and ego development, than on self-development throughout the life cycle.

Self Psychology evolves out of explorations of narcissism and Kohut's (1971) presentation of conceptions of self-object transference: specifically, mirroring, merging, and idealizing transferences. This differs from the classic conceptions of displacement in which feelings related to past objects are transferred onto the analyst. Kohut's sensitivity to patients who suffered from a lack of parental empathy and the absence of parental appreciation has heightened our sensitivity to pre-oedipal deficits which are often the source of unstable self-esteem, or low self-regard. Traditionally transference occurred via displacement and connoted stable self and object distinctions, boundaries, and a sense of the other as separate and distinct. Kohut, in contrast, describes patients who may have a cohesive sense of self, but whose self-regard fluctuates within his postulated framework of two distinct lines of development—namely, an object line of development and a narcissistic line of development. Thus, in terms of narcissistic instability, the therapist is mirrored and idealized; he or she lends support as a self-object, rather than as a separate object.

Spirited discourse centers around such questions as the relationship of Self Psychology to classic psychoanalytic theory. Is Self Psychology based on deficits—at odds therefore with traditional theory based on conflict, for example, Tragic Man versus Guilty Man? What is the significance in Self Psychology of insight, interpretation, and work with oedipal conflicts and castration disorders? The prominent focus of Self Psychologists is on empathic data-gathering by the therapist regarding the patient's feelings. Transference in a treatment relationship is based on optimal empathy, rather than the traditional optimal frustration, embodied by the "blank screen" analyst. Self psychologists attempt to sensitively understand the patients' subjective states and their vulnerability in the face of missing structures. By offering themselves as a part object, they hope to facilitate structure building.

Many critics of Self Psychology claim that it is hardly revolutionary and that the "new" practice focus is merely a presentation of skilled sensitive work psychologists have always known and striven for. Others suggest that Self Psychology is not a separate field; that, in fact, it affords us only different descriptions of what traditional theory has presented regarding drives, object relations, ego development and arrests, and the narcissistic reactions to stress and trauma. Many critics suggest that Kohut and his followers have paid scant attention to major life traumas in the childhood of patients. Instead, they claim he focuses excessively on parental empathic ruptures, and in treatment, recommends that the analyst play a reflective listening role rather than the traditional interpretive one.

In the patient population they describe, Kohut (1978) and other Self Psychologists emphasize thwarted development, which creates deficits, and suggest that pre-oedipal injuries are more profoundly damaging to self-esteem than unresolved oedipal conflicts. The parents of these children have not successfully and consistently reflected pleasure, pride, and delight in their children. Ideally, treatment would focus on patients' ambitions, ideals, values, humor, and events in their daily lives, rather than transference interpretations, drive manifestations, and insight-induced restructuring. Self Psychologists note that traditional approaches have labeled large populations of patients untreatable and unresponsive. Often these populations have remained in therapy forever with no evident changes. These same populations are the ones with which social workers and psychologists most frequently work in public clinical settings. Self Psychologists suggest that their approach, which embodies more activity, articulation, and demonstrable empathy reaches such clients more often than traditional analytic models.

Much has been written about pathological narcissism, a constant variable in the borderline population. Freudian theory and Ego Psychology present its development in object terms, whereby profound self-investment is the consequence of defensive withdrawal of libidinal cathexis to others, following injury and trauma. Van der Waals (1965) argues that severe narcissism does not simply reflect a fixation in early narcissistic stages of development and an absence of the development of object love, but that it is characterized by the simultaneous development of pathological forms of self-love and pathological forms of object love. Moreover, he states that normal narcissism develops simultaneously with normal object relationships, pathological narcissism with pathological object relationships. Kernberg (1970) describes a process of refusion of the internal self and object images that occurs in the narcissistic personality at a developmental level at which ego boundaries have already become stable. Thus this population is not subject to psychotic regression. He postulates a fusion of ideal self, ideal object, and actual self images as a defense against intolerable reality in the interpersonal realm, with a concomitant devaluation and destruction of object images, as well as external objects. The normal tension between actual self on the one hand, and ideal self and ideal object on the other, is eliminated by the construction of an inflated self-concept within which the hostile mother's narcissistic use of the child—which makes the child feel privileged—sets he or she off on a search for compensatory admiration and greatness. Many of these patients have occupied a pivotal place in their family structure as either the only and/or brilliant child, or the one expected to fulfill the family aspirations.

In contrast to these theorist/clinicians, Kohut (1971) advances an alternative view of the etiology of the narcissistic personality disordered patient. As mentioned previously, he describes two separate lines of development. The object line of development is the accepted Ego Psychology view, encompassing stranger anxiety, symbiosis, separation-individuation, object constancy, the oedipal conflict, and oedipal love, that is, attachment to others. Kohut's second line of development of the self, narcissism, does not depict defensive withdrawal, but illustrates a normal developmental unfolding that parallels the object line of development.

When patients evidence disturbances in the realm of the self, their archaic objects, still connected with narcissistic libido (self-objects), remain unchanged, intimately linked with the archaic self. These patients remain fixated on archaic grandiose self configurations and/or archaic overestimated narcissistically cathected objects. Under optimum developmental conditions the exhibitionism and grandiosity of the archaic self are gradually tamed, and the entire structure is ultimately integrated into the total personality. The idealized superego is introjected, and it becomes an important component of psychic organization by providing leadership. If the child, however, suffers severe narcissistic trauma, then the grandiose self does not merge into the relevant ego content; retained in its unaltered form, the self strives for the fulfillment of its archaic aims. If the child experiences severe disappointment in the admired adult then the idealized parent image is also retained in its unaltered, grandiose form. It is not transformed into tension-regulating psychic structure, but remains an archaic, transitional object that is required for the maintenance of narcissistic homeostasis (Kohut 1968).

A full elaboration of the differences between Kohut, Kernberg, and other theorists is beyond the scope of this text. Concisely stated, their differences are as follows. Kohut establishes a continuity of pathological and normal narcissism, with treatment focusing almost exclusively on the vicissitudes of development of libidinal cathexis, so that his analysis of pathological narcissism is essentially unrelated to any examination of the vicissitudes of aggression, and of internalized object relations. Kernberg, on the other hand, likens his view to those of Jacobson, Mahler, and Van der Waals. He states that pathological narcissism can only be understood in terms of the combined analysis of the vicissitudes of libidinal and aggressive drive derivatives. Pathological narcissism does not simply reflect libidinal investment in a pathological self-structure. The pathological self has defensive functions against underlying libidinally invested and aggressively invested primitive self and object images which reflect intense, predominantly pre-genital conflicts centered around both love and aggression.

Kernberg, like Mahler and others, believes that the development of normal and pathological narcissism always involves the relationship of the self to object representations and external objects, whereas Kohut "stands alone in his proposition of a separate developmental course for narcissistic libido and object libido," according to Rothstein (1979, p. 903). In addition, Rothstein suggests that the differences between Kernberg, et al., and Kohut arise from the various types of patients they encounter. Thus Kohut's perspective centers on those who present cohesive and more or less stable narcissistic configurations, which is, perhaps, the reason for his insistence that "the strengthening of ideals, and the achievement, even to a modest degree, of such wholesome transformations of narcissism as humor, creativity, empathy and wisdom—must be rated as a more genuine and valid result of therapy than the patient's precarious compliance with demands for a change of his narcissism into object love" (1966, p. 270). This attitude differs markedly from Kernberg's. Kernberg reserves the term "narcissistic personality" for patients who present what he terms a culture of pathological narcissism characterized, he claims, by rage toward the maternal object, coldness, ruthlessness, a lack of genuine sadness, and the incapacity for empathy and depressive reactions.

Of particular concern to us are the supposedly untreatable individuals for whom we believe Kohut's optimistic approach affords the most realistic therapeutic opportunities. These individuals are frequently bombarded by confrontation and authoritarianism in group treatment which "is, in effect, honesty and candor with a vengeance" (Levy 1976, p. 141). What is so often lacking is the empathic stance of the clinician, emphasized by Self Psychologists, one which we see as of critical importance to group therapy. Identification with the aggressor can and often does result in scapegoating. Appreciation for narcissistic vulnerabilities, on the other hand, has direct relevance for therapeutic empathic intervention, and is, we believe, more effective than interpretation, uncovering, clarification, or probing (the more traditional approaches). Essential to the Self Psychology approach "is the understanding of the early response to parents both as libidinal objects and 'self objects' which mirror and enhance the developing self. The developmental concept of narcissism and that of narcissistic transference which leads to idealization, mirroring needs, twinship, and merger sheds light on a variety of interactions taking place in group therapy. The leaders, other group members, or the group as a whole supply a missing part of the self rather than functioning as separate objects with whom there is conflict" (Stone and Whitman 1977, p. 357). The formulations of the Self Psychologists posit clear implications for clinicians working with groups. Nonjudgmental acceptance of the individual's needs—to idealize the leader, or the group, to receive recognition and admiration—provides a theoretical basis for empathic intervention; in addition, it offers support to frequently damaged client populations, who need to experience the therapist "as a selfobject mother who exists primarily for the needs of the patient (or client)" (p. 358). We offer the Self Psychology perspective as an innovative approach to practice technique, despite the ongoing controversy, in psychoanalytic circles, over development and etiology.

Regardless of the contributions of current theories, group therapy should not be perceived as a panacea, or "the best" intervention. In the consideration of group treatment, two questions inevitably arise: What are the indications and counterindications for group treatment, and which candidates should be selected for group therapy? Diagnostic criteria are essential determinants for selecting any form of therapy. Josselyn (1972) warns against professional bias, commitment to a single modality of intervention deemed suitable for all patients. She relates an "... experience with adolescent patients who had participated in a group for which there had not been an initial screening and/or, in which the leader of the group believed group therapy was the therapy of choice for all adolescents" (p. 4). This erroneous assessment caused members to become acutely disturbed by the group experience. Some acted out previously repressed conflicts; all manifested seriously depleted ego strength; the factor that brought on ego exhaustion was the group therapy sessions.

Criteria for determining indications and contraindications for group therapy are varied. In considering potential candidates one must be clear as to how they have handled previous developmental tasks. Berkovitz and Sugar (1975) list useful guidelines for this determination: "(1) emancipation (or lack of emancipation) from parental attachments, (2) development of satisfying and self-realizing personal attachments, with ability to love and appreciate the worth of others as well as one's self (versus excessive self reference, and superficial attachments), (3) an endurable and sustaining sense of identity in the family, social, sexual, and work-creative areas, and a flexible set of hopes and life goals for the future (or a cohesive self, but unstable sense of self-esteem) (p. 3). These authors further suggest that recommendations for group treatment depend to a great extent on the availability of a suitable group. For example, there is a danger in mixing adolescents who do not act out with those who act out severely. In other words, the common practice of grouping individuals of all ages together on the basis of a common label, for example, foster children, obese adults, and delinquent youth, should be reexamined. We have recommended that assessment measures include ego functions, developmental level, and the stability, or lack thereof, of self-regard.

The severely narcissistic and withdrawn individual, totally lacking in empathy, fixated in struggles and issues regarding his or her self-esteem or self-regard, is, most frequently, an inappropriate candidate for an immediate group therapy experience. Such individuals may require individual therapy first, to enable them to make successful relationships in a group. Clients with deficient control such as the hospitalized patient, still immersed in resistance, and lacking therapeutic identifications with staff, may create resistance among other members. Heacock (1966) notes, as unsuitable for group therapy, "the severely delinquent and hyperactive boy who 'acts in' during the sessions. His disruptive behavior spreads to the others who are quite responsive to this, and so therapy becomes impossible. Suggestible patients who are easily led should be eliminated, as they are frequently stimulated to more acting out by the therapy" (p. 41). Ginott (1961) enumerates several criteria to exclude specific children from group therapy, for example: children experiencing intense sibling rivalry, shallow, sociopathic children, cruel children, children who persistently steal, selfish children, impulsive children, and those who lack empathy. (We would refer to the sociopathic child as the narcissistically disordered child.) However, we believe that these children, in light of the newer theories, can benefit from group treatment via empathic leader responses and careful groupings. Ginott also excludes children with accelerated drive expression and children who are highly sexualized and/or extremely aggressive. Children who have been eroticized via exposure to perverse sexual activities are probably not suitable for group treatment at first. Similarly children who have been traumatized by overt catastrophe need the more supportive individual modality, promptly and immediately.

Freud thought that groups cause libidinal factors and old patterns to surface in members; for instance, when members seek consolation and reassurance for infantile anxieties, they can experience transference phenomena to peers as siblings, and to the leader as parent, manifesting either blind devotion, or profound disappointment. Freud's (1922) cautious approach does not negate the value of group experiences. He thought successful immersion in a well-functioning group would inhibit and even cure neurotic functioning. Buxbaum (1945), who emphasizes the submission and rebellion phenomena in group process, claims that group experiences are crucial in development as a "medium between the dependence of the child and the independence of the adult" (p. 365). Agreeing that group experience is valuable for children, adolescents, and adults, we underscore the importance of selectivity, based upon assessment.

There are specific advantages of group therapy. Certainly the person who is threatened by one-to-one relationships will feel safer in the group medium. Adolescents still engaged in struggles for independence and autonomy often feel freer and more protected in groups rather than in a dyadic treatment mode. Fluctuations between rebellion and submission are allowed in groups. Independence and identification with the leader are encouraged; relationship problems not evident, or touched on, in individual therapy are often uncovered in a group setting. Distortions about self and others can be modulated when there is opportunity for members to act as co-therapists in preparation for self-parenting—that is, self-directed independent insight and enhanced ego functioning.

Highlighting the crucial importance of the early mother-child interactions first studied by Ego Psychologists, and now, by Self Psychologists, this text begins by focusing on early intervention, prevention, and work with new mothers and their children, in the hope that this immediate intervention can somewhat curtail developing psychopathology. Parent education and parent guidance is offered to aid in child rearing during the vulnerable and formative years.

Little that has been written to date integrates group therapy in terms of Ego and Self Psychology. The goal of this book is to analyze a variety of group work cases according to Ego and Self Psychological theory, and to provide, for students and supervisors, both the theory and the technique for intervention in parents' and childrens' groups. The papers included have been contributed by people who have been working with groups for many years, as well as by graduate students. Our primary goal was to demonstrate the applicability of Ego and Self theoretical perspectives to a varied client population. In some instances we have applied the Ego and Self Psychology perspective where our contributors did not, opening the door for reformulation of traditional conceptions. Each paper is introduced in light of certain variables that are significant to group organization and functioning. These include: group composition, setting and purpose, level of intervention (i.e., clinical techniques), group process, and group dynamics. It is our opinion that each of these is essential to group process and to group outcome. Some of our authors have already incorporated and integrated these newer models. The volume as a whole represents both traditional and more contemporary viewpoints; the text as a whole mirrors the current clinical scene.

Specifically, there is a wide range in the various groups' characteristics. Members of groups may be psychologically intact or psychologically fragmented. Variables such as setting, ego strength and age of participants, and directness of treatment determine which techniques are used. In spite of the diversification among groups, we feel that Ego and Self Psychological theories offer a unifying foundation.

Psychoanalytic theory is dedicated to exploring and explaining normal as well as pathological and symptomatic development. We therefore emphasize work with both children and their parents. Application of this perspective can have far-reaching effects, as Kohut notes "... each resolution of a deeply grounded psychic disturbance of an individual father or mother may benefit a whole series of generations—an analogy to (and a reversal of) the biblical punishment leveled against the children and children's children of the sinner" (1978, p. 514). We believe that this applied analytic approach clarifies directions to take in early intervention, prevention, and direct ongoing group therapy with troubled populations.

REFERENCES

Anthony, E. J. (1971). The history of group psychotherapy. In *Comprehensive Group Psychotherapy*, eds. H. Kaplan and B. Sadock, pp. 4–31. Baltimore: Williams and Wilkins.

Berkovitz, I. H., ed. (1972). *Adolescents Grow in Groups*. New York: Brunner/Mazel.

Berkovitz, I. H. and Sugar, M. (1975). Indications and contraindications for adolescent group psychotherapy. In *The Adolescent in Group and Family Therapy*, ed. M. Sugar, pp. 3–26. New York: Brunner/Mazel.

Blanck, G. and Blanck, R. (1974). *Ego Psychology: Theory and Practice*. New York: Columbia University Press.

Brody, S. (1964). Aims and methods in child therapy. *Journal of the American Academy of Child Psychiatry* 3:385–412.

Buxbaum, E. (1945). Transference and group formation in children and adolescents. *The Psychoanalytic Study of the Child* 1:351–365. New York: International Universities Press.

Eubank, E. E. (1932). *The Concepts of Sociology*. Boston: D. D. Heath.

Freud, A. (1965). *Normality and Pathology in Childhood. The Writings of Anna Freud*, 6. New York: International Universities Press.

Freud, S. (1921). Introduction. *Group psychology and the analysis of the ego. Standard Edition* 18:67–134.

Ginott, H. (1961). *Group Psychotherapy with Children*. New York: McGraw–Hill.

Hartmann, H. (1958). *Ego Psychology and the Problem of Adaptation*. New York: International Universities Press.

Heacock. D. R. (1966). Modifications of the standard techniques for out-patient group psychotherapy with delinquent boys. *Journal of the National Medical Association* 58:41–47.

Josselyn, I. M. (1972). Prelude—adolescent group therapy: why, when and a caution. In *Adolescents Grow in Groups*, ed. I. H. Berkowitz, pp. 1–28. New York: Brunner/Mazel.

Kaplan, H. and Sadock, B., eds. (1971). Introduction. *Comprehensive Group Psychotherapy*. Baltimore: Williams and Wilkins.

Kernberg, O. F. (1970). Factors in the psychoanalytic treatment of narcissistic personalities. *Journal of the American Psychoanalytic Association* 18:51–85.

Kohut, H. (1966). Forms and transformations of narcissism. *Journal of the American Psychoanalytic Association* 14:243–272.

———(1968). The psychoanalytic treatment of narcissistic personality disorders. *The Psychoanalytic Study of the Child* 23. New York: International Universities Press.

———(1971). *The Analysis of the Self*. New York: International Universities Press.

———(1978). Psychoanalysis in a troubled world. In *The Search For Self*, ed. P. Ornstein. New York: International Universities Press.

Levy, C. S. (1976). *Social Work Ethics*. New York: Human Sciences Press.

Ross, N. (1974). Foreword. In *Ego Psychology: Theory and Practice*, eds. G. Blanck and R. Blanck. New York: Columbia University Press.

Rothstein, A. (1979). An exploration of the diagnostic term "narcissistic personality disorder." *Journal of the American Psychoanalytic Association* 27(4):893–912.

Scheidlinger, S. (1968). The concept of regression in group psychotherapy. In *Psychoanalytic Group Dynamics: Basic Readings*, ed. S. Scheidlinger, pp. 233–254. New York: International Universities Press, 1980.

Slavson, S. R. (1958). *Child-Centered Group Guidance of Parents*. New York: International Universities Press.

Stone, W. N. and Whitman, R. M. (1977). Contributions of the psychology of the self to group process and group therapy. *International Journal of Group Psychology* 27(3):343–359.

Van der Waals, J. G. (1965). Problems of narcissism. *Bulletin of the Menninger Clinic* 29:293–311.

Winnicott, D. W. (1953). Transitional objects and transactional phenomena. *International Journal of Psycho-Analysis* 34:89–97.

Wolf, A. and Schwartz, E. (1971). Psychoanalysis in groups. In *Comprehensive Group Psychotherapy*, eds. H. Kaplan and B. Sadock. Baltimore: Williams and Wilkins.

CHAPTER 1

Principles of Group Practice

ESTER BUCHHOLZ, PH. D.
JUDITH MISHNE, D.S.W.

GROUP COMPOSITION

The importance of employing diagnostic criteria for determining the composition of groups cannot be overemphasized. "The very fact of group mixture in itself may sometimes play a great part in what happens in a group, even when the best of conditions and the best and most skillful adult leadership are taken for granted" (Redl 1966, p. 239). In other words, group membership may take precedence over all other group factors. Therefore, it is necessary to assess group members to allow group workers better control over what occurs.

Composition, however, does not depend entirely on diagnostic factors; the group's meeting place and purpose influence the selection of participants. In addition, individuals seek out particular groups in particular settings. A pre-screening assessment interview is critical. Beginning therapists especially may have difficulty establishing this prerequisite because they often do not have sufficient people to populate their groups. At other times clinicians are pressured by work conditions to recruit individuals randomly to join the group. Glass (1969) believes a small group cluster is preferable to large numbers poorly matched. For example, a group consisting of all the troublemakers from a class may find it hard to outlive its designation. The pressures of supervisors or agencies, however, are not always surmountable. In such situations, understanding ego development through assessment of ego functioning can serve as a guide to interactions between members.

ASSESSMENT OF EGO FUNCTION. We have referred to ego functions several times. How are they assessed? Following the developmental lines established by a particular group of neo-Freudians including A. Freud, Mahler, Erikson, and Hartmann, Ego Psychologists such as Bellak, Hurvich and Gediman (1973), and Blanck and Blanck (1974, 1979), clearly depict various ego functions that can be assessed through interviews and testing procedures. Specifically, the individual is viewed in terms of object relations, ability to withstand anxiety and frustration, degree of conflict-free autonomous functioning, extent of reality testing, defensive functions, thought processes, and synthetic ability.

OBJECT RELATIONS. Level of object relations, considered by many to be the surest indicator of the structure of the ego (Kernberg 1976) is manifest in the type of friendships and interactions people have with others, though as Blanck and Blanck note, it "is not always easy to ascertain" (1974, p. 108). On the most primitive psychotic level we speak of individuals dealing fundamentally with negative introjects that cause continuous rage reactions or total withdrawal. Descriptions of borderline functioning typically emphasize inconsistencies and fluctuations; people are liked only in terms of how well they gratify the needs of others; objects do not take on stable, permanent meaning. There are many levels of neurotic exchange. Sado-masochism, for example, results in painful, fixed attachments.

A withdrawn individual may sit in a group and never participate. There have been occasions when individuals with the defensive symptom of withdrawal remain quietly aware of group transactions. In turn, the group responds to them. At other times withdrawal is predicated on a deep mistrust and anger which prohibit involvement with external objects. Ginott (1961) regards children who suffer intense sibling rivalry as poor candidates for group work. These characteristics typically are revealed in initial clinical interviews and on TAT, CAT, and Rorschach tests. If not using diagnostic tests, the therapist may find guidelines by observing the client's behavior in therapy. Total lack of curiosity or excessive interest in the therapist, absence of relationships in the person's life, tendencies to indiscriminately latch on to others for short periods, all may indicate a borderline personality. Parents who move from place to place and person to person may be functioning at a narcissistic level of involvement and may be instructing their children to make similar types of connections. This parent population would benefit from a confirmation of self through mirror transference by other group members and/or the leader.

DRIVE MODULATION. An ability to withstand anxiety and frustration is related to regulation of the libidinal and aggressive drives. There are at least two interpretations of this intrapsychic regulation. One is that high order defense mechanisms such as repression and sublimination are working well. Another explanation suggests that individuals with acceptable self-images have learned, through empathic relationships with parents, to employ self-soothing mechanisms that allay anxiety and drive expression. "Acting-out" behavior that is difficult to control within the group (or outside the group in response to group experiences) may be a result of excessive drive stimulation. Slavson's activity groups for latency age and adolescent boys, as well as his activity therapy groups, offer an outlet for drive derivatives which may not always be facilitated through verbal expression (Slavson and Schiffer 1975). Groups have been described as providing a more permissive atmosphere than individual consultations (Ginott 1961). Concurring, in general, with this viewpoint, we also emphasize that impulsive individuals in groups might not receive the limit-setting necessary for their maturation. Whereas group treatment might be conducive to growth for the repressed individual, it might, at times, be counterproductive for the impulsive client.

AUTONOMOUS EGO FUNCTIONS. Hartmann (1958) hypothesizes, in contrast to early Freudian theory, that the ego and id develop from an undifferentiated matrix. This perspective in psychoanalytic theory implies that the ego and id are potentially separate and that autonomous functions develop without conflict. Perceptual skills, motility, intention, and cognitive functions, for example, need not, unless the individual is under stress, show evidence of secondary interference. The most obvious disturbances in these autonomous functions occur in individuals with intellectual retardation, physical handicaps, or organic dysfunction. The disorders may range from mild to severe. Mainstreaming of mildly impaired people in groups usually does not cause them any special problem, unless they are unused to socializing. Severe fear of bodily injury in nonimpaired group members can create strong anxiety in such situations. The leader needs to be attuned to this underlying dynamic as it may be manifested in indirect ways through anger, oversolicitousness, or rejection.

With individuals who are moderately handicapped, group suitability is a more difficult issue. The first consideration, though, is the leader's training. Therapists intending to work with special populations should be experienced and knowledgeable. Without such a background unintentional mistakes are made. In one such situation, a learning disabled child with organic impairment continuously repeated all statements and questions. Everyone in the group became irritated. The leader interpreted the behavior as an attempt to get attention. In this instance the leader was uninformed that perseveration was a particular characteristic of organic impairment.

REALITY TESTING. Appropriate reality testing implies good judgment and a sense of separation between what occurs inside the individual and what is happening in the external world. Concomitantly, individuals are able to correctly appraise meanings and intentions in acts performed by themselves and others. Opportunities for reality testing are prevalent in group treatment because the group is a microcosm of the real world. Feedback, an avenue for personal change, is an ongoing component of group process.

In part the degree to which group members focus on reality is a function of the type of group and the age of group members. For example, psychoanalytic groups frequently pay primary attention to dream and fantasy material. Young children in play groups engage in make-believe. Reality testing is fostered in groups through exchanges among members. Inappropriate responses receive rapid reactions from group members. New types of behavior can be tested out in comparatively safe surroundings. Because feelings and thoughts are shared, those uncertain of the basis for their own emotions or ideas often find clarification. There are many opportunities for unsatisfactory old self-object experiences to be replaced by new self-object relationships.

EGO DEFENSES. The earliest ego function described by Freud was the defensive system. Defenses are mechanisms used to deal with unconscious drive derivatives. Although they are employed unconsciously, they are recognizable in behavior. Defenses can be understood developmentally. The young child employs primitive defenses such as splitting. Splitting would also be apparent in an individual who was unable to contain disparate feelings about others simultaneously. Perhaps the clearest delineation of this defense comes from Kernberg's (1976) writing. He states that when we are young, positive and negative internal pictures or introjects of our parents (principally, the primary caretaker) are separate because our emotions—which are related to libidinal and negative aggressive drives—are associated with disparate perceptual constellations in the ego; and we are unable to integrate them. This inability to integrate disparate forms parallels what Piaget describes as that which occurs with inanimate objects prior to object permanence.

The anxiety connected with negative introjects may ultimately overpower positive introjects. Splitting, an active "keeping apart," prevents the anxiety from becoming generalized. Excessive splitting may interfere with later integration of affects, as well as self and object images. Synthesis does not take place either in those with low tolerance for anxiety or in people who are unusually aggressive. It is in these cases that splitting serves a purpose similar to repression, especially in the young, as a defense against anxiety.

Adults typically use the more sophisticated operations of repression and intellectualization. The type of defense employed is an important indicator of ego structure. As people interact in groups and feel more comfortable, defensive styles become apparent. Earlier, it was deemed useful to immediately expose and confront defenses and "remove" them in order to reveal the underlying conflict. The adaptive aspect of defenses has been clarified, and a more cautious, nonassaultive approach is becoming increasingly prevalent among clinicians.

THOUGHT PROCESSES. Diagnosis of psychotic functioning was previously determined on the basis of thinking disorders. In an Ego Psychological approach, individual symptoms are not relied upon so heavily for making assessments. They are considered rather as personality characteristics. Disturbances in thinking, however, are more likely to be part of a pathological picture. The abilities to classify, make sense of perceptions, and think logically are features of mature thinking. Children's thought is, initially, nonverbal. When language first develops, abstractions are beyond a child's comprehension. This is sometimes the cause for misinterpretations between adults and children. Formal thinking is a higher order function, first apparent in adolescence, according to Piaget (1955). The importance of avoiding differences in comprehension and thinking patterns that may occur between individuals whose development is unmatched is usually a significant reason for grouping together people who are at similar cognitive and chronological levels. When group members have to struggle very hard to have others understand them, or are unable to grasp the meaning of exchanges, the impact for change is lessened.

SYNTHETIC EGO FUNCTIONS. Without the ability to organize and unite incongruent elements of ourselves, functioning would be fragmented and incoherent. The synthetic or integrative process serves that role. What Sander (1980) refers to as an overview of the self, and what Ego Psychologists describe as the individual's "observing ego," presume an ability to integrate and stand apart simultaneously.

We have already discussed this integrative function in our description of splitting. The synthetic process also underlies the orderly associations people make in conversations in groups. An overly zealous defense system can cause blocking of associations and retard synthetic operations.

FORMATION OF THE GROUP. Toplin notes the difficulty of distinguishing between individuals with "neurotic-like superstructures... deficiency illness, impairment of individuation, or a disorder of the self" (1978, p. 173) and people with basic neurotic conflict disorders. Characteristics of disturbances of cohesiveness are manifest in "... free floating... anxiety, depletion, and (empty) depression" (p. 176). Therefore, in terms of symptoms, one may see inhibited functioning, phobias and fears, and perverse sexual practices comparable to neurotic manifestations, in a "less than neurotic" client.

An examination of ego functioning was suggested as a strategy for assessing level of development. Once the potential group members are assessed in this manner, how is group composition determined? Some evidence supports both homogeneous and hetereogeneous groups, but for different purposes (Yalom 1970). Heterogeneous groups have advantages over homogeneous groups for intensive interactional group therapy. Homogeneous groups traditionally were composed according to a single variable, such as "presenting problems." These groups were thought to cohere quickly, to offer members a large measure of support, and to presumably provide rapid symptom relief. In contrast, the heterogeneous groups are conducive to conflict and provide more fertile ground for effecting alterations of character defenses and manifest behavior. Therefore, one aspect of determining group composition depends on the group's purpose. Grouping people homogeneously, however, may not result in a genuinely similar mix. To understand why this is so, we return to levels of ego functioning and other developmental factors. In many groups organized along a single dimension such as alcoholism, single parenting, or acting-out children, each individual is discovered to be different in terms of dynamic conflicts, descriptive diagnosis, and psychosexual stage of development. Depending on the goals of the group, a single criterion may or may not be helpful.

Glass (1969) believes that beginners should start with more homogeneous groups made up of individuals with at least "average" or "above average" intelligence, as this usually ensures interaction and interest in the group. Homogeneity should be provided for children's groups in terms of age and grade level. In all groups, when it is possible, there should be some matching of intellectual strength and interests. Yalom (1970) reports on a technique for eliminating group isolates and allowing for heterogeneity which includes matching. This is called the "Noah's Ark" principle of forming groups. Every individual is paired with a comparable peer.

What happens when groups are composed of people who know one another? Different clinicians take different points of view. Axline (1947) actually encouraged children to bring their playmates with them to form a play therapy group. Glass (1969), on the other hand, warns against the difficulty in running groups when members have serious loyalties to one another and advises counselors to avoid what he calls "the neighborhood effect." Ginott (1961) advises against intermingling family or friends together for both practical and theoretical reasons. From an Ego Psychological framework, development could be blocked if group members simply reinforced habitual patterns of behavior.

Ginott (1961) formulates certain criteria for selection which transcend the play therapy milieu. Group composition is optimal if it allows for corrective identifications, such as the meek with the brave. Relief from ridicule is necessary to ensure that minimal recapitulation of past shaming occurs. Leaders provide optimal tension, by including the quiet with the aggressive. Some individuals of higher order ego functioning, are always necessary, to balance out lower functioning borderline individuals.

Whether groups should be open or closed to new members is another issue that divides therapists. Dinkmeyer and Muro (1979) mention the positive and negative aspects of the opposing policies. The open group may lack cohesiveness. Undoubtedly, there is a sense of interruption each time a new member joins the group. Older members will form an alliance or coalition while new members, who may be anxious, may either withdraw or attempt to dominate the group. The reactions can be likened to the arrival of a sibling in the family. Viewed in this manner, reactions to new members may be advantageously interpreted. In educative groups this interpretation of sibling rivalry may be contraindicated. The flexibility of an open group may stimulate change within certain individuals. Changing group composition, however, is always disruptive, and thus, ideally, members should be given preparation and time for feelings to be expressed. Disruptions are not always avoidable. Adding new members as old ones drop out may be necessary to insure survival of the group. In general, group survival frequently is given precedence over principles of group composition. To the practiced eye however, group survival is not at stake as often as one may assume.

SETTING AND PURPOSE

Groups conducted by clinicians for rehabilitation purposes are located in such varied settings as public schools, mental health clinics, correctional institutions, hospitals, child welfare agencies, settlement houses, community centers, and offices of private practitioners. A rehabilitation approach seeks to help members make changes to alleviate specific handicaps from effecting their functioning in social, interpersonal, and occupational roles. Where the group is offered forms an integral part of the experience insofar as setting determines group purpose—delineating services that are long- or short-term, problem-focused, or open-ended. Schwartz and Zaba (1971) note that the agency or host setting has a stake in the proceedings, in that its own tasks and focus are involved. They suggest the convergence of two sets of tasks — "those of the clients (or patients) and those of the agency, [which] creates the terms of the contract that is made between the client group and the agency. This contract openly reflecting both stakes provides the frame of reference for the work that follows, and for understanding when the work is in process, when it is being evaded and when it is finished. The moving dynamic in the group experience is work" (p. 8). Agency function is clearly articulated by Smally: "The first task in the use of agency function is to determine through initiating the process whether the purpose or purposes of those [it] seeks to service and the purpose of the agency or institution or service to be represented, can come together in a fruitful engagement towards a common end" (1970, p. 114).

Every group has a purpose for being. Purpose means any ultimate aim, end, or intention that is latent or manifest, unconscious or conscious. "Some of the purposes may be rooted in the person's unconscious needs. Almost always there is a subtle and complex combination of individual purposes which may agree or be in conflict with the stated purpose of the group" (Northern 1969, p. 19). Agency function introduces a focus, a particularization that serves as a dynamic in the clinician-client relationship; it suggests the kind of services offered and the kinds of clients served, be they psychiatric patients, public welfare recipients, children in foster care or in hospitals and residential treatment centers, or middle-class, psychologically minded adults seeking therapy. Recently, group approaches have been used in an attempt to prevent deviant behavior among groups of children or adults via discussion groups, parent education groups, drug abuse education in schools, and so forth.

The concepts of agency function and focus suggest a spectrum of approaches, though generally groups offer clinical, educational, or management interaction. Examples of each category are suggested. An educational group may include six to ten parents in an ongoing group examining early childhood development, or a group of unwed adolescent mothers participating in a group devoted to discussion and consideration of birth control. Management groups are frequently used in hospitals and residential centers for discussion of patients' admission, discharge, examination of day-to-day program planning, or group problems such as scapegoating or vandalism. Clinical groups with insight-oriented treatment should be carefully selected to ensure an appropriate balance; meetings should occur at regular intervals on specified days to ensure the development of group interaction. Improvement of specific psychological or interpersonal problems should be the goal. Educational groups and management groups often provide therapeutic input and contribute to the well-being of the members, the predictability of a setting's structure, and the enhancement of communication. Although the boundary lines between these types of groups are often blurred, we believe that these distinctions help the practitioner clarify a group's focus and purpose.

THE MILIEU. The physical surroundings and staffing patterns of agencies merit consideration. Initially, we will present optimal conditions; later we will address ourselves to the practical realities and limitations routinely encountered in clinical settings, social agencies, and schools. Meeting rooms should be in a location comfortable for the group members and leader. The setting should facilitate group exchange. This would include a cheery and sufficiently large room with comfortable seating arrangements, and well cared for furnishings. Rooms that are too small force members into close proximity, a potential cause of frustration and irritation. In planning for children's groups, Ginott (1961) states that "... forced propinquity engenders hostility and intensifies defenses; in cramped quarters isolated children withdraw further into themselves and aggressive children attack others. A very large playroom is also undesirable; a big room invites wild running and rough play in aggressive children and permits withdrawn children to avoid contact with the therapist and the group members" (pp. 63–64). Adults also fare badly in a crowded room or in one that is excessively large.

Furniture should be sturdy, and for children's groups, creative materials, and a sufficient number of tables and chairs should be provided. A bathroom nearby is crucial. We would not recommend seeing adults in children's therapy rooms. The small size furniture and the toys prompt regression and feelings of childishness and exacerbate the conflict between authority and submission in member/leader relations. Groups should not convene in messy, disheveled rooms left in disarray by a prior session as outer chaos can disrupt clients who lack sufficient inner structure and stability.

Our comments on ideal physical facilities do not mean we are oblivious to practical realities. One may be forced to utilize a less than optimal setting, and the professional must compromise and accommodate to the host setting. It is not unusual for a mental health clinic, a school, or social agency to lack suitable space. One must judge whether to begin or not by considering the ecology and the environment. It is unsound to begin a venture doomed to fail. Beginnings must frequently be delayed until organizational procedures, like requisition of necessary furniture, are accomplished—or until the needed arrangements can be completed. Budgetary constraints are often a part of environmental reality. For example, in a settlement house, or mental health clinic, one must often be creative and innovative while struggling with precarious funding. Engaging adolescents in the creation of an attractive meeting space may prove to be an effective therapeutic tool—thus the improvement of the physical surroundings serves several therapeutic goals. Minimally, one should aim for a closed area to insure confidentiality, the absence of disruptions and interruptions by other staff and clients, and/or a minimum of distracting noise and chaos.

LENGTH OF SESSIONS. We suggest the length of meeting time be tailored in accord with setting, group purpose, and the age and ego structure of the clients. For instance, pre-school children and impulsive young latency age children might well not be able to tolerate more than 45 minutes of meeting time. Adolescent and adult clients may well benefit from an hour-and-a-half session. However, there are obvious exceptions. Acutely psychotic adult patients may become too agitated in sessions that last beyond a 40-minute meeting. Practice wisdom, experience, and consultation must provide guidelines. We would recommend that members be expected to prepare and clean up, before and after any creative activity or the serving of some refreshment. Time needs to be allocated for these procedures.

LEVEL OF INTERVENTION—CLINICAL TECHNIQUES

Practice art and practice wisdom require the differential use of self by the skilled clinician. Criteria such as ego strength of members and group purpose should dictate the use or avoidance of therapeutic regression.

TECHNIQUE. Scheidlinger (1968) suggested a classification scheme in which the degree of regression promoted deliberately by the therapist is delineated according to specific criteria: activity–catharsis–mastery focus; cognitive–informational focus; interpersonal–socialization focus; relationship–experiential focus; and uncovering–introspective focus. The more intact the patient, the less support, direction, and advice required of the leader; a more introspective focus is possible. With less intact patients, treatment requires an ego and reality oriented method that utilizes activity–catharsis and cognitive–informational focus. Clinics and agencies are seeing fewer and fewer "classic" neurotic patients. Thus, for these "less than neurotic" patients, extensive uncovering psychoanalytic procedures are contraindicated. Treatment, for example, of the borderline patient requires providing "... experience which will reinforce secondary ego processes in order to help the patient develop more effective means of meeting his own needs in a socially acceptable manner" (Stuart 1964, p. 40). Ongoing empathic exchange replaces challenging techniques that lead to confrontation.

EGO SUPPORT. Blanck and Blanck note that "... ego support is probably one of the most mentioned and yet most misunderstood tools in psychotherapy" (1974, p. 345). These authors cite mistaken simplistic praise, pats on the back, and suppression as erroneously presumed to be the opposite of "uncovering." They stress diagnostic understanding of ego functioning, searching for the highest level of development, and resonating to the patients offered material within the context of patients' accomplishments. In addition, interventions are aimed at improving the defensive functions of the ego to facilitate better coping with depression and anxiety.

These same authors stress verbalization in semantic communication, as this aids in the neutralization of drives, enhances reality testing, and diminishes magical thinking (Blanck and Blanck, 1974). The importance of verbalization in early childhood is stressed by Katan who states "... verbalization increases for the ego the possibility of distinguishing between wishes and fantasies on the one hand, and reality on the other. In short, verbalization leads to the integrating process, which in turn results in reality testing and this helps to establish the secondary process" (1961, p. 185). Blanck and Blanck stress the same point and note that neutralization of the drives is "... promoted principally by verbalization which replaces, or at least, postpones action" (1974, p. 349). "While neutralized libido builds object relations, neutralized aggression powers the developmental thrust toward separation-individuation" (p. 350).

CONFRONTATION. Another frequently mentioned technique in individual and group treatment is that of confrontation. This approach is based on external presentation of group members' behavior and attitudes, with the goal being the desirability of changing behavior, for better social adaptation, to retain love, etc. Requested and/or demanded change usually does not become internalized or signify genuine growth. Blanck suggests a different intent, i.e., "... to help the observing part of the ego look at the experiencing part and confront itself intrasystemically. While the most obvious advantage of such internal confrontation is that the patient is less likely to refute and reject internally perceived insight ... the most valuable aspect of confrontation from within is that it is, in and of itself, therapeutic because it promotes the ego's capacity via exercise of function" (1970, pp. 507–508).

Self Psychologists avoid confrontation and refrain from anticipating rapid change. Insight, per se, is not expected to ameliorate or temper faulty self-esteem, the grandiose self, or perfectionistic strivings. The therapist needs to be patient and content to be a mirror, and to allow the patient to idealize the therapist. Frequently the therapist is called upon to listen closely to the individual's subjective state where the self as an agent is undeveloped, withered or deficient (Stolerow 1980).

As emphasized, techniques vary from group to group, depending on clients' ego development. The varying states and stages of ego development are inevitable in comparing and contrasting adult groups, child groups, and adolescent groups. Commonly, in working with adolescents, the therapist must be more actively involved with the group, talking and offering more, providing interventions and reality oriented instruction. Directiveness may not only be allowable, but necessary. With adults the same techniques could be inappropriate or even harmful. When and how to intervene are matters of judgment, experience, sensitivity, and style. With adolescents one is often more open with one's own thoughts, values, and range of emotions. With adult groups, good technique often requires containing one's emotional reactions in order to aid in transference reactions in the more fixed character structure that distinguishes the adult from the adolescent. In contrast to adults, adolescents generally struggle with separation anxiety; because they are seeking identifications, they often need the therapist to act as a teacher and/or parent.

Adolescents may commonly present acting-out behavior in group meetings and thus need limits from the therapist. Additionally, they need direct counseling on drug use, sexual activity, birth control information, and venereal disease. As the adolescents' therapist, one must be prepared to fill some parent/teacher role model functions; self-revelation, provision of limits, education and information, in a benign environment that promotes insight and understanding can accomplish this. Caution is required so that the therapist does not impose his or her personal needs, beliefs, or values in an intrusive fashion.

Overall, no matter the age or the ego structure of the group members, the "...unwavering reliability of the therapist is essential to building object relations. The therapist is there, predictable, in the same kindly mood each time" (Blanck and Blanck 1974, p. 339). Whoever the clients, or patients, and wherever the treatment or work is undertaken, consistency and predictability is essential. "The therapist and the setting take on the task of auxiliary stimulus barrier and soother...interpretation is of less value than empathic relatedness" (p. 355). Client self-determination or "...guardianship of autonomy is not an active technique; it is rather an attitude" (p. 357), integral to skilled practice in all educational or therapeutic endeavors.

GROUP PROCESS

Group process is a term used both generally and specifically. Sometimes it has the same connotation as group dynamics. Here, group process is linked to interactions and used as it was intended when first coined by Foulkes in 1957 (Fried 1971). Interaction, whether positive or negative, always occurs in groups. Through this interaction, group processes begin. The intrapsychic life of each member is challenged and perhaps begins to change. Group interaction is largely responsible for the process that creates the climate necessary for change. Of course, the particular kind of process that occurs depends upon the therapist's approach and the type of group. Methods can be employed in groups to encourage particular interactions. Foulkes (1965) believes the need to relate is fundamental to group members. Moreover, within this relating " . . . it is the process of communication rather than the information it conveys that is important to us" (1965, p. 152).

EGO PSYCHOLOGY APPLIED TO GROUP PROCESS. An Ego Psychological orientation can illuminate group process from at least three perspectives. First, the evolution of a group can be viewed in terms of developmental stages. Second, individual group members can be guided in terms of their transitions in ego development. Last, developmental psychology offers practical and technical guidance for group intervention.

Fried (1971) articulates the phases of group development in a way that models Mahler's individuation and Erikson's psychosocial theories. Fried's descriptions of the initial interactions between group members can be seen as representative of dependent feelings arising from symbiotic wishes. These initial encounters are significant in that they may or may not elicit trust. As group members reveal more information about themselves, issues of autonomy and power arise in the group. The group leader is often likened to a father or mother. Scheidlinger (1980) sees membership in a group as tied to a deep wish to reconstitute a conflict-free relationship to a need-gratifying mother. Fried sees the early transferences in groups as narcissistic, with members seeking approval and inclusion from overevaluated and admired leaders. Parallel to the optimal achievement of object constancy in individual development is the growth of attachments in groups. The most advanced stage of group functioning would be commensurate to an individual's achieving individuation and mutuality. At this point object relations between members are at an empathic level in which giving as well as taking occurs.

When groups as a whole are analyzed, the process is viewed in an undivided way. Group functioning in its entirety is paramount. However, individual development is yet another point of reference when scrutinizing group process. Erikson saw ego identity and group identity as complementary processes (Scheidlinger 1980). Individuals maintain less fragmented selves if their own ideals can be synthesized without unduly compromising group ideals. The feeling of identity, in part, can build from the identifications that are made in the group in two ways. The identification can be similar to the selective identification described by Jacobson (1964). In this process, as individuals identify with different group members they begin to build a more coherent picture of themselves. In discussing this process in the developing child, Blanck and Blanck state that "... selective identifications become enduring and consistent parts of the ego, permanently modifying it to the point where the child becomes aware of having a coherent, continuous self" (1974, p. 66). This is identification used in the normal developmental process.

Identification is also a prevalent defense used by group members. When the process is used defensively it is an attempt to obtain gratification or withstand anxiety through identification with others who possess either desired or feared attributes. This type of identification is frequently seen when one member sides with another, overly aggressive member. In contrast, for Self Psychologists, identifications could serve to reinforce good self-object representations. Negative aspects of the self could also undergo change through identification.

Many people will enter groups without differentiated self and object images; that is, without having attained object constancy, a fusion between the good and bad object. Rather than feeling whole, the person will feel part of another on an unconscious level. Blanck and Blanck (1979) describe several types of relationships common among borderline patients; for example, individuals fantasize others as necessary to complete themselves, fear merger and engulfment as potential loss of identity, or fantasize union with another in an imaginary world. Typically, others are not seen as separate, autonomous people. When fusion of the good and bad objects has not occurred, splitting is still a major defense. The young child needs this separation of good and bad objects to keep aggressive feelings from overwhelming ego functions. In the developing child and adult this defense mars object relationships, interferes with reality testing, and, in fact, jeopardizes all ego functioning.

How does the group experience affect faulty object relations? Basically, groups offer a place to work out some of these problems. For example, the type of "joining-in" experience which is helpful in the early stages of promoting a better tie with the omnipotent other occurs spontaneously in groups because there is ample opportunity to find an omnipotent partner with whom to merge. If the developmental stage of group members is understood, the interactions are clarified and appropriate interventions can be made.

In groups of schizophrenics, splitting occurs on an extremely pathological level. Rage reactions often accompany excessive acting-out behavior. One patient who saw the therapist as a bad object could not tolerate the therapist's reflections. In the middle of a session the schizophrenic member jumped up, cursed, and stomped about. The leader and group members reflected on the irate patient's fear of merger. The nonassaultive interventions soothed the upset patient and gradually, over weeks, improved his ego functioning.

Many of the phenomena so beneficial for support of the borderline patient's ego can happen spontaneously through group process. Some of the mechanics of effective group therapy that promote ego growth are outlined by Dinkmeyer and Muro (1979). Those which seem to prove most influential in changing borderline functioning, and which are also significant for children needing group therapy, are: group acceptance, which promotes a sense of belonging; universalization, which encourages a sense of connectedness with others; altruism, which fosters a desire to help others through being helped; and ventilation, which affords an opportunity for self-expression. But in regard to self-expression the Blancks stress that the clinician must differentiate "... between encouraging the use of neutralized aggression for growth, on the one hand, and ventilation which goes nowhere, on the other" (1974, p. 157).

There are processes described as techniques in group therapy that are in harmony with Ego Psychological practice. The importance of the corrective emotional experience, reality testing, and certain types of confrontation have already been pointed out. An element particular to group interactions is group cohesion: the connectedness or mutual bond experienced among group members. Cohesion is, of course, what keeps individuals attending group sessions. Cohesion stems from many different sources (Fried 1971). It can arise from the shared characteristics or goals of members, from the unconscious needs directed toward the leader, or even from the mere wish of all to get well. Another way to appreciate the phenomenon of group bonding is to view it as a means of satisfying the symbiotic wish. Silverman (1978) looks at the relationship between therapist and patient as a sanctioned method of gratifying early desires for dependency.

There are, of course, important ways in which dyadic and multiple relationships differ. The comparison between individual and group therapy has been spelled out before (Anthony 1971). Our thesis is that many of the organizing principles of Ego and Self Psychology, used primarily in work with individuals, are useful and beneficial in group treatment. "Perhaps we should not be too competitive about who should learn from whom, provided we make sure that we learn from each other..." (p. 116).

GROUP DYNAMICS—RESISTANCE, ALLIANCE, TRANSFERENCE, AND COUNTERTRANSFERENCE

The dynamics of treatment include resistance, alliance, transference, and countertransference. Traditional definitions of these phenomena will be offered in this section, as well as recent revisions suggested by Ego and Self Psychology.

RESISTANCE. Resistance implies the existence of psychological organization and the capacity to use defense mechanisms; according to Blanck and Blanck "Defense and therefore resistance are intrapsychic phenomena dependent upon the existence of structure. Resistance-like behavior is often viewed erroneously" (1979, p. 145). In this review of theorists who regard resistance as aggressive, self-destructive behavior that opposes treatment, they note that traditionally, lateness, silence, negativism, withholding, and hostility are regarded as resistance. However, as Blanck and Blanck further explain, silence does not always have to represent hostile withholding; it can also arise out of a wish for empathic closeness. Ego Psychology "forces reconsideration of the concept of resistance to include those behavioral manifestations classically regarded as such, but which really present opportunity to use the drives and affects for structure building and for strengthening self and object images by means of promoting selective identification" (pp. 159, 169). Aggressive adolescents are not necessarily negativistic and resistant; possibly they are asserting appropriate separation needs. For the less structured patient population, i.e. borderline clients, aggressivity and negativism might not reflect resistance, but rather, distortions and subphase inadequacies.

THERAPEUTIC ALLIANCE. For a less structured population, Blanck and Blanck suggest that "... the therapeutic alliance constitutes a relationship in which the major technical task is to illustrate the affective distortions caused by subphase inadequacies arising from the relationship with the primary object" (1979, p. 160). "Working alliance" is one of the many terms borrowed from the field of adult analysis; it evolved from the phrase "treatment or therapeutic alliance," first introduced by Zetzel (Zetzel and Neissner 1973) in 1956 and used by Greenson in 1965. Originally Freud referred to an alliance between the analyst and the healthy part of the patient's ego. Many analysts (e.g., Sterba, Zetzel, Stone, and Loewenstein) have emphasized that the readiness to form an alliance with the analyst is not transference and should be clearly distinguished from it, yet a number of authors do not accept the distinction between alliance and transference. In addition, they do not believe that alliance should only be perceived as the conscious and rational wish to be rid of suffering, or that once alliance has been established, it remains stable, in evidence even at times of intense resistance or transference. Novick states that "The emphasis on conscious rational motives for the alliance departs radically from the clinical reality" (1970, p. 254).

Lane (1980) suggests that emphasis on particular aspects of traditional concepts of therapeutic alliance must be modified for interpretive work with children. She notes the immature object capacity of children whose continued reliance on multiple self-objects in the psychic system reflects the quality of the therapeutic alliance. "Simply put, the most normal child has not undergone many transformations of narcissism. Concomitant to this developmental reality, are heightened aspects of the therapeutic alliance involving idealization, mirroring and merger; and while they may reflect psychopathology in the child's self-system, ... they also reflect a normal mode of relating in childhood" (p. 133).

Keith (1968) defines therapeutic alliance as a state of ego functioning that connotes increased self-awareness of internal psychological processes, made possible by a splitting of the ego which allows the perceptual processes to turn back upon the self (Jacobson 1954). In other words, during treatment, one part of the ego is looking and listening, while another is feeling and experiencing. Not all clients have such well-developed inner ego structure to be able to effect the above noted split. For example, "... most psychotic and borderline children are able to form a symbiotic relationship with the therapist. This merging of ego boundaries means that for a long period of therapy the patient will use the therapist's ego as his own observing and synthesizing ego.... This merging of the therapist's and child's ego can be called a 'pseudo-alliance' since it does not represent a true therapeutic splitting of the child's own ego. The therapist consistently and repetitively interjects his own secondary process and rational behavior into the treatment situation" (Keith 1968, p. 38). The occurrence of this same pseudo-alliance phenomenon with less structured adolescent and adult client populations must be underscored. Concern about the merger phenomenon should dictate careful composition of groups. The phenomenon of contagion with clients whose ego boundaries are blurred and inadequate has been previously noted.

TRANSFERENCE. The development of psychoanalysis as a method of treating neurotic patients has been largely determined by knowledge of the nature of transference. Greenson offers a working definition of transference: "By transference we refer to a special kind of relationship toward a person; it is a distinctive type of object relationship. The main characteristic is the experience of feelings to a person which does not befit that person and which actually apply to another. Essentially, a person in the present is reacted to as though he were a person in the past" (1967, pp. 151, 152). Transference is a repetition, a new edition of an old object relationship (Freud 1905). It consists of any of the components of a significant object relationship, expressed as wishes, fears, fantasies, attitudes, drives, or defenses against them. Obviously, it also occurs outside of the treatment situation. The people who are the original sources of transference reactions are those who were meaningful and significant people in early childhood (S. Freud 1912, A. Freud 1946). Transference responses and reactions, inappropriate in the current context, relate to someone in the past; they are repetitions of a past object relationship. This very feature connotes object constancy, when self and others are distinct and separate. The achievement of object constancy signifies a successful separation and subsequent individuation; child and mother (self and other) are no longer fused, or split objects, all good or all bad. Self and object cathexis is stable and permanent.

The "less than neurotic" population has not achieved object constancy as a result of arrests or regression during various phases of the separation-individuation phenomenon. This population of clients requires reexamination of the concept of transference. Blanck and Blanck, in examining the interpretable transference note the following:

> Where there is impairment of: ego organization, level of object relations, degree of internalization, development of autonomous ego functions, then it follows that neurosis proper cannot be organized. In that condition, there is impaired capacity to receive and utilize interpretation of transference. Where the therapist is perceived as a potential gratifier of symbiotic need, for example, or as narcissistically perceived parts of a self-object unit, then long held formulations of transference do not apply in the traditional way. Often the analyst is neither a true transference object nor a real external one but only a potential gratifier of a subphase need (1979, p. 99).

This conceptualization highlights the more recent findings of A. Freud, Kohut, and Greenacre, among others, who note developmental deficits and deficiencies in structure formation that transcend the infantile neurosis. Greenacre (1971) made a distinction between patients with psychoneurotic conflicts and a delimited subgroup of patients with developmental deficits attributed to parental pathology. Paraphrasing A. Freud (1968, 1970), Greenacre describes a "neurotic superstructure" that proliferates on failures, defects, deficits, and structural faults so that neurotic problems more or less obscure the critical pathology. Greenacre (1971) and Kohut (1971, 1972, 1977) emphasize the importance of distinguishing conflicts resulting from infantile sexual drives from inadequate conflict solutions resulting from an immature ego; the latter, they claim, are caused by inadequate structure formation.

In discussing symptom formation in disorders of the self, Tolpin (1978) specifically emphasizes the distinction between symptoms that are truly neurotic and those that are simply imitative. She notes that "... symptom formation begins when the cohesive self is threatened by the danger of psychological fragmentation and/or the danger of psychological depletion, enfeeblement and loss of vitality" (p. 175). Tolpin lists the following manifestations of disturbances in a sense of cohesiveness: free-floating anxiety, depletion, depression, separation problems, marked propensity for narcissistic rage, clinging, demanding, coercive and manipulative behavior, and developmental arrests.

She also notes a breakdown of self as seen in phobias such as fear of noise, desertion, illness, robbers, witches, monsters, animals, insects, and so on. Habit disorders, also found as symptoms, take the form of fecal retention, soiling, masturbation, addiction, overeating, or perverse fantasies.

Behavioral disorders such as voyeurism, exhibitionism, or promiscuity, comprise another area of disturbance. Toplin emphasizes the following: "For patients with structural deficits, genetic reconstructions and interpretations of conflicts are ineffectual because these interpretations bypass and obscure the central psychopathology; and they inadvertently repeat childhood psychological injuries which lead to artifacts and regressive transferences" (1978, p. 181). Patients suffering faulty self-esteem, missing sense of direction, anxiety, depression, and shaky values and ideals develop various self-object transferences that must be distinguished from our classic definition of transference. The discovery that the analyst is a new edition of the child's pre-structural self-objects thus bears directly on the notion of the nonanalytic corrective emotional experience wherein the analyst is a new object. Ritvo (1974), and Berger and Kennedy (1976), present the notion that improved self-esteem as well as the acquisition of purpose and ideals and a sense of direction are beneficial byproducts of treatment.

In summary, the transference phenomenon with neurotic and more intact clients involves three people: a subject, a past object, and a present object. It is based on two achievements, the patient's capacity to differentiate between the self and the object world and his or her ability to displace reactions from past object representations to objects in the present. The healthier patient has an organized, differentiated self. This is in distinct contrast to the population Tolpin describes above. With severely ill and regressed patients, those that are borderline and psychotic, transient psychotic reactions to the therapist may result from a lack of self-other distinctions. The concept of working or therapeutic alliance described by Greenson, Zetzel, etcetera, designates the reliable working relationship as the relatively nonneurotic rational rapport between patient and therapist. It centers on the patient's ability and desire to work purposefully, utilizing the observing rather than the experiencing part of the ego.

The most essential ingredients of successful work with children and adolescents include realistic perceptions, genuine feelings of respect, compassion, empathy, and friendliness. In individual intensive psychotherapy, these qualities generally are reserved for the termination phase of treatment, when patient and therapist savor the special, private, and meaningful work accomplished together. Hurn, in discussing the termination phase, notes "the tendency to perceive the analyst objectively and without transference distortion . . . " and suggests that " . . . reactions emotionally appropriate to each other are expectable and have either a mourning like character or one that portends mourning" (1971, p. 80). Blanck and Blanck ask the basic questions: "When is the analyst real, when is he truly a transference figure, when is he [or she] experienced as part of a self-object unit fantasied to be a potential gratifier of unfulfilled need" (1979, p. 101). Referring to transference with neurotic patients, they answer that the analyst " . . . may also be experienced as potential gratifier of symbiosis, differentiation, rapproachement," i.e., meeting unmet needs of early pre-oedipal subphases of ego organization (p. 101).

COUNTERTRANSFERENCE. Countertransference is distinguished by unconscious forces within the therapist, whereby the therapist reacts to the patient in inappropriate ways, displacing earlier relationship and experiences from the therapist's own life (DeWald 1964). Thus the patient may be unconsciously used by the therapist in relationship to professional colleagues; the patient may become a source of pride or shame for the therapist. Groups of generalized countertransference reactions may include such drive derivatives as a therapist's need to be needed, to have the dependency of others, or to feel omnipotent. Patients may be used to satisfy drives of voyeurism and curiosity, or to gratify unconscious aggressive or masochistic needs. All of these feelings could be connected to controlling, manipulative behavior by the therapist. If a therapist is not conscious of his or her own unconscious and unresolved earlier conflicts, his or her competence will be greatly undermined. In addition to considerations of countertransference as reflections of blind spots in the analyst, countertransference is also regarded as a means of understanding the patient and the patient's communication. The affective reactions stirred up in the analyst may contribute important information on patient's feelings.

Proctor (1959) notes that countertransference problems become progressively greater in work with the impulsive narcissistic client who acts out. Such patients tax therapists who attempt to defend themselves with counterresistance. Frequently therapists are tempted to counterattack or mobilize infantile aspects of their superego against the patient's id. This mobilization of the therapist's superego can result in rejection, punishment, or hostile demands for conformity by the patient. Proctor's use of the term countertransference is the reverse of transference, with the progressive, fixed patterns set by infantile object relations displaced by the therapist onto the patient. "Interpretation to the patient of the therapist's own countertransference can be a highly effective tool, but requires some finesse. Such interpretation must be correctly timed, and should be aimed at the most superficial level that is effective" (p. 305). This use of self in the patient's behalf, with the less than neurotic population, expands the concept of countertransference. Blanck and Blanck state that the therapist " . . . takes on more of an interpersonal role than was understood when countertransference, defined in its strictest sense applied to neurosis alone . . . . Especially now that we understand that the therapeutic need for reorganization of the patient's subphase inadequacies calls for some sort of experiential interaction with the therapist, must the therapist be in communication with his own phase and subphase adequacies and inadequacies" (1979, pp. 135–136).

APPLICATIONS TO GROUP TREATMENT. Groups introduce new therapeutic and conceptual paradigms. Transference and countertransference become most complex in groups. "Although a group consists of individual patients with individual problems we must now focus on the whole multi-person unit, and, where applicable, conceive of the group as the patient" (Stierlin 1975, p. 163). As in individual therapy, transference and countertransference phenomena in groups are formed and delineated by the patients' and therapists' contributions. Frequently these include typical group fantasies that will mirror and shape certain kinds of recurrent group behavior. "These group fantasies or basic assumptions in turn structure the group's attitudes, perceptions, and expectations of the leader. Such group attitude we may then call the group transference" (p. 165). Thus the leader or therapist is perceived as the all-giving, all-knowing superparent—with the power to satisfy and gratify the exorbitant and regressive needs of the group.

Yet, the leader may also be viewed as the intrusive enemy whom the group must fight or flee. A more benign, neutralized view depicts the leader as partner or someone who enables growth. Countertransference responses might develop from omnipotent, manipulative responses on the part of the therapist who wishes to be the charismatic leader. Deviating from the role of neutral observer, the leader may then become excessively seductive and overgratifying or else a controlling authoritarian figure who demands compliance. All of the pitfalls cited by Proctor (1959) in work with children and adolescents who act out are magnified in group treatment. The impact of countertransference is intensified by the pressures inherent in a group. Additionally, members of the group project their unconscious fantasy objects not only onto the leader but onto group members as well and try to manipulate them accordingly. "Each member will stay in a role assigned to him by another, only if it happens to coincide with his own unconscious fantasy and if it allows him to manipulate others into appropriate roles. Otherwise, he will try to twist the discussion until the real group does correspond to his fantasy group. The result of each member's doing this is that there will be established a common denominator, a common group tension out of each member's individual dominant unconscious tension" (Scheidlinger 1950, p. 132). Ezriel recommends interpretations of what transpires in the group on a moment by moment basis, and in fact "... pays minimal attention to member-to-member relationships except insofar as they reflect the fantasied concerns regarding the leader" (Scheidlinger 1980, p. 287).

Another interesting concept of transference dynamics of the therapeutic group experience has been formulated by Grotjahn (1972). He notes the following:

The transference aspects in the therapeutic group situation are experienced similarly and at the same time quite differently from the transference neurosis in psychoanalysis. In the psychoanalytic group experience a three-fold transference development can be observed: the transference relationship to the therapist or central figure is patterned according to the transference neurosis as it is known from psychoanalysis. A second important transference relationship develops between the members of the group to each other. According to clinical experience it is this peer-transference which exhibits the greatest therapeutic pressure in groups ....A third transference relationship develops to the group as a pre-oedipal mother. This third transference relationship is of decisive importance in groups of adolescents since the central conflict of adolescence takes place between the need for dependency and the drive for individuation and identity (1972, p. 173).

Grotjahn and many adolescent group therapists recommend that a therapist team include a male and a female as this is seen as having beneficial influence on the therapists' countertransference. Presented is a stance of active, honest, frank, spontaneity by the central figures, who also at times, in a transient fashion, known only to the therapist take turns becoming one of the group.

The conception of the group as the pre-oedipal mother, and the design of co-therapists seems to us particularly useful in formulating group treatment with "less than neurotic" populations who have neither achieved object constancy nor mastered separation-individuation, and who frequently use splitting as a defense. Two therapists permit the splitting of good and bad mother and hopefully insure the eventual fusion of these views. Blanck and Blanck's discussion of the "Real Object" is a particularly useful contribution to group as well as individual treatment with clients with subphase maldevelopment. By permitting himself or herself to be experienced as a nontransference object, "the analysts or therapists do become real to the patient but in a circumscribed way, not really themselves but as a representative of the object world, especially when the patient's connection with the real world is uncertain. Many analysts are finding that they cannot validly sustain the image of nonparticipant observer and interpreter even in the psychoanalysis of neurosis" (1979, p. 115). By assuming the roles of catalysts and leaders into the object world, therapists and members alike facilitate growth through selective identifications.

As previously noted, original conceptualizations and models of therapy groups emphasize the "object love" relationships with the leader and members, based on the model of transference neurosis. Stone and Whitman suggest that the recent contributions of Kohut and his co-workers to the psychology of the self (Kohut 1966, 1968, 1971, 1972) have direct relevance to the understanding of " . . . aspects of relationships of group members with one another and the leader, as well as group formation (group) cohesion and (group) fragmentation" (1977, p. 343). These authors suggest that " . . . pre-oedipal issues of nuclei, self and self-objects [are] useful conceptual tools in both individual and group psychology. In group psychology when this model is used, the leader and/or the group is seen as a 'self object' which maintains the cohesion of the individual by confirming the archaic grandiose self or by offering itself as an idealized vehicle for archaic fantasies or greatness" (p. 345). Therefore, on the level of the group-as-group, we see that each individual and especially the leader, becomes not only a love object but also a necessary part of the self of each individual. Concepts of narcissism and self require the formulation of objects as self objects, parts of the self whose only function is to supply missing or needed parts of the self. "Both the leader and the group can be usefully conceptualized this way, and this understanding leads to a second major observation: two basic forms of transference may exist for the individual: object-narcissism or an idealizing transference (my group or leader is the greatest) or subject-narcissism, thus keeping the original perfection of a grandiose self-concept" (p. 346).

Primitive forms of the grandiose self can be seen in twinship and merger fantasies. "Merger fantasies, an even earlier developmental stage of grandiosity, arise often in the beginning phases in groups, but may be present throughout the life of the group and may only be exposed after a period of therapy" (p. 349). When projection of primitive grandiosity onto others occurs, the result is an idealizing transference that expects all protective caretaking to be done by the leader. Thus we can hypothesize that "less than neurotic" clients or patients are not conventionally dependent upon the leader; rather, the leader is not viewed as a separate object, but, in fact, an idealized self object. Patients' rage is the frequent response to the de-idealization of the leaders. The leader must respect these conceptualizations and accept the role of a narcissistic object because of patients' need for the therapist (and co-members) to function as parts of themselves (Goldberg 1973). Mirroring responses and accepting idealization are crucial. Idealizing transferences frequently cause clinicians discomfort, and the traditional approach has been to admonish patients to give up unrealistic expectations of the leader, to take a more realistic view. "This debunking of the idealizations has left patients confused since most appreciate their unrealistic expectations but are unaware of the function they serve in their insistent seeking for an idealized self-object" (Stone and Whitman 1977, p. 356).

There are many additional implications for leader behavior. "In mirror transferences appreciation of the individual's contribution to the functioning of the group needs attention by the therapist. For instance, excessive adherence to group-as-a-whole interpretations may leave the individual patient with the feeling of being a cog in a machine and therefore depersonalized" (ibid., p. 355). "We are not suggesting that central group issues be avoided because of the potential for narcissistic blows to the individual, but, rather, that the therapist be alerted to the possibility that group-as-a-whole interpretations may be experienced by a particular patient as a nonrecognition of his uniqueness" (p. 355).

In conclusion we underscore our view that Ego and Self Psychology and the study of narcissism have much to offer to group work and group therapy interventions. What is required is the nonjudgmental acceptance of patients' needs to idealize and be idealized, or to deidealize both the leader or the group. Recognition and admiration provide a basis for soothing and empathic interventions.

REFERENCES

Anthony, E. J. (1971). Comparison between individual and group psychotherapy. In *Comprehensive Group Psychotherapy*, eds. H. Kaplan and B. Sadock, pp. 104–117. Baltimore: Williams and Wilkins.

Axline, V. M. (1947). *Play Therapy*. Boston: Houghton Mifflin.

Bellack, L., Hurvich, M., and Gediman, H. (1973). *Ego Functions in Schizophrenics, Neurotics, and Normals: A Systematic Study of Conceptual, Diagnostic, and Therapeutic Aspects*. New York: Wiley.

Berger, M. and Kennedy, H. (1976). Pseudobackwardness in children. *The Psychoanalytic Study of the Child* 31:279–306. New Haven: Yale University Press.

Blanck, G. (1970). Crossroads in the technique of psychotherapy. *Psychoanalytic Review* 56:498–510.

———, G. and Blanck, R. (1974). *Ego Psychology: Theory and Practice*. New York: Columbia University Press.

———, G. and ———, R. (1979). *Ego Psychology–II. Psychoanalytic Developmental Psychology*. New York: Columbia University Press.

DeWald, P. A. (1964). *Psychotherapy: A Dynamic Approach*. New York: Basic Books.

Dinkmeyer, D. C. and Muro, J. J. (1979). *Group Counseling: Theory and Practice*. Itasca, Illinois: Peacock.

Ezriel, H. (1950). A Psychoanalytic Approach to Group Treatment. In *Psychoanalytic Group Dynamics: Basic Reading*, ed. S. Scheidlinger, 1980, pp. 109–146. New York: International Universities Press.

Foulkes, S. H. (1965). Psychodynamic Process in the Light of Psychoanalysis and Group Analysis. In *Psychoanalytic Group Dynamics: Basic Readings*, ed. S. Scheidlinger, 1980, pp. 147–162. New York: International Universities Press.

Freid, H. (1971). Basic concepts in group psychotherapy. In *Comprehensive Group Psychotherapy*, eds. H. Kaplan and B. Saddock, pp. 47–71. Baltimore: Williams and Wilkins.

Freud, A. (1946). *The Ego and the Mechanisms of Defense.* New York: International Universities Press.

———, A. (1968). Indications and contraindications for child analysis. *The Psychoanalytic Study of the Child* 23:37–46. New York: International Universities Press.

———, A. (1970). The symptomatology of childhood: A preliminary attempt at classification. *The Psychoanalytic Study of the Child* 25:19–41. New York: International Universities Press.

Freud, S. (1905). Psychical (or mental) treatment. *Standard Edition* 7:283–302. London: Hogarth Press.

———, S. (1912). The Dynamics of Transference. *Standard Edition* 12:97-108. London: Hogarth Press.

Ginott, H. (1961). *Group Psychotherapy with Children.* New York: McGraw-Hill.

Glass, S. (1969). *The Practical Handbook of Group Counseling.* Baltimore: BCS Publishing.

Goldberg, A. (1973). Psychotherapy of narcissistic injuries. *Arch. Gen. Psychiat.* 28:722–726.

Greenacre, P. (1971). Notes on the influence and contributions of ego psychology to the practice of psychoanalysis. In *Emotional Growth Psychoanalytic Studies of the Gifted and a Great Variety of Other Individuals Volume II*, pp. 776–806. New York: International Universities Press.

Greenson, R. R. (1967). *The Technique and Practice of Psychoanalysis*, Vol. I. New York: International Universities Press.

Grotjahn, M. (1972). The transference dynamics of the therapeutic group experience. In *Adolescents Grow in Groups: Experiences in Adolescent Group Psychotherapy*, ed. I. H. Berkowitz, pp. 173–178. New York: Brunner/Mazel.

Hartmann, H. (1958). *Ego Psychology and the Problem of Adaptation.* New York: International Universities Press.

Hurn, H. T. (1971). Toward a paradigm of the terminal phase: the current status of the terminal phase. *Journal of the American Psychoanalytic Association* 19:332–348.

Jacobson, E. (1954). The self and the object world: Vicissitudes of their infantile cathexes and their influence on ideational and affective development. *The Psychoanalytic Study of the Child* 9:75–127. New York: International Universities Press.

Jacobson, E. (1964). *The Self and the Object World.* New York: International Universities Press.

Katan, A. (1961). Some thoughts about the role of verbalization in early childhood. *The Psychoanalytic Study of the Child* 16:184–188. New York: International Universities Press.

Keith, C. R. (1968). The therapeutic alliance in child psychotherapy. *Journal of Child Psychiatry* 7:31–53.

Kernberg, O. F. (1976). *Object Relations Theory and Clinical Psychoanalysis.* New York: Jason Aronson.

Kohut, H. (1966). Forms and transformations of narcissism. *Journal of the American Psychoanalytic Association* 14:243–272.

——— (1968). The psychoanalytic treatment of narcissistic personality disorders. *The Psychoanalytic Study of the Child* 23:86–113. New York: International Universities Press.

——— (1971). *The Analysis of the Self.* New York: International Universities Press.

——— (1972). Thoughts on narcissism and narcissistic rage. *The Psychoanalytic Study of the Child* 27:360–400. New York: Quadrangle Books.

——— (1977). *The Restoration of the Self.* New York: International Universities Press.

Lane, B. (1980). Some vicissitudes of the therapeutic alliance in child psychotherapy. In *Psychotherapy and Training in Clinical Social Work,* ed. J. Mishne, pp. 119–134. New York: Gardner Press.

Novick, J. (1970). "The vicissitudes of the working alliance" in the analysis of a latency girl. *The Psychoanalytic Study of the Child* 25:231–256. New York: International Universities Press.

Piaget, J. (1955). *The Language and Thought of the Child.* New York: Macmillan.

Proctor, J. T. (1959). Countertransference Phenomena in the treatment of severe character disorders in children and adolescents. In: *Dynamics of Psychopathology in Childhood,* eds. L. Jessner and E. Pavenstedt. New York: Grune and Stratton.

Redl, F. (1966). Art of Group Composition. In *When We Deal with Children,* pp. 236–253. New York: Free Press.

Ritvo, S. (1974). Current status of the concept of infantile neurosis. *The Psychoanalytic Study of the Child* 29:159–182. New Haven: Yale University Press.

Sander, L. W. The development of the self: infancy research. Reflections on Self Psychology Conference, Boston, October 3, 1980.

Schwartz, W. and Zalba, S. R. (1971). *The Practice of Group Work.* New York: Columbia University Press.

Scheidlinger, S. (1968). Therapeutic approaches in community health. *Social Work* 13:87–95.

——— (1980). *Psychoanalytic Group Dynamics: Basic Readings*, New York: International University Press.

Silverman, L. H. (1978). The unconscious symbiotic fantasy as a ubiquitous therapeutic agent. *International Journal of Psychoanalytic Psychotherapy* 1:562–585.

Slavson, S. R. and Schiffer, M. (1975). *Group Psychotherapies for Children.* New York: International Universities Press.

Smally, R. (1970). The Functional Approach to Casework Practice. In *Theories of Social Casework,* eds. R. Roberts and R. Nee, pp. 79–128. Chicago: University of Chicago Press.

Stierlin, H. (1975). Countertransference in family therapy with adolescents. In *The Adolescent in Group and Family Therapy,* ed. M. Sugar, pp. 161–177. New York: Brunner/Mazel.

Stolerow, Robert D. Self psychology: Implications for psychoanalytic theory. Reflections on Self Psychology Psychoanalytic Society Meeting, Boston, November 1, 1980.

Stone, W. N. and Whitman, R. M. (1977). Contributions of the Psychology of the self to group process and group therapy. *International Journal of Group Psychology* 27 (3):343–359.

Stuart, R. (1964). Supportive casework with borderline patients. *Social Work* 9:38–44.

Tolpin, M. (1978). Self objects and oedipal objects: A crucial developmental distinction. *The Psychoanalytic Study of the Child* 33:167–184. New Haven: Yale University Press.

Yalom, I. D. (1970). *The Theory and Practice of Group Psychotherapy.* New York: Basic Books.

Zetzel, E. and Meissner, W. W. (1973). *Basic Concepts of Psychoanalytic Psychiatry.* New York: Basic Books, Inc.

PART 2
Early Intervention

Introduction: The Rationale for Early Intervention and Preventative Work with Parents

Parenthood, according to Erikson (1959), is a normal developmental phase in which biological and psychological factors play complex and interrelated roles. Benedek states that parents "live with the real child at the same time that they are fostering the intrapsychic child as a hope of their self realization" (1970, p. 125). It is difficult to imagine the presumed emotional security of the Victorian parent-child relationship given our awareness of modern parents' anxieties. We cannot enumerate all the causes of worry and anxiety that so absorb contemporary parents. Clearly, the external societal conditions, changing values, role delineation, altered patterns of employment, economics, and the pervasive breakdown of authority and traditional sources of order all contribute to our "Age of Anxiety."

It may be that certain changes in present-day society and in child-rearing practice can account for some of the problems. Thus, for example, the role played by the family organization in development, has been gradually undermined, distorted and interrupted. Many factors are of influence here. Sometimes they act in isolation; at other times they are reinforced by a number of other variables. Consider for example the significant increases in the number of broken marriages and divorces....The affluence of present-day society may be a significant subtle factor capable of influencing human development in negative directions....Similarly there has been a marked change in the attitude of many parents regarding the setting of limits and controls for their children. Many parents have gone to extremes that seem highly questionable in their wisdom. Frequently they have chosen to abandon many of their obligations and prerogatives as parents and are hesitant in setting the necessary controls and limits (Nagera 1973, pp. 49–51).

In light of this catalogue of stresses and newer, more sophisticated methods of diagnosis, it is not surprising that clinical findings show an increase in child psychopathology. Given this reality, we would underscore the values of treatment aimed at prevention, education of parents, and early intervention. The critical periods of parenthood, the earliest transactional processes between mother and infant, deserve special attention.

Whether early educative intervention in the lives of parents and children should take place is a controversial matter. Counseling non-disturbed families with procedures and theory extrapolated from treatment means, to some, reliance on a disease model when a healthy perspective is required. In actuality, many of the Ego Psychological assumptions arise from research and observations of untroubled infants and toddlers.

Another criticism of parent education comes from those worried that a scientific approach toward parenthood will destroy the natural, spontaneous relationship that should exist between parents and children. Even those dedicated to increasing the understanding of typical interactions between parents and children raise the question of whether empathy can be tutored. Benedek (1970) suggests that empathy is probably an intuitive response but, as such, can be encouraged. Empathy " ... implies also the parent's spontaneous or *well-thought-out insight* [italics ours] into motivations of the child's behavior. Only the empathic understanding of the ongoing process (between parent and child) can guide the parent's interaction with the child toward a successful end....Parents, being adults, could often help themselves and their children, if they would attempt to understand the motivation of their own responses to their children's needs and behavior" (p. 121).

RATIONALE FOR EARLY INTERVENTION

A frequently cited reason for why there is a need for early educative intervention with parents, regardless of the well-being of family members, is that today's parents are too often left alone while raising children. Rarely is an extended family present to teach beginning parents how to cope effectively. A group setting may be particularly useful for counteracting a parent's sense of isolation. Parents can share problems, issues, and feelings relative to child rearing with peers and receive guidance from the leader. For Slavson (1958) the importance of parents learning through exchanging experiences is the paramount feature of such groups.

To be effective, early preventative work with parents must supply them with psychological data on the evolving child that will enhance their parenting and the child's emotional development. Groups offer a relatively unthreatening milieu in which information can be exchanged, discussed, and integrated. What information is basic to analytically oriented parent groups? Anthony suggests that self-objects, that is archaic objects " . . .which are not experienced as separate and independent from the self, . . .are mainly need-satisfying, function performing and part-objects" (1976, p. 34). Parents need to assist children in learning to view others not as self-objects but as separate, whole objects. Children need to be helped to develop beyond the "dangerously archaic stages of objecthood. The prevention of narcissistic starvation and injury is at the core of the parenting task" (p. 35). The most important maturational phase according to Kohut (1971) is the developmental period when the beginnings of a cohesive self materialize. Anthony recommends that " . . . the greatest preventative opportunities will be in the original crystalization of the cohesive self" (1976, p. 40).

Anthony (1976) reminds us of an infrequently stressed term, self-constancy, which Mahler (1975) refers to as integral to optimal separation-individuation. Some of the identifying characteristics of self-constancy in the young child are stable moods, maintenance of play, appreciation of bodily functions, and ability to postpone refueling, all in the absence of the primary love objects. In the early years object-constancy and self-constancy are interrelated. The parents are needed to provide "extrauterine protection" against narcissistic assault for many years. Therefore, the parental self has to be considered as important a focus as the child's self in early intervention (Kliman 1976).

Information to parents about children's ego and self development might eliminate distress both in children and parents. The following vignette illustrates how a parent education group proved helpful, but one can imagine how much more helpful it would have been if parents had been alerted to the psychological issues earlier in their child's development.

A pre-adolescent child was placed in treatment for uncontrollable and unpredictable rage reactions. The therapist, concerned by the degree of narcissistic rage and the repetitiveness of the symptom, referred the child for psychological evaluation. The most significant finding was that the child had been adopted at five months after having lived happily in a foster home. The initial reaction to the new parents was two days of nonstop angry crying. We are all familiar with Spitz's (1945) descriptions of "anaclitic depression" in babies following mother's total absence. Typically, this occurs when mother's presence has been only partly internalized, yet the mothering has been satisfactory. This child did not go into a severely depressed state probably because the adoptive parents were constantly present and extremely nurturing. However, at no time were they made aware of the critical period in which they were removing the child to new surroundings. When the parents were told the importance of the adoption's timing, in an educative group setting, they were able to discuss with the child some of the child's history in a nonthreatening manner. The rage reactions eventually subsided, which substantiated the parents' group leader's view that the symptoms were linked to this crucial early experience. Parental guilt was alleviated by group support and understanding. If the adoptive agency and parents had been better informed, the situation could have been handled earlier.

The group cases in chapter two illustrate how parents can become informed, "well qualified," and "well functioning." Kliman (1976) pinpoints self-concepts that enable parents to function adequately in their roles. Healthy narcissism is exemplified by attitudes that are " . . .basically self-approving and basically self-trustful, and as a result, free of the need to project malice and feel mirrored archaic harshness of self-mocking, self-humiliating, and self-critical attitudes. During the earliest period of extrauterine life the psychological gestation process must be directed at supplying the infant, rather than using the infant mainly as a gymnasium for strengthening weak narcissistic processes" (p. 22).

REFERENCES

Anthony, J. The Self and Congenital Defects: Prevention of Emotional Disabilities. Association of Child and Adolescent.

Psychotherapists Fall Meeting, October, 1976, Chicago, Illinois.

Benedek, T. (1970). The family as a psychological field. In: *Parenthood: Its Psychology and Psychopathology,* eds. T. Benedek and E. J. Anthony, pp. 109–136. Boston: Little Brown.

Erikson, E. H. (1959). *Identity and the Life Cycle. Psychological Issues,* Monograph I. New York: International Universities Press.

Kliman, G. The self-concept: Its significance in preventative psychiatry. Association of Child and Adolescent Psychotherapists Fall Meeting. October, 1976, Chicago, Illinois.

Kohut, H. (1971). *The Analysis of the Self.* New York: International Universities Press.

——— (1971). Thoughts on narcissism and narcissistic rage. *The Psychoanalytic Study of the Child,* pp. 360–400.

Mahler, M., Pine, F., and Bergman, A. (1975). *The Psychological Birth of the Human Infant–Symbiosis and Individuation.* New York: Basic Books.

Nagera, H. (1973). Adolescence: Some diagnostic, prognostic and developmental considerations. In *Adolescent Psychiatry* pp. 44–55. New York: Basic Books.

Slavson, S. R. (1958). *Child-Centered Group Guidance of Parents.* New York: International Universities Press.

Spitz, R. A. (1945). Hospitalism: An inquiry into the genesis of psychiatric conditions in early childhood I. In *The Psychoanalytic Study of the Child* 1:53–74. New York: International Universities Press.

CHAPTER 2

The Technique of Psychoanalytically Oriented Parent Education

LAWRENCE BALTER, PH.D.

EDITORS' NOTES
Dr. Balter presents a technique of parent education that integrates traditional psychoanalytic theory with more recent psychoanalytic ideas and locates the development of the empathic parent in a group atmosphere in which acceptance, support, and insight are provided by the ego capacities and self-esteem of group members.

The psychoanalytic method was originally designed for the treatment of neurotic individuals. Gradually, psychoanalysts undertook to widen the application of the technique; modifications were introduced so that delinquents, children, and groups, could benefit from the psychoanalytic method (Aichhorn 1936, Slavson 1950). Freud (1909) himself was a pioneer in an "indirect" treatment mode for a child. The evolution of a modified psychoanalytic method for the education of parents thus has a long history (Fries 1946, Furman 1969, Jacobs 1949, Ruben 1960).

Working with small groups of parents to enhance their child-rearing skills is now popular. Psychoanalysis, as a theory of human development as well as a problem-solving technique, is a particularly well suited paradigm for work with parents. However, its application to the education of parents requires particular modifications and a measure of prudence, as the participants in the groups are not patients, and the expressed purpose is the amelioration of the developmental difficulties involved in raising essentially healthy children (Balter 1977).

As a theory of personality development, psychoanalysis provides guidelines for understanding behavior patterns, emotional concerns, and ego skills of children during various stages. Moreover, the theoretical framework suggests that there is continuity from childhood experiences to later adult personality characteristics. Helping a child to successfully navigate the many developmental stages encountered in growing up should provide some assurance that the child will perform as a competent, viable adult. Reliance on parental "intuition" for this task is insufficient for a number of reasons. The enormous success of parent aids such as magazine articles, instructional kits, radio and television programs, and countless books written by mental health workers and others bears witness to this fact.[1]

Psychoanalytically oriented parent education emphasizes the intimate connections between the emotional lives of child and parent. It promotes insight into the meaning of behavior, so that child management is enhanced by an increased awareness of underlying motivations. Furthermore, uncovering the reciprocal needs and satisfactions that constitute a major part of the parent-child system is an important aim of this dynamic approach. This objective requires a good deal of courage on the part of the parent, especially where the parent's expectations are on a par with the primitive demands of the child. The parent's ability to accept his or her primitive feelings, rather than repress them, enables constructive options to be found. Increased awareness, in turn, facilitates the acceptance of similar feelings in one's offspring.

The tactful unmasking of the children we were (and, therefore, the children we have subordinated within ourselves) is another of the tasks for discussion groups. *Grattez l'adult et vous y trouverez l'infant!* (Ferenczi 1956). Revelations of this sort are, of course, not ends in themselves but springboards for more growth-promoting, child-rearing practices. Usually, explorations of this kind evoke memories of how the adult participants were treated as children. Discussions of "discipline" problems, for instance, almost always prompt recollec-

---

[1] The many problems arising from the parent-child relationship have been the subject of lifelong work by writers such as Winnicott, Mahler, Spitz, and the Balints, to name a few.

tions of how the parents themselves had been disciplined (more often than not, this means punished). Recalling relevant past memories is an important ingredient in psychoanalytically oriented group education: hopefully, it keeps parents from blindly repeating past lessons and increases their empathic understanding of the child's perspective (Balter 1976).

Parenthood itself has been referred to as a developmental phase in human development, during which the parents' attitudes toward their child that originated in their own childhoods are " ... reanimated by the emotions of the current experience ... " (Benedek 1959). Benedek details the parent-child relation in an interesting way. She states that there is a " ... reciprocal interaction between mother and child" referred to as " ... emotional symbiosis which enables the creation of structural changes in each of the participants" (p. 392). As the child grows, he or she encounters conflicts that awaken memories of past conflicts in the parents; reworking these can bring about personality changes in the adult. Thus, an insight-directed educational procedure for parents can help to facilitate further development of the adult's personality and simultaneously promote healthful growth for the child.

Psychoanalytically oriented parent education is partly supportive, partly insight directed, and partly didactic. One of the primary goals of the parent education group is to support growth rather than to lessen pathology. Accordingly, as in any educational process, communication and continual self-examination are facilitated; psychoanalytic procedures that are employed in both individual and group work are necessarily modified for application to parent education groups. The therapist must avoid mobilizing guilt or shame in the parents as they disclose the intimate details of their interactions with their children. Furthermore, as the participants do not think of themselves as patients, a collaborative working arrangement that does not probe for the latent "problems" works best. An optimistic atmosphere that supports the accomplishments of children and the innovative practices of parents should be maintained. Techniques for conducting psychoanalytically oriented parent education groups can be organized around the following psychoanalytic concepts.

Transference refers to the attachment of feelings and attitudes to a therapist that derive from a patient's early childhood. Attitudes toward authority, for example, may unfold in the transference aspect of the patient-therapist relationship. A patient may unwittingly "test" the analyst by talking provocatively or failing to arrive on time for appointments. In psychoanalytic therapy these trends are routinely exploited in order to illuminate particular features of the patient's personality. In order to do so, therapists usually keep their personal beliefs to themselves. However, this is not a vital aspect of psychoanalytically oriented parent education groups. Without making authoritative pronouncements, the consultant may point out how particular child behaviors reflect intrapsychic struggles. Similarly, some self-disclosure on the part of the consultant may actually stimulate further exploration by lowering anxiety in the members of the group. Transference relationships to persons outside of the group such as family members or teachers, however, may be explored insofar as they relate to an issue under discussion.

Externalization is a concept that has recently been described as a subspecies of transference within the context of school consultation (Kris 1978). It also has relevance to the process of psychoanalytically oriented work with parents. Externalization differs from the phenomenon of transference in that it refers to the process of ascribing a part of an inner conflict to the person of the consultant. Externalization must be dealt with by clarifying the opposing sides of the issue rather than interpreting it as a transference reaction.

Group process—interpersonal dynamics among the group's members—is regularly analyzed in group therapy settings. In the parent group setting, it is advisable to avoid exploration of these dynamics. Emphasizing relationships among group members can have destructive consequences since the participants in parent groups do not conceive of themselves as patients. In fact, such an emphasis may be perceived as a diversion from the group's goal. An exception is a situation where the group's survival is threatened by interpersonal tensions.

Resistance and defense are central to psychoanalytic investigation. Typically a patient's resistance to self-exploration is carefully and deliberately dealt with in a number of ways. Usually the therapist attempts to make the patient aware of his or her self-protective measures by verbalizing these attempts to the patient. In parent group settings, a similar though less personal approach is advisable. A friendly, directive, comment with a light interpretive touch is helpful in returning the group to its task: "we seem to have strayed from the topic," or "I guess we're joking about it because it's actually a pretty upsetting (or serious) matter," and "sometimes this topic is a difficult one for a group to talk openly about!" On the other hand, it is beneficial to teach parents to recognize defensive measures in their children.

Abstinence in psychoanalytic terminology, refers to the method of withholding certain gratifications in the analyst–patient relationship; these can include the patient's wish to be taken care of and "cured" by the authority figure, or the desire for praise and encouragement. Abstinence encourages tolerance of frustration which, in turn, enhances problem-solving abilities. However, since the parents' goal is to improve techniques for child management, suggestions and common experiences are naturally shared among the group's members. Therapists are cautioned here to time any advice-giving so as to not impede the uncovering of underlying thoughts and feelings. The therapist's use of silence to heighten tension, thereby promoting further exploration, should be used sparingly, if at all, in parent education groups. Silence for the purpose of thoughtful deliberation and introspection is always desirable, but using it to increase anxiety may have a degenerating effect on this type of motivated, task-oriented group. Of course, if silence occurs among group members, its meaning must be ascertained and managed accordingly.

With regard to the mechanical issues concerning arrangements for discussion groups, experience suggests numerous viable variations. While volunteers are generally better participants, it should not be assumed that assigned participants (as in certain mental health facilities) present insuperable problems. Compulsory attendance by no means dooms a group to failure, but the obligatory nature of the membership should become part of the group's work. The frequency of sessions may be decided upon jointly unless dictated by practical constraints such as the consultant's availability to the facility. Continuity does not appear to be damaged even by meetings held twice a month. Time between discussions can be used to try out techniques discussed. Consensus, or perhaps ritual, has set the average length of a session at somewhere between one and two hours. Ten members per group is probably optimal, but here too, various contingencies must be accounted for. The tenure of the meetings may be prearranged or assessed periodically. In school settings, for example, it is often convenient to make arrangements on a semester basis.

In conclusion, it might be useful to refer to the notion of "the parental imperative" which suggests that "as individuals we are all finally part of a species, products of evolutionary sequences that long predate our individuality and our particular social situation" (Guttman 1973, p. 62). Furthermore, we are all "to a greater or lesser degree the agents of a species purpose, which is the raising of viable children —children who can in their turn rear viable children" (p. 63).

If insight directed parent training is to be an effective means of improving child-rearing practices, continuous attempts must be made to codify the most suitable procedures. Optimally, the techniques should be derived from an organized body of knowledge such as psychoanalytic theory, and should withstand the test of experience.

REFERENCES

Aichhorn, A. (1936). *Wayward Youth.* London: Putnam.

Balter, L. (1976). Psychological consultation for pre-school parent groups. *Children Today* 5:19–22.

——— (1977). Parent education and the school psychologist. *International Encyclopedia of Neurology, Psychoanalysis, Psychology, and Psychiatry,* ed. B. Wolman. Volume 8, pp. 194–196. Cincinnati, Ohio: Van Nostrand and Reinhold.

Benedek, T. (1959). Parenthood as a developmental phase. *Journal of the American Psychoanalytic Association* 7:389–417.

Ferenczi, S. (1956). Introjection and transference. In *Sex in Psychoanalysis.* New York: Dover.

Freud, S. (1909). Analysis of a phobia in a five-year-old boy. *Standard Edition* 10:1–148.

Fries, M. (1946). The child's ego development and the training of adults in his environment. *The Psychoanalytic Study of the Child* 2:85–112.

Furman, E. (1969). Treatment via the mother. In *The Therapeutic Nursery School,* eds. E. Furman and A. Katan. New York: International Universities Press.

Guttman, D. (1973). Men, women, and the parental imperative. *Commentary.* 56:59–64.

Jacobs, L. (1949). Methods used in the education of the mother: A contribution to the handling and treatment of developmental difficulties in children under five years of age. *The Psychoanalytic Study of the Child* 3/4:409–422.

Kris, K. (1978). The school consultant as an object for externalization. *The Psychoanalytic Study of the Child* 33:641–651.

Ruben, M. (1960). *Parent Guidance in the Nursery School.* New York: International Universities Press.

Slavson, S. R. (1950). *Analytic Group Psychotherapy.* New York: Columbia University Press.

EDITORS' DISCUSSION

GROUP COMPOSITION AND POPULATION. Parents, not patients, are the participants in these groups. There is no outline of how or where to organize such groups, though school settings are mentioned. Balter does say that volunteer membership is more desirable, but "compulsory attendance by no means dooms a group to failure." Ten is considered an optimal number of members, with room for flexibility according to circumstances.

SETTING AND PURPOSE. Time and place for meetings can be determined by the group or by factors such as availability of the consultant. As few as two sessions a month are enough to maintain continuity, if the intervening time is used to put suggestions made to parents into practice. Meetings last from one to two hours.

The major goal is to encourage parental insight into children's behavior. Balter gives special recognition to the courage of parents who are able to pursue their own primitive feelings in an attempt to understand those of their children.

LEVEL OF INTERVENTION AND STANCE OF THE WORKER. Clinicians support development rather than the removal of pathology; they are supportive, partly insight directed, and didactic. Balter believes in a modification of analytic individual and group technique. The developmental psychoanalytic theories remain intact, and modifications are only with regard to practice principles.

GROUP PROCESS. Balter refers to process as interpersonal dynamics. He does not believe in exploring those tensions in a parent education group unless they undermine the group's survival. Abstinence is not used to further development; advice giving is the norm. Removing parental guilt and anxiety improves child management. This is typically true for mature parents. When dealing with less well-functioning groups, enabling individuals to tolerate guilt and anxiety may be a primary goal.

GROUP DYNAMICS. Balter makes specific comments on the role of transference and resistance in parents' groups. Interpretations are minimal and intended to help the group progress rather than uncover material. The therapist's self-disclosure can be an effective means of reducing anxiety.

GENERAL CONSIDERATIONS. In contrast to the paper by Weissburger, in which she takes a strictly educational, Ego Psychology perspective, Balter's delineation of parent education groups adheres to more experiential, traditional, psychoanalytic descriptions of technique. Nevertheless, his reliance on Ego Psychology theory is apparent in his orientation as well as his references. To elaborate on Balter's focus on the defense of externalization: when conflict is seen by patients as emanating from the consultant, his approach sounds similar to the Kleinian idea of projective identification that some ego and self psychologists have adopted. In this process the "bad" part of oneself is unconsciously cast off into the other person. Then the "bad" part is located in the other person rather than in oneself. The use of Kohutian theory is implicit in the unconditional positive regard Balter shows toward struggling parents.

The techniques in Balter's paper provide a helpful foundation for implementing this type of group work. It is worth noting, too, that Balter addresses his comments to parents without signifying gender. Especially in today's society, there is a great need for fathers as well as mothers to participate in educative groups.

CHAPTER 3

Early Interventive Work with New Mothers
FAY SHUTZER, M.A.

EDITORS' NOTES
An educative group for postnatal mothers is an appropriate setting for applying principles of Ego and Self Psychology. Typically these are groups available to expectant parents or parents of older children. Shutzer's paper exposes all the uncertainties of leader-member interactions. The link between actual content and methods of group technique is so clearly spelled out that the reader will easily discern where these techniques are congruent with Ego and Self Psychology.

The postpartum period for mothers may be characterized by uncertainty, "baby-blues," and loneliness. The postpartum period as discussed is the one that immediately follows delivery. We are *not* referring to postpartum depressed mothers. There are few resources for parents who need support during the early trying months of child rearing. This paper describes one group conducted for postpartum mothers.

ORGANIZATION

Organizing a group of new mothers is a difficult task: some postpartum mothers are too disturbed for group treatment; and in many cases hospitals are not free to recommend patients. Numerous institutions and hospitals including the Maternity Center, La Leche League, and Lamaze teachers were consulted in the effort to contact potential group participants. An officer of the American Society for Psycho-Prophylaxis in Obstetrics (ASPO) made available a list of Lamaze teachers who later helped to organize the group. The group provided a forum for participants to share life styles, and feelings about motherhood.

This promoted a better understanding of the emotional changes experienced by the postpartum women and showed participants that their feelings were shared by others. One of the group's main objectives was to provide referrals for participants needing more individualized treatment.

ADVANTAGES OF THE GROUP SETTING

The first few months of motherhood are often isolating. Meeting with women who are undergoing similar experiences can dispel that feeling of isolation; by sharing ideas, feelings, and problems, each woman gains insight into her own role as a mother.

Although the mothers could receive support in an individual setting, the possibility for mutual sharing and learning would be reduced. While most mothers do not seek structural change, they are likely to benefit more from the different types of support offered by a group setting than from an individual treatment approach.

Finally, though women differ in their child-rearing approaches, group members gain an understanding of the emotional and physical changes each woman is experiencing, and this offers individuals the opportunity for individual growth. These three outcomes, support, understanding, and growth, are all possible in a group setting (Berkovitz 1975).

THE LEADER'S ROLE

In order to understand the mechanics of a group (Glass 1969), the leader's influence on the group must be examined closely. Leaders must be as objective as possible when examining their influence, both positive and negative, on the group. Nevertheless, self-criticism is a difficult task.

Although the leadership in this group was essentially nondirective, there were times when control was assumed. Early sessions required guidance and control in order to establish group cohesiveness. Since new members joined until the fourth session, the position of the leader as "organizer" lasted longer than intended. As the group developed, the leader's influence was needed when the group became anxious.

The group's autonomy was lessened on the occasions when members were instructed in a group exercise or assigned questions to think about during the week. At these times, the leader was often challenged by the group. Three factors may have been responsible for this testing: (1) the group may have felt comfortable enough with the leadership to challenge it (Glass 1969); or (2) the group may have been reacting negatively to what seemed a change in the leader's style from less to more structure; or (3) the membership may have felt in a dependent position when given assignments.

It is possible that some of the group members often felt a need for stronger leadership. Early attempts to involve the group in defining their goals were not as successful as might be expected in an adult group. At that stage in the group's development they may have felt a need for greater direction. This fluctuation between dependency and autonomy is not unusual in short-term work. Levels of development among participants in an educative group differ, and members exhibit varying degrees of mastery over their internal conflicts. The leader needs to recognize these differences and allow for the development of different degrees of attachment. Moreover, selectively presenting participants with psychological hurdles to surmount offers members possibilities for ego growth. If group members are encouraged to support each other, they may act as auxiliary leaders. Attention directed toward a number of individuals rather than just one does not necessarily diminish involvement in each individual's case.

WEEK #1 — INTRODUCTORY PHASE

The first meeting of the group was characterized by much tension and anxiety. Individuals were concerned with gaining acceptance from other group members. These feelings are to be expected in the beginning of a new group and should be viewed as a necessary catalyst for change (Dinkmeyer 1971).

With the convening of members, the group entered into the Introductory Phase (Glass 1969), also known as the Inclusion Phase (Fried 1971). The group began by assessing the rationale for the group's organization and the membership goals. Members introduced themselves to each other by describing whatever they felt the others should know about their pregnancy and delivery experiences. In this early phase of the group's existence, which Fried (1971) compares to the stage in human development characterized by narcissism and symbiosis, group members generally spoke directly to the leader, rather than to each other. At first, conversation did not flow easily, and often it was necessary for the leader to promote discussion by asking specific questions. Freud (Anthony 1971) points out that the need for dominant leadership lessens as the members develop into a group and the group becomes more cohesive. This phenomenon was apparent as the members began questioning one another more spontaneously and speaking less directly to the leader.

In discussing the nature of the beginning group, Freud (1922) refers to five conditions, based on McDougall, for promoting a collective mental experience. They are continuity, awareness of goals, similarity, customs and habits, and definite functions. In the group for postpartum mothers, (1) some degree of continuity was established after the first group meeting as seven more meetings were scheduled to follow; (2) the individual members became aware of the nature and goals of the group; (3) the group members had been in Lamaze classes— somewhat similar in nature to this group; (4) the group began to establish customs and habits such as the place and time of meeting, and preferred seats; and (5) the group members began to have definite functions and roles that differentiated them from each other.

Roles as described by Newman (1974) began to evolve in the first session. One person, Karen, became both the "pathetic needy one" and the "monopolizer," taking up much of the time with a nonstop personal monologue. Her neediness was expressed in the topics she wished to pursue, namely, her perception that the baby gets all the attention, while the mother is deprived of love. By the conclusion of the session, the leader determined that Karen needed a therapeutic referral and could benefit little from an educational approach.

Another type suggested by Newman (1974), apparent in this group, is the "doctor" who actively avoids being a "helpless one or patient." This individual is usually independent and offers precise, pat answers and "cures." In this group, the role seemed to be taken by Linda who needed to prevent the others from looking too closely at her own vulnerability.

WEEKS #2 AND 3 — POWER PHASE

During the second and third weeks, new members were added; while they were in the Introductory Phase, the rest of the group began to move into the stage of Resistance (Glass 1969) where they struggled, challenging the leadership. Linda showed her autonomy, a characteristic sign of this stage (Fried 1971), by answering questions for the entire group that previously had been answered by the leader. Another, Diana, questioned the reasons for initiating the group, testing the validity of the leader's role. A new member, Maureen, still at the Inclusion Phase, struggled with her desire for acceptance and belonging. Although the group was quite ready to accept her, she kept her distance, using the mechanism of flight, by maintaining that she would not be able to come all the time. Initial dependence on the leader, a sign of the Inclusion Phase, was evident in the other new member, Carol, who was concerned with breastfeeding. She directed all comments and questions to the leader, ignoring members.

The process of transference, though less important than in a non-therapy group, was evident. Fried (1971) describes the early signs of transference as a desire for acceptance. Defenses against transference at this stage often take the form of timidity, submission, or placation. Signs of early transference were apparent in both new members' behavior. Both expressed their desire for acceptance through submissiveness. Fried (1971) describes later signs of transference as competition with and challenge of the leader, though she notes that these behaviors are often masked by defenses.

Members' roles can be expected to alter when the group undertakes new tasks (Newman 1974). For example, Maureen took several roles, ranging from the "oh-so-sorry one," apologizing for taking up the group's time, to the "outsider," continually emphasizing that her membership might not continue. However, her predominant role was as the "helpless, needy one." Another member, Linda, had become the "competitor," consistently disagreeing with the leader's support of breastfeeding.

Although discussions often included anxiety provoking material, issues that the group was not yet ready to handle were specifically avoided. Members exhibited a pattern of asking nonthreatening questions that masked more anxiety laden areas. For example, Diana's concern with finding the time to get things done, seemed to translate into the more profound fear that she no longer had a life of her own. She could not admit that she sometimes wished the baby were not around until others expressed similar feelings. Another member avoided initiating discussions of her breastfeeding problems for many weeks. It was not until she was questioned directly that she poured out her feelings and confusion.

Topics of concern gradually were articulated: everyone seemed anxious about milk supply and the ability to breastfeed; a more pervasive anxiety seemed to be a fear of postpartum depression, and if and when it would hit. The group seemed to be relieved when told why the member who had dominated the first meeting had not returned. Her presence the first evening had been unsettling for the group and heightened their concern about depressions. They felt relief that she had decided that the group was inappropriate for her and hoped she would seek help.

WEEKS #4–7 — PRODUCTIVE PHASE

Although the group did not enter the Productive Phase (Glass 1969) at the fourth session per se, it seemed that members had reached a level of intimacy at which they found they were able to both give and take (Fried 1971). There were signs of the Productive Phase in earlier meetings (and regression to earlier phases in later ones). Being able to accept Adrienne, a new member, warmly indicated the degree to which the group had progressed. In contrast, members of the same ongoing Lamaze class had greeted each other coolly in this setting the first night (week #1). The group's cohesiveness enabled them to greet a new person with trust and affection.

For Adrienne, the entry was not easy. She came to the group with mistrust and anxiety. While the group had progressed to the Productive Phase, she was going through the Introductory and Resistance Phases. In the seventh session, she still felt the need to challenge both the leader and other group members. Perhaps because she was unable to quite catch up, she became somewhat of a scapegoat (particularly in the final session when she was absent), though she seemed to choose this role for herself by differing with the group on most issues. The group itself did not isolate her, yet group opinion frequently sided against her.

At the Productive Phase in group development, it seems appropriate to examine the mechanisms that affect group change. The potential for these particular mechanisms as described by Dinkmeyer (1971) hopefully exists in each group; however, they do not automatically occur. The first group mechanism, acceptance, is based on respect for the opinions and feelings of others.

The mechanism of ventilation requires an accepting atmosphere. Group members frequently tend to hold back, revealing their problems and fears only after being questioned. For instance, Carol alluded to the time when she cried all night, but had difficulty talking openly about it. Another member could never bring up breastfeeding problems without first being questioned. For Adrienne everything was fine—the "baby blues" were nothing serious, and everyone had them.

Intellectualization and feedback as a mechanism for learning strongly influences the development of an educational group. The leader's support of intellectualization was employed throughout, as the members verbalized particular problems and feelings. Reality testing, another group mechanism, fosters the development of empathy and altruism in educative groups. In this case, mothers were reassured that their experiences were normal and common to others.

WEEK #8 — TERMINATION

Prior to the final session, it was anticipated that certain phenomena would occur. Predictable circumstances include (1) the absence of members at the final session who cannot deal with the separation; (2) pressure on the leader to continue the group or talk among members concerning how they might get together; (3) members becoming depressed in an unconscious attempt to make the leader feel guilty for abandoning them.

To some degree, several of the above phenomena occurred in this group. After we carefully selected a meeting time convenient to Adrienne, she cancelled for reasons that could have been circumvented. This suggests that she may have felt too much anxiety in separation. She had relied on denial previously as a defense mechanism ("I feel guilty being here—my baby's so good," "I think there is too much emphasis on the postpartum experience") and now seemed to be using flight as well. The desire to continue the group was strongly manifest in the final session. In a cancellation phone call, a member asked for a future meeting though the unspecified nature of "in a few months" may have been her way of distancing that desire. One member, particularly reluctant to end, offered her apartment for continuation. She settled for a reunion meeting in February. Finally, the group accepted termination, reviewing the group experience, the reasons for its existence, and the positive effects that may have resulted.

Other dynamics were also present in termination: group members talked about the group, its structure, and its past and present members. This approach enabled the group members to cope with the pain of losing the group (Yalom 1970). The leader who is prepared for the sentimentality and the desire to continue, can remain firm in handling the termination, thus enabling group members to better handle the separation themselves. The tenderness and affection that were evident in this session indicated the degree of mutuality and shared learning that had evolved in the group (Fried 1971).

Group Log

WEEK #1 — FIRST MEETING

MEMBERS PRESENT. Lee, Karen, Diana, Linda

CANCELLATIONS. Adrienne—called to say stitches too painful and will join later. Bonnie—husband called. Baby too cranky, so won't come this week. Maureen—did not call. When I phoned her after the meeting, her husband said she was asleep.

Lee and Linda arrived a few minutes late. They both recognized each other from their Lamaze class as they had the same teacher. They compared notes on births, babies, and so forth while waiting for other members to arrive. Karen came at 7:45 and Diana at 7:50. I was nervous about the late arrivals and decided not to wait any longer for Maureen. I began by asking everyone to introduce herself and tell a little bit about her baby and birth experience. Karen, seated on my left, began first. She said that her name was *now* Karen D. because she had had such a horrible three weeks after her baby was born in May that it resulted in divorce from her husband. She spoke rapidly and seemed tense. Lee was next (it appeared that they were taking turns in order of seating). She explained that her birth experience had been a positive one. Her baby, a girl born ten days earlier, was very good and easy to care for. Lee added that she had help from her own mother during the day, and that she was enjoying the motherhood experience thus far. Linda introduced herself next. She spoke perfunctorily, saying that she was a nurse and had had a very easy labor and delivery at the hospital where she worked.

Diana, seeing that Linda seemed to be finished speaking, began speaking in a soft and trembling voice. She said that all had gone well during the birth of her daughter and that she had left the hospital after the first twenty-four hours, but that she was having problems breastfeeding. When questioned by the others, she explained that she had both sore nipples and mastitis, perhaps because the baby did not suck long enough. The cures for the two different problems were opposite in nature and Diana was having difficulty clearing up either problem. This information was provoked by the questioning of the group members. Members were concerned about Diana's problem and how she might resolve it. She seemed to blame the baby's lack of interest in sucking, but at the same time she described the baby as being interested in pacifiers and bottle nipples—thus blaming herself as well. A few predictable suggestions were made; nevertheless, Diana seemed to be relieved to have brought up the problem.

A lull in the conversation resulted once everyone had fulfilled my request. I then asked the group to think about what they would like to cover in these sessions, adding that I had plenty of topics of my own, but that I'd rather talk about things that were important to them. Karen mentioned several problems that she wanted to talk about: her feeling that the baby gets all the attention and the mother is put in second place; handling strangers in the street who tell you what to do; and the feeling of being left out and needing love yourself. She also wanted to know about jaundice, since her baby had it at birth. Here Linda was helpful in explaining to the entire group that jaundice was common among newborns. By explaining how it happened she was able to put the problem in perspective and allay a few fears. Lee said she'd like to talk about how to involve her husband more, but defensively added that otherwise things were good. Linda and Diana said that they didn't have anything specific that they wanted to talk about, but that maybe later they'd like to approach the topic of going back to work.

Diana then asked Karen if she had received any help when she first brought the baby home. Karen did not respond directly to the question, but unleashed a long story about her own family, her mother-in-law, apartments, etcetera. She rambled somewhat and was not always clear, but the structure of her story became evident. On the night that her baby was born, her father-in-law had died. Her husband took his father's death very badly, even though his father had been sick for some time. Karen never saw her husband while she was in the hospital. He lavished love and affection on the baby, but he didn't seem to care about either her or his mother. Because her husband had beaten her up several times during the next few weeks, she left him. She claimed that he wanted her to come back but that she had refused. They had since been legally separated, though her husband's family had not been told.

Intertwined with the story, Karen alluded to her mother-in-law's instability and described her as schizophrenic. Karen's story was a lengthy outpouring, during which the rest of the group sat silently and seemed somewhat in shock. I waited for a chance to interrupt and change the flow of the conversation without cutting Karen off totally, but found it difficult to do so. At the conclusion Karen apologized for taking so much time but said she felt much better for it.

At about 8:30 Diana said that she had to leave right on time. I agreed that everyone had responsibilities and probably needed to leave on time. I said I regretted that we had started off so late. Karen asked the others if they were feeling depression. (Big things at the last minute?) Trying for closure and to alleviate the tension of those who had undergone a positive experience, I said that the postpartum experience took many forms and that one doesn't have to experience a real depression. I added that there are lots of changes going on from week to week, and even those who experience no depression at all find that there is some adjustment to be made to a new way of life.

WEEK #8 — LAST MEETING

MEMBERS PRESENT. Lee, Diana, Carol

CANCELLATIONS. Adrienne—called to cancel because some repairmen were coming, and she had to be there to let them in. She asked about the possibility of a reunion group in about three months, and she said to tell everyone she was sorry not to be there. Lee and Diana arrived first, both with their babies—and, to my surprise, five minutes early. Carol arrived with Timmy just on time. Diana brought me a gift—a lithograph her husband was printing—and I thanked her and told her I was going to have it framed.

Carol asked about a conference I had attended and I related to them my experience and impressions. One of the speakers, an obstetrician, talked about her feeling that women were neglected in the hospital after the baby was born. When I mentioned this to the group, it sparked a conversation about length of stay in the hospital. Carol felt she needed those few days to relax and recover, whereas Diana, who had only stayed for twenty four hours in the hospital, felt the traditional stay was too long. We discussed the trend toward having mothers spend less time in the hospital, which developed during World War II when the beds were needed, and maternity patients were sent home sooner than their usual 10-day stay. I pointed out that at that time women were given some childcare training while in the hospital, but owing to the abbreviated stays now, this training was no longer possible. I described the doctor's feeling about the six week check-up and told the group that she felt this visit was needed sooner and that the doctor should give the patient an opportunity to discuss at length the choices of birth control. She also felt six weeks was an unnecessarily long period to prevent the postpartum mother from returning to sexual activity. Diana said that her doctor told her as she left the hospital that whenever she felt like having intercourse she could begin. Lee said her doctor saw her at three and six weeks postpartum, and then again, at three months, so she felt she did not suffer from neglect.

I was asked if the director of Lamaze spoke, and I told them that she was Master of Ceremonies. I mentioned her parent workshops and displayed a handout that I'd been given, describing the workshops as "preventative family therapy." I then described our group as an early form of a parent workshop. I thought everyone was very detached in this discussion of parent workshops.

Diana talked about the group, saying she wished it could continue, though she felt it might be difficult for me as the leader to schedule it, and she even volunteered her apartment, if I wanted to meet there. I said they should all keep close contact with each other. Diana said she would definitely like to have a reunion group (I had previously delivered Adrienne's message, including her wish to get together again in a few months). Diana mentioned that she had seen Pat and told Pat that she would have liked to meet with her after the baby's birth, rather than see the doctor at six weeks. We talked about the value of reunion groups (reunion of Lamaze classes) and Carol said she had one, but she hadn't gone. She added that she wondered why she had not attended.

At this point I was sensing that Diana felt the need for the group to continue and was having problems separating. She said she had learned a great deal from the group. Then she said she would have liked Pat to have had a reunion group. I commented that I was sorry Adrienne was not with us because she might be able to answer whether or not she would have preferred a group led by a nurse or doctor at the early stages. I talked about Linda's presence being very helpful with health-related questions. Carol said she felt that there was a cultural difference for Adrienne and that the French did not share Americans' concerns about feelings. Diana added that Adrienne had not come to all the sessions.

Carol asked me what I had learned from the group. I said I had learned quite a lot about running a group and being a leader. I explained that, as an adult, when one leads a children's group, one is automatically the leader. I said I thought our group was a quiet one and that I had been able to be a part of the group as a nondirective leader most of the time. I also said that the group had convinced me that I would like to continue working with new mothers because their experiences and questions interested me. I felt that I had learned how these meetings helped the mothers and their babies.

We then talked about the timing of our group. Everyone felt it was good to have started early, and Diana said she liked having the ages of the babies close together. I said that I had learned for my next group to stress at the outset that the members need not anticipate depression. Then I mentioned Karen, who had felt she didn't belong. Someone asked about Linda, and I explained again why she had not come back. Diana said Karen really didn't belong, because her baby was so much older. I also mentioned that it was difficult for her since she had had such an unhappy situation. Diana commented that as a leader I was very sensitive to the needs and feelings of the individuals in the group, which every leader might not have been.

I raised a question from last session about why each of them had chosen to have a baby. Diana said she had thought about it and decided that it was part of her relationship with her husband. She just wanted his baby, and they both felt it would fill out their relationship. Lee said she wanted to go through everything her body could do, and Carol said she wanted that experience too. I asked if we (as women) were still influenced by society—that to be a success one must bear a child. They did not agree. Diana said she had friends who had decided not to have children.

At this point Carol was bouncing Timmy around, and Lee and Diana both commented that he looked like a real boy. Diana asked Carol if she was conscious of his being a boy. Diana said she was much more gentle with her baby. Carol said that she was very aware that he was a boy and probably did treat him differently. I mentioned the study where women who were mothers of girls tend to talk to their babies much more, and mothers of boys tend to cuddle them more.

Since it was time to go, and I sensed some anxiety, I set a reunion date for February. I sensed some relief after that. Everyone got up to leave, slowly dressing their babies, talking, and prolonging the departure. I felt a warm feeling when everyone said good-bye, and they all left together.

REFERENCES

Anthony, E. J. (1971). The history of group psychotherapy. In *Comprehensive Group Psychotherapy*, eds. H. Kaplan and B. Sadock, pp. 4–31. Baltimore: Williams and Wilkins.

Berkovitz, I. H. (1975). Caring and the relevance of small groups in secondary schools, but with a caution. In *When Schools Care*, ed. I. H. Berkovitz, pp. 3–8. New York: Brunner/Mazel.

Dinkmeyer, D. C. (1971). Therapeutic forces in the group. In *Group Counseling: Theory and Practice*, eds. D. C. Dinkmeyer and J. J. Muro. Itasca, Illinois: Peacock Publishers.

Fried, E. (1971). Basic concepts in group psychotherapy. In *Comprehensive Group Psychotherapy*, eds. H. Kaplan and B. Sadock, pp. 47–71. Baltimore: Williams and Wilkins.

Glass, S. D. (1969). *The Practical Handbook of Group Counseling*. Baltimore: BCS Publishing.

Newman, R. G. (1974). *Groups in School.* New York: Simon and Schuster.

Yalom, I. D. (1970). *The Theory and Practice of Group Psychotherapy.* New York: Basic Books.

EDITORS' DISCUSSION

COMPOSITION AND POPULATION. Postnatal mothers were solicited through phone calls upon the recommendation of obstetrical organizations. The women, for the most part, were typical of a healthy population, and, except in one instance, asymptomatic. That mother was referred out for individual therapy. No formal assessments were made.

SETTING AND PURPOSE. The group was run under supervision as part of an academic course assignment for the graduate student leader. The meetings were held in a home where the atmosphere was personal and informal. From the outset, members were told the length of time for sessions and the number of sessions.

LEVEL OF INTERVENTION AND STANCE OF WORKER. The framework for the group was educative. The leader was at a beginning level in terms of group experience and skill. In addition to her clinical course work, the leader drew from the events in her own life, having had a child, being a new parent, in order to demonstrate empathy with members' feelings and attitudes. From Shutzer's comments, it is clear that she was relatively nondirective, kept deliberately to manifest issues, and gave advice cautiously. The challenging behavior of some group members may have been evoked by Shutzer's fluctuation between directiveness and nondirectiveness.

GROUP PROCESS. Techniques employed encouraged mutuality, acceptance, and ventilation. Group attendance and cohesion were difficult to obtain. Shutzer encouraged group interrelation and tried to minimize her position as an authority figure.

GROUP DYNAMICS. The leader, though alert to some of the issues of resistance and transference, purposefully did not deal with them, and maintained her stance as a catalyst and the object for selective identification. Shutzer capitalized on her own successful navigation of the early postnatal phase. Although denial was manifested by members, she did not interpret their defensive style. Interpersonal issues were given an educational emphasis.

Benedek and Anthony (1970) and Mahler, Pine, and Bergman (1975) have focused on the mother-child dyad not only in terms of the child's development, but also from the point of view of the mother's ego development. They stress that involvement with the needs of babies revives in a mother feelings stemming from her earliest experiences in infancy and childhood. The success of the mother's passage through her symbiotic period influences her reactions to the symbiotic position of the child. At its best, the mother-child relationship evokes a pleasant memory of a former symbiotic union. The mother is then able to reciprocate by giving her child the necessary warmth and protection. If the mothers in an educative group have experienced basic satisfactory ties with their caretakers during their first two years of life and are not suffering disappointments from a lack of positive, complimentary experiences with their own mothers, then only minor reparative work is necessary. This is accomplished as parents feel some of their dependency needs being met through group support. The person in Shutzer's group referred to as "the monopolizer" was not just in need of attention but was obviously suffering from earlier, unfulfilled dependency needs.

It is not surprising that one of the members of this group could not benefit from group mutuality. Typically, when people are selected for educative groups the important initial screening phase does not take place, though this aspect of group practice is as critical for this method of intervention as for any other. Still the feelings of the depressed group member were handled tactfully when the suggestion was made to her to receive individual treatment.

Many beginning groups function unevenly. Here there was some difficulty in maintaining a topic and exploring themes with some depth. Strong transference reactions were apparent in members' reactions to the time limits established for the group. One member showed her unresolved ambivalence, a probable reaction toward significant others from the past, by expressing her desire to attend a last meeting yet being unable to do so. The need for acceptance and attachment, described in this paper as transference, which could have partial roots in earlier object relations, was probably related in actuality to conscious attempts to form a working alliance. Another factor influencing group behavior was the members' resistance toward becoming involved. In part, this may have resulted from the knowledge that the group was to be of short duration. When dependency needs are strong, as they were here, and long-term gratification of those needs is ruled out, as it had to be in such a short-term group, deeper commitment may be withheld. The only two members with consistent attendance had formed a personal friendship. Shutzer's depiction of educative group process is especially valuable insofar as she describes exchanges between members and leader.

Anthony, James. (1970). The reaction of parents to adolescents and to their behavior. In *Parenthood, Its Psychology and Psychopathology*, eds. J. Anthony and T. Benedek. Boston: Little Brown.

Mahler, M., Pine, F., and Bergman, A. (1975). *Psychological Birth of the Human Infant–Symbiosis and Individuation*. New York: Basic Books.

CHAPTER 4

Mother Guidance Groups—An Aid in the Ego Development of Pre-School Children
ELEANOR WEISBERGER, M.S.W.

EDITORS' NOTES
This chapter focuses on nonworking mothers from intact, middle-class families. Parenthood is viewed as a developmental phase. Weisberger is most interested in exploring motherhood within the framework of the child's point of view. She perceives child development as an ongoing struggle between ego, id and superego, and the parent's role as being supportive to the developing ego of the child. Further details of the author's experiences can be found in *Your Young Child and You*, Dutton, NY, 1975.

Some years ago, as a social worker in the Child Psychiatry Clinic, University Hospital, Cleveland, Ohio, this author was impressed by the help parents were given by professionals from a variety of disciplines. The major work of guiding parents at that time was done by social workers and social work students, though both child psychiatrists and psychologists also participated. The clinic was organized around principles derived from the child guidance movement; its approach was interdisciplinary; its primary focus was on the child. As was true of other clinics then, social workers' efforts concentrated on the task of helping parents help their children. Psychologists' efforts focused primarily on helping the child directly.

Skillful group support for parents was recognized even then as an essential element in helping children. For the pre-schooler, work with the parents is especially important for, to a large extent, parents are the environment. Theory underlying group work with parents of pre-schoolers is predicated on certain developmental assumptions common to the field of child development. Phases such as the oral, anal, phallic, and genital are seen as developmental sequences that overlap and influence succeeding phases. The child younger than five needs the help of his or her parents (or those taking on parental responsibilities), to master these powerful, instinctual impulses.

Since the ego of the very young child is relatively unstructured, and the self is still crystalizing, the help adults provide children in handling primitive feelings and impulses is of great importance. The manner in which such basic issues as toilet training, separation, sibling rivalry, discipline, and sex education are handled have a significant impact on the development of the young child's emerging ego.

Since the beginning of the child guidance movement in the twenties, parents have found themselves on the receiving end of limitless and conflicting advice. This has been a mixed blessing; the advice has frequently contained partial truths; elementary solutions to complex issues have been proposed. Today there is a wealth of conflicting "how-to" advice from professionals, books, magazines, and television. This has put parents in the unenviable position of not knowing who to believe or how to approach a given problem.

I wanted to work with groups of mothers to see if they could support each other and address common issues in a group setting. Mothers of pre-schoolers were chosen in light of professional information acknowledging the significant development which takes place in the early years. Mothers rather than fathers were invited because they were able to attend meetings held during the day. The purpose was to evaluate the influence of socio-cultural factors on normal parents and to observe, however crudely, what pressures children under five exert on their parents. Pediatricians were asked to refer mothers. No screenings were done. The first ten mothers who applied were accepted.

Since that time, several hundred mothers have participated in these informal weekly sessions. Now, almost without exception they are referred by friends. In effect, a grapevine of mothers has been established. Although a physician occasionally will refer a mother, membership, for the most part, has relied on word of mouth.

Most of the mothers in these groups were in their 20s and early 30s, college-educated, and dedicated to the raising of their children. Careers had been set aside despite the pressure of the times to have women return to work and school. They did not seem to question their decision to remain at home. They were a self-selected group of women who attended meetings voluntarily. "How to help the children grow up, not just grow" was one mother's explanation for her presence at the first meeting. Implicit in that remark was the recognition of children's need for guidance if they are to achieve maturity.

The goal of the first meetings was to learn directly from the mothers which issues concerned them most. In educational terms, the function of the group was to help parents help the child and to promote parents' primary role as educators of the young. Answers to direct questions and recommendations were related to developmental theory. At no time did therapeutic goals usurp the primary educational task. In the instances where the mothers' emotional difficulties interfered, referrals were made to other professionals.

Surprisingly, everyone was having some degree of difficulty in child rearing. The nonjudgmental tone in the group undoubtedly contributed to the freedom with which the parents chose to discuss their most pressing problems. It was apparent to all that confusion about normal development contributed to mothers' feelings of inadequacy. This confusion was true both of mothers who had read a lot about child rearing and of those who had read little or nothing. An underlying theme, heard again and again, was "If I were handling my child better, this would not be happening." Clearly something was amiss if so many parents burdened themselves with constant self-criticism. The mothers in every group appeared to have an almost overwhelming sense of responsibility for their children's behavior and seemed not to know when, if ever, the children should be held accountable.

It was as though the child were a blank slate, and the parents' handling was solely responsible for the child's behavior. They seemed to feel that their child's conduct put them on public trial. They thought that other households were better run, more serene, more tranquil, and only they suffered from suppertime squabbles, messy pants, and sibling rivalry. These young mothers had been led to expect that children evoke the best in parents; the fact that they also evoke the worst was apparently the best kept secret in the United States.

Many of the mothers appeared to be paying a price for their sophistication. Since they knew the early years were important to their children's future stability, they were often prevented from acting by their fear of making mistakes. It seemed that previous generations of parents, if often misguided, had been more sure of themselves. They appeared to have little difficulty in handling authority. If children experienced emotional stress in their adult years, parents in these earlier years did not appear to feel responsible. This is not meant to suggest that the old way was better; yet it was certainly easier.

Many of the mothers in the groups operated under assumptions they presumed to be scientific. Many seemed to share what this author labelled the "understanding fallacy"; in other words, if a child had a reason to act in a certain way, and psychology could explain his right to that reason, then parents felt that they had to be understanding (or, as interpreted by the group members, tolerant). What they could not comprehend was that children often seemed to behave in worse ways when faced with understanding and patience. The "a reason is an excuse" phenomenon seemed to weigh heavily on these conscientious parents. Psychological insights meant to increase parental understanding of the child's world appeared to offer the child license for unacceptable behavior. A favorite theme, "this too will pass," had often left parents waiting indefinitely.

Attempts to modify behavior by treats or punishment (the historical carrot and stick methods all parents have used from time to time) did not seem to work with any consistency. Children did not appear to respond as the books had inferred. "When I grow up," said one 3½-year-old, "I want to be a baby." Efforts to have her toilet trained were thwarted by the logic of a toddler who thought that being changed and waited on was the ultimate human pleasure. Another child who was suffering from the heat on a hot day turned to his mother as he stepped out of the air-conditioned supermarket and said accusingly, "You didn't cool the outside!" Mothers frequently reported behavior that seemed illogical and irrational to them. "Why does he refuse to put his hat and coat on when we go out when I've told him how cold it is?" "Why does she run in happily to nursery school and then turn around crying and say she wants to go home?"

The egocentricity of the very young surprised and startled the mothers as they exchanged stories. "I want to be biggest, most loved, and most important," announced a 5-year-old. Parents were bewildered by their children's negativism, by their cruelty, resistance, and selfishness. "Why won't he eat nicely? We try to set a good example," said one distraught mother. "I put her to bed twenty times," said another. "First it's a kiss, then water, then the bathroom, then a book, then a hug to grandma, etcetera . . . etcetera . . . . What does she want?

Why isn't she satisfied?" Misunderstanding of the child's conflicting nature was apparent in all of these examples. The parents obviously believed that children are inherently reasonable creatures if properly nurtured and cared for.

In an effort to give their children self-esteem, mothers provided praise and more praise. They struggled with the fact that a child could tear up a picture, just as doting relatives claimed it was marvelous.

The little girl described earlier, who was sent to bed twenty times in a row ("I was trying to be reasonable," said the mother, "and I was hoping she would be"), saw the mother explode in a rage. "If you'd only said 'no' in the first place," the child said piously a few minutes later, "this wouldn't have happened." These vignettes caused mothers to perceive a "no win" proposition for themselves. They had heard of the terrible twos, but the stubborn threes, fearful fours, and trying fives?

Theories of child development apparently needed to be reexplained. The infant in Freudian terms is a being who starts out in the world wanting immediate and total satisfaction of needs. Since parents are the child's first educators, it is they who have to support a more mature level of functioning by helping the child come to terms with inner conflicts. Conflict, therefore, is inevitable. While some children seem to have an easier time accepting life's demands than others, all, undoubtedly, would prefer to have things go their way.

The idea that the children are subject to instinctual pressures of their own was new. The fact that infantile behavior on the part of the young causes parents to behave less maturely proved an astonishing insight. Once this was understood, the mothers seemed to better understand their own responses.

The regressive pull of infantile demands had made them privately ashamed. To learn that others had been affected similarly was a relief. The most significant insight into their children's infantile behavior was the recognition of instinct as a fact of childhood. Understanding the nature of childhood—its impulses, erratic behaviors, and beginning struggles of conscience—gave each parent knowledge and, therefore, power.

If this was more complicated than any of the mothers had envisioned, it was also far simpler. By clarifying "who started what," parents had the information necessary to intervene appropriately. Acts could be judged on their merits.

Before this insight, guilt had often obscured responsibility. When mothers felt guilty about becoming angry, for example, they were operating on the assumption that they were responsible for the behavior they were seeing, that their parenting had caused the infractions they witnessed. This interfered with their common sense and good judgment. The child's need for reasonable limits was forgotten in light of anxious self-questioning.

Children are upset by ambivalence, and uncertainty was the message these children were receiving. For the children who were struggling with developmental strains of their own, the guilty and anxious inconsistency of the parents, unable to discern their role clearly, heightened their own anxiety.

The mothers in the group gained a more realistic perspective on the behavior of their young. There was an intellectual effort involved in this educational process. The group fostered the position that parents have a responsibility to help a child manage his libidinal and aggressive drives. Fostering a sensible discipline, which balances indulgence and frustration to encourage progressive development, the parents, in effect, lend children ego support. The parent's ability to allow the child appropriate independence as he or she becomes more competent, is part of the process. The underlying message to mothers was that "they [the children] have the motor power. You do the steering until they can take over for themselves." The child is not viewed as bad or good, but as incomplete, in need of a relationship with a loved person to develop properly.

No topic of interest to a parent was off limits in these groups. The ages of the children, however, caused certain topics to surface repeatedly. Toilet training was a topic in all the groups because it was seen as the first major educational task. Before this, the mother is largely concerned with what the baby needs. Now she is asking the child to do something *her* way for the first time. Since the child is the final arbiter in what often becomes a contest of wills, he or she acquires a new power.

The child is ready to start toilet training when the sphincter muscles are fully developed (at about 18 months), so that physiological control is present; the child should be able to walk; he or she should have a basic vocabulary and have shown the ability (urethral control) to stay dry for several hours at a time. The introduction of the potty and training pants is preliminary and requires a month of taking the child to the potty and emptying diapers into it. Everything must be done gradually so that the mind and emotions of the child have time to grasp what is asked, and to struggle with the conflicting emotions this educational task evokes. Helping mothers to understand that toddlers are conflicted people (often they cannot agree with themselves) enabled them to be more patient with accidents. The training was really an education in body mastery. The expectations were increased in graduated steps—from potty to toilet, from diaper to training pants. The child was slowly encouraged to handle the whole process. All of this is gradual and takes place over many months.

What was new to mothers (many of whom knew and/or had used props like the potty and training pants before) was the role this process played in future development. Many of the child's feelings about toilet training influence his or her response to future life expectations. Increased self-sufficiency is the reward for this effort. The recommendation that parents refrain from overreacting to success or failure is based on the recognition that this is the child's job. A child's success increases his or her self-esteem enormously; it is a victory "of self over self, not parent over self." That is why rewards, treats, and punishments are ineffective. Finally, it may be seen as a useful educational measure which aids in the development of causal reasoning. A cause-effect relation is always visible and every mistake has a consequence. The issue of discipline was a common thread in the fabric of every group meeting. This was also true of aggression which was seen as a force which could be positive or negative. Helping the child to use aggression constructively is central to the idea of discipline.

In groups there is a risk involved in giving management advice. The leader does not have the kind of information that is available from individual interviews. Getting parents to take a simple position was the initial aim—"Stop the upsetting behavior; we will learn more about it after it is stopped." By sending children to their room until they could manage, mothers were able to keep from becoming so angry that their actions were punitive. Also, they were able to avoid the guilt that resulted from explosions of anger when they had waited too long to act.

The difference between discipline and punishment was a related issue. There was the tendency, when the children became active, to become too punitive in response to aggression: "You stay there all afternoon" or, "Wait until daddy comes home." The idea that the child should be allowed to make the decision about when to come out of the room was foreign to them. Most of the mothers had been raised in an adversary system that pitted parent against child. A parent-child alliance suggests that a parent can say: "You can come out whenever *you* can manage." As with toilet training, it is a victory of self over self. Because it allows the child to save face, it decreases his or her humiliation, and desire for retaliation.

As the mothers reported to the group successes or failures, they gained a more in-depth understanding of their children. By listening to each other and watching a recommendation work over time, they clarified many of their own confusions for each other and were relieved to learn that others shared similar problems.

Children's competitiveness was another topic of common concern. Could mothers let them win in areas where it didn't matter? Could parents find ways of allowing the developing sense of self to achieve some autonomy? The mothers struggled with this. Many seemed to operate on an all or nothing approach. "We discipline firmly to drill out badness" or "we allow anything, as love conquers all." The need to hold the line on some things while yielding on others appeared to make sense.

A "more firm—less firm" principle evolved. Mothers attempted to be more firm only about matters that genuinely concerned them. (Each family varied in this regard, and this leader was supportive of the right to order their own priorities.) Did it really matter if the red cap was worn instead of the blue? In order to arrive at tactful alternatives that provide an outlet for impulse, sensitivity to the individual child's interests is necessary.

Ways of preventing arguments were sought. The effort was made to change the climate in the home so that the children's need to control would not make the home into a battlefield. Rather, it was hoped that the children would become increasingly cooperative as their wishes, too, were considered.

Parents, as benevolent autocrats, can allow children some power if they assume that the interplay of freedom and restraint will free the child to find solutions to the good/bad conflict inside of them. Parents can lend weight to the good side (as in toilet training) without denying the anti-social impulses that also exist.

Freedom is seen as providing the child with room to struggle with a contradictory self in a way that is ultimately more consonant with the duality in one's nature. The sessions were described by one mother as a how-to course in "civilizing your children without taking the joy out of them or out of us either."

Since the issues were complex, the leader was in the position of acknowledging many truths at once. Some developmental stresses are so great for the child (for example, the negativism of the terrible twos) that good handling may or may not yield a happy result immediately (what you do is not necessarily what you get). These are the times to let many things pass, knowing that time will inevitably result in development. As the child's intelligence develops, the inner conflicts will gradually subside. Listening to other mothers whose children were a bit older was a great comfort for mothers who had to endure days of protracted negativism.

The oedipal phase of development was a foreign concept to these mothers. Normality in their own development had resulted in normal repression. Although they could only understand the leader's description of oedipal development on an intellectual basis, they were relieved to learn that it was not something of their making. This freed them from entering the struggle and helped them help the child to contain the conflict. Knowing where one's behavior as a parent can make a difference and where it cannot helps clarify parental disciplinary decisions. Certain absolutes were necessary: "You cannot hurt me, the family or yourself. You cannot destroy things." Having sensible barriers countered developmental aggressive upsurges. Beyond that, there was room for leniency about small issues that parents were able to tolerate. Substitutes were found useful. Kicking stools were invented; punching pillows were allowed. Deflection, substitution, verbalization, and restraint were effectively employed. These parents were open in their discussions about their own rearing. It was evident that group support enabled them to do things differently with their children, despite the pull their own histories exerted.

The mothers learned that limits encourage rather than limit a child's emotional development by supporting the child's developing conscience. By saying no, the parents relieve the child of unnecessary guilt. This point led full circle to the issue of modesty and privacy. These mothers seemed to reflect the prevailing American view that openness is the best way to educate children to sex differences. They were astonished to hear this questioned. They wanted to help children feel comfortable with, and unashamed of, their own sexuality. The feelings expressed by the parents was that what is natural should be accepted as natural; children should not be made to feel guilty about normal body functions. The assumption here was that if these are accepted calmly from the start, the child will not regard his or her body as dirty or embarrassing.

This thinking was reflected in every group. It assumed that input from the environment was the most significant factor in sex education.

The idea that seeing is believing, and therefore educational, appeared to be widespread. Mothers hope that children, after seeing their parents—and each other—undressed, would ask questions which could be answered directly. Guilt, thought to have been inspired by the attitudes of a sexually inhibited society, would then be eliminated.

The point was raised that this thinking, though seemingly logical, had effects not anticipated by its advocates. Observers of young children who were raised with this open approach found to their dismay that children were not freer, but often more excitable and less educable because of it. It was thought that exposure to adult nudity and its attendant size discrepancies could be too stimulating for the child who is attempting to contend with dimly understood drives. The leader stressed that this was not a moral issue but simply a matter of what the child could handle. Invoking privacy did not mean a return to Victorian secretiveness and hypocrisy. It is important for parents to answer their children's questions and thereby allow learning to occur in manageable doses. Open discussion of sexual issues can allow parents to correct the massive amount of misinformation readily available. Children are relieved by privacy. The leader shared her observation that children question more what they do not see. In treating children it is found that they often do not ask questions because they do not know where to begin. Thus, the recommendation was for privacy, honest discussion, and repeated responsiveness as the children got older and asked over again.

The need to examine the way the child's mind works was implicit in these recommendations. A simple question in response to the child's own question, such as "What do you think?" "What have you heard?" evoked interesting answers. From one 4-year-old: "My daddy's pee pee is higher than the sky"; from a 3½-year-old: "Everybody has a penis. You cut mine off and gave it to the baby"; a 5-year-old-girl: "What's a vagina anyhow? Hardly nothing." Instead of merely being amused at these infantile misperceptions, it was important to try to understand where they came from. Literature and research suggest that these "peculiar" notions come from the children themselves! What Selma Fraiberg (1959) describes as magical thinking is particularly characteristic of the thought processes of pre-schoolers. They believe their thoughts make things happen; they have an unrealistic view of size. Anything can and does happen in the world of their imagination.

This focus made the leader's recommendations more comprehendible. Modesty was a not easily resolved issue. Some parents were overreacting to the prudery of their own parents by "enlightened" exhibitionism. To them, the recommendations were a step backward. Other mothers raised with an open-door policy felt their adequacy was a telling rebuttal to this strange theory. The leader did not press the issue, conceding that some children are more easily stimulated than others, and that it is impossible to predict how individual development occurs. In general, decreased stimulation calms children and allows progressive development to occur with less strain. Technically one sees this as the support of the ego rather than id.

Another important issue regarding magical thinking in the young child is the question of time. It seems to stretch forever for the very young. Having the mothers remember how slowly time passed when they were young allowed them to catch a glimpse of how different time is for the toddler. "When you leave, it feels like for always," said a 4-year-old to his mother. The tears at nursery school or with a sitter were thus seen not just as provocative, controlling behavior, but rather, as a real response to separation and what was perceived as a loss "forever." Knowing children live in a magical land where the clock never moves helped parents to educate children to real time by planning small, assimilable separations. Slowly the time sequence is increased as they get older. Underlying all of this is the recognition that the young child develops and matures over a continuum, within the framework of a relationship with a parent or caretaker.

Helping parents see the necessity of preparing children for important events was found to be useful. A step-by-step approach was taken. The child was told of the event—for example, the first day of school or an impending hospitalization—before it took place. After it was over there was further discussion of what happened. This allowed the child to ruminate about the event and to absorb the feelings aroused by the event. It was, in effect, a safety valve for "feeling pleasure." Verbalization, with its ability to anticipate and clarify, was also useful in the parallel story.

The parallel story was offered to mothers as a way of helping children recognize unique feelings and make sense of experiences. Thus mothers were encouraged to tell stories about other children who face situations similar to their own. The telling of a parallel story that the child can relate to legitimizes emotions. Having learned something of the normal distresses that children are subject to in the course of growing up, the mothers were able to make up stories that went right to the heart of things. Many wished to have the stories end happily, for instance, "and then he loved his baby brother." However, the leader suggested that these tailormade stories should not be overly optimistic. Negative feelings take time to unfold. The story provides room for hostility and makes children less self-critical. This helps preserve self-esteem. Rather than acting these feelings out, they were expressed in words.

Each group lasted ten weeks, despite protests and wishes to continue. This was done deliberately as the leader felt that mothers should be given a chance to put into practice what they had learned on their own. Organized in an effort to impart information about child development, the group was not intended to offer long-term discussion and support.

Six months later, the group convened to see how things had progressed. While practical successes and failures were candidly reported ("John toilet trained but regressed with illness"; "Susie seemed to mature when she expressed jealousy of the baby"), what was most significant was the fundamental nature of the principles the mothers had absorbed. The idea that behavior had meaning seemed to have struck home. "It's not that the theories were so new or revolutionary," said one mother, "it's that I started to observe and really listen to my child. When I responded I was more in tune with what was going on."

Anna Freud (1965) describes four areas of difference between children and adults. First she describes children's egocentricity, their relationship to the world in terms of their own needs. Second, she describes the sexual confusion that arises when the immature infantile sexual apparatus encounters genital issues in terms commensurate with pre-genital experience. Third, she describes the relative weakness of secondary process thinking (e.g., reality thinking) compared with magical (e.g., impulse and fantasy) thinking. Finally, she features the difference in the children's evaluation of time.

These four areas were the very ones which elicited most thought on the part of the mothers in every group. The mothers were concerned with their children's selfishness and aggression, and hence felt much work on discipline essential. They were involved in clarifying sexual issues for children who distorted what they saw. The magical thinking which dominated the youngsters' viewpoint required much in the way of realistic explanation and clarification. Finally the issue of the children's inability to view mothers correctly led to much discussion regarding the issue of separation from their primary caretakers.

Obviously the women in these groups came to the task of motherhood with a genuine wish to mother successfully. Yet many did not experience in their own childhoods the kind of "good mothering" talked about in our sessions. Nonetheless, they lent the strength of their own egos (buttressed by new insight) to their children and were gratified to see better results than they had hoped for.

REFERENCES

Fraiberg, S. (1959). *The Magic Years*. New York: Charles Scribner's Sons.

Freud, A. (1965). *Normality and Pathology in Childhood, Assessments of Development*. New York: International Universities Press. Vol. VI.

EDITORS' DISCUSSION

GROUP COMPOSITION OR POPULATION. Weisberger's mothers' groups were composed of women initially referred by pediatricians, and later via the grapevine and self-referral. No screening or diagnostic assessment was done by the therapist. This referral process brought together a self-selected and motivated group of homogeneous women who were not employed; they had postponed work and careers until their toddlers were in school. They were all college-educated young mothers in their 20s and 30s. The population was similar to that studied in the research project with Mahler, Pine, and Bergman, as reported in *The Psychological Birth of the Human Infant*.

SETTING AND PURPOSE. During weekly sessions young mothers met informally with a clinician in private practice. The clinician's purpose and goals for the mothers' groups evolved from her prior work in the child psychiatry clinic of a large metropolitan teaching hospital where she had engaged in the practice of, and teaching of, parent guidance. Her focus was further stimulated by her concern about piecemeal "how-to" advice in the media. Her purpose was educational; she explicitly avoided a group therapy experience. In instances where mothers' emotional problems interfered, they were referred to other professionals.

LEVEL OF INTERVENTION AND STANCE OF CLINICIAN. The level of intervention is best defined as an educative stance; group activities included clarifying, enabling, facilitating, advising, and teaching mothers about child development. It was hoped that knowledge of age-appropriate achievements would promote the mothers' confidence and allow them to function comfortably in the role of primary educators of their children. Questions were answered and recommendations offered in the context of developmental theory. The educational, nontherapeutic purpose of the group meetings was clearly stated. The clinician's stance was nonjudgmental, active, and supportive. Ego Psychological developmental tenets of "average expectable environment" (Hartmann 1958), "optimal frustration" (Spitz 1965), and "developmental lines" (A. Freud 1963) were emphasized.

GROUP PROCESS.   On the basis of the contract set at the time of engagement, the groups were terminated after ten weeks, despite members' protests and wishes to continue. This was decided by the leader, based on her view that mothers should be given a chance to practice independently what they had learned. There was a follow-up meeting six months later where members shared their reactions to the group and to what they had learned. Cohesiveness generally remained constant.

GROUP DYNAMICS.   Because of the educational, nontherapeutic purpose of the groups, the author does not address herself to such phenomena as transference, countertransference, and alliance. She focused solely on the achievement of an educational alliance. Implicit in the paper is the author's awareness of resistance, transference, etc. when she refers to members' emotional problems and referral out, for individual treatment.

Freud, A. (1963). The concept of developmental lines. *Psychoanalytic Study of the Child* 18:245–265.

Hartmann, H. (1958). *Ego Psychology and the Problem of Adaptation.* New York: International Universities Press.

Mahler, M., Pine, F. and Bergman, A. (1975). *The Psychological Birth of the Human Infant–Separation and Individuation.* New York: Basic Books.

Spitz, R. (1965). *The First Year of Life.* New York: International Universities Press.

Winnicott, D.W. (1958). *The Maturational Processes and the Faciliting Environment.* New York: International Universities Press.

CHAPTER 5

Group Work with Single Mothers
AVA L. SIEGLER, PH.D.

EDITORS' NOTES
Dr. Siegler is working with a challenging population: women who work and raise children without consistent help from a father figure. These women have to support their families, in contrast to the middle-class mothers described in the preceding chapter. Some of the single parents Siegler describes are from backgrounds that lacked adequate emotional nurturance. Had Dr. Siegler not understood their narcissistic and ego deficits so well, the groups may not have been as well attended or successful.

CULTURAL CHANGES: THE SINGLE WORKING MOTHER

In New York City alone, more than 100,000 single working mothers are raising children under six years of age. They represent the growing trend toward single-parent families noted in the past decade (Lasch 1977). The majority are *not* middle-class women who choose to work, or, who return to work after a divorce (bolstered by household help, child-support payments, and the father's weekend visits with the children). Most are women who *must* work, because they are the sole support of their families. The fathers are not usually available as emotional, social, or financial partners. The mothers must face the complex responsibilities of parenthood alone. The frenetic rhythms of urban life often intensify feelings of uncertainty, apprehension, and isolation, and they feel caught in a web of tangled stresses.

For many of these mothers, the day care system provides an alternative to transient caretakers, unreliable family arrangements, or, in some cases, locking a child in the apartment while the mother goes to work. When psychological problems arise, these mothers are least likely to take advantage of mental health facilities because of a lack of knowledge, time, or finances. Their children do not often attract the attention of any specific child advocacy group: they are neither psychotic, nor retarded, nor physically handicapped, nor orphaned. Yet they frequently suffer from a wide range of emotional and cognitive difficulties. When these mothers and their children began to claim clinical attention, the need to study the problems of this special population and to create an intervention program that would provide psychological support for these families became apparent. In light of this, an early intervention pilot project was developed within a day care center in Manhattan. This center serves a multi-racial, multi-ethnic group of working parents, 80 percent of whom are young mothers raising a single child, alone. Roughly 65 3–6-year-olds are enrolled in the preschool nursery and kindergarten program. The project offers direct, on-site psychological services to the families at the day care center.

Group intervention models were developed that were based on psychoanalytic developmental Ego Psychology. The aim of these models was to understand the function of the family, the nature of mother-child interactions in the absence of the father, and the special demands placed upon the single mother during the oedipal phase of development.

THE FUNCTION OF THE FAMILY

It is the family that forges the link between character and culture. Through family interactions and patterns the child's personality is fashioned. Though family composition and style varies in accord with class and geographic differences, its function, socialization of its young, remains the same.

According to psychoanalytic theory, the family's cultural task is accomplished through a series of complex object-relations and object-representations established in early childhood, and crystallized by the outcomes of normal oedipal struggles between parents and child (Blanck and Blanck 1974, Neubauer 1960). It follows then, that alterations in family structure, whether caused by individual or cultural variables, will resound and reverberate throughout development.

In our culture and in this century, the dominant family structure has been the nuclear family (that is, a family containing a father, a mother, and more than one child). However, the absence of a father in the child's formative years and the presence of a working mother have become increasing realities since World War II (Aries 1962, Isaacs 1949, Lasch 1977, Rutter 1974). While many observers are alarmed about the social and economic effects of "fatherlessness," little research exists that either documents the psychic consequences of this altered family structure or examines the psychic resources that mothers and their children rely on in order to cope with the loss or absence of a father.

MOTHER-CHILD RECIPROCITIES IN THE ABSENCE OF THE FATHER

The existing analytic literature that discusses the one-parent family has emphasized the potentially destructive effects of the father's absence on the development of the child (Isaacs 1949, Loewald 1951, Neubauer 1960). Most writers focus their concern upon the preoedipal and oedipal distortions that are inherent in this altered family structure and maintain that the presence of both parents is essential to a satisfactory oedipal outcome. Over twenty years ago, Neubauer blamed "the lack of oedipal stimulation, normally found in the continuous day-to-day interplay between the child and each parent, and especially as evidenced by the relationship of the parents to each other" for causing what he called "a primary imbalance" (1960, p. 305). It is obvious that the "continuous day-to-day interplay" between the child and the parent, and between the parents themselves is a widely varying exchange, influenced by many factors, some of which have nothing to do with the actual physical presence of the father.

In our clinical investigations we repeatedly have found that the effects of the father's absence on the child's development are determined by the ways in which the mother experiences and defines this event for the child. Mothers have countless ways of keeping the image of the father alive, or, conversely, destroying his image, if that is their wish. While there is no question that it makes a difference when a child is raised in the absence of a father, the more interesting question focuses on what sort of a difference it makes. The meaning of the loss of the father in both the life of the mother and that of the child depends on whether the loss was incurred through death, illness, separation, divorce, or abandonment.

Any of the families studied in our project experienced a severe rejection concurrent with object loss. Many of the young mothers were abandoned by the biological father of the child before or shortly after the baby's birth. Other fathers left later. In charting the course of mother-child interactions during the father's absence, the following variables were found to be critical:

1. the mother's personality and level of maturity
2. the sex of the child
3. the age of the child and the developmental stage in which the father left the home
4. the existence of other supports for the family at the time of losing the father
5. the degree to which the father remained available to the family after the separation
6. the mother's experience of her partnership with the father and her reaction to his departure
7. the child's experience of the father and reaction to the loss
8. the mother's capacity to explain the father's departure to the child
9. the mother's understanding of the special stresses associated with single-parenthood

A descriptive profile, drawn from experiences with these mothers, may be helpful in conveying the impact of raising a child alone.

All of the mothers in the project had considerable difficulty being a single parent. They were deeply concerned about the developmental implications that the lack of a father was likely to have upon their child, and this was especially noted in the mothers of male children. Even those mothers who had made new and steady alliances with another man felt some apprehension about the fact that, "It can't be the same...I mean he's not his *real* father." Those women who had not made a new alliance often felt torn between their wish to act sensitively, responsibly, and knowledgeably about their children, and their desires to have a life of their own, and to seek out a new male partner. They were acutely aware of the intensity of their bonds to their children. One mother expressed the tie this way: "Tommy and me are a matched set, you know, you can't break us apart." The mothers would often choose relationships with men that were based upon the man's capacity to display affection and protection toward their child. The connection to such a man was often maintained in the face of clearly expressed dissatisfaction with him on other grounds: "He's not what I want in a man, but I hate to leave him because he's good to the baby."

For most of the women, the early years of infant care had been difficult and demanding. They were usually quite young when the baby was born, and the birth itself had often been an unexpected and/or unwelcome event in their lives, interrupting their late-adolescent search for identity and intimacy. Despite the abrupt onset of parenthood, most of the mothers in the project described a surge in self-esteem when they became parents. They felt that they were necessary to the baby, and indeed, many believed themselves capable of being responsible parents at this point in their lives, even in the total absence of the father.

THE SPECIAL TASK OF THE MOTHER DURING OEDIPAL DEVELOPMENT

Interestingly enough, many mothers began to experience increased apprehension about raising the child alone with the onset of the oedipal years. This differed from the ease and self-confidence they felt when the child was younger.

Their increased anxiety seemed to signal their awareness on some level of the psychic meaning of the oedipal triangle, and their recognition that it was going to be particularly difficult to negotiate this phase of development alone. Their concerns clustered remarkably about the issues that are recognized as crucial to oedipal resolutions:

1. Sexual differentiation and the development of sexual identity, e.g., "Will my son grow up to be homosexual with no man around?"

2. Object choice, e.g., "My daughter goes to any man on the subway and asks him to be her daddy. Isn't that bad for her?"

3. Superego formation, e.g., "I really worry that with no man around, he won't learn to listen." . . . "I try to be really tough on the kids, so they'll have self-control and respect for me, because I'm alone."

4. The crystalizing of ego ideals, e.g., "I don't know what to tell him about his father. I mean, when he was little, it didn't

matter, but now he asks me all the time, was he good or bad?"... "Her father is a real bastard. He never sees her except to give her an expensive toy so he can feel like a big-shot, while I pay the bills. But I'm afraid to tell her the truth, 'cause he is her father."

The parent of an oedipal age child must disengage him or herself from the child's seductive attempts to include the parent in the fulfillment of erotic desires (Anthony and Benedek 1970, Freud, A. 1960, Freud, S. 1905, Kestenberg 1975). To accomplish this, appropriate limitations and restraints must be placed upon the child. In the one-parent family the mother must absorb the entire role of "frustrator." This increases the child's ambivalence toward her. Single mothers often try to delay taking on this restrictive role; or they attempt to shift the responsibility onto a male figure in their lives, even a transient partner. In this way they may succeed in creating a makeshift oedipal triangle in which the child can experience exclusion. These mothers are often attempting, with whatever resources they have at their disposal, to create a more complete oedipal drama. Additionally, the discrepancy between the pre-oedipal mother who permitted the child to sleep with her as a comfort to both of them, and the oedipal mother who abruptly permits a man to displace the child in her bed, insisting that the child sleep alone—produces bewilderment, sadness, and rage in the oedipal age child. The mother's sudden change seems to the child to be without warning.

In the normal oedipal phase of development (3 to 6 years old), the child would ordinarily become aware of his or her parents as a couple. This perception represents a developmental achievement. Children begin to perceive the triangular nature of their position vis-à-vis the parents in a unique way that emphasizes their exclusion from the parental relationship. That is, their sense of themselves as singular is, in some senses, synchronized and dependent upon a perception of the parents as a couple. The oedipal age child from a one-parent family does not have this perception of "coupling" available in a continuous and reliable manner. Child and mother must therefore compensate for the resultant blind spot in their vision of the oedipal dilemma. They do this by fantasizing about what is missing in reality, so that the shadow of a father falls upon the developmental path.

Both parent and child struggle valiantly to create an exchange between them that will accommodate the surge of impulses that accompany the oedipal phase. How they enter this phase has, of course, already been partially influenced by distorted and unresolved pre-oedipal issues. Nonetheless, development proceeds, integrating the old, imperfect resolutions with the new challenges.

Certain "pairings" between mother and child that represented a type of generalized response to the oedipal dilemma were observed in the project. These pairings should be seen as types of reactions in extreme form. They are meant for descriptive use only, and should not reduce our sense of the complexity of intra-psychic conflict for either parent or child.

THE EROTIC PAIR.   In this coupling, the mother of the child permits and encourages the child's oedipal overtures, while retaining pre-oedipal modes of relating. She feeds the child's fantasy that he is, in fact, the mother's one and only love. This pairing has quite different implications with a male child than with a female child, and varies from those rare instances (in our population) of incestuous sexual exchange to the mild erotic feelings expressed in the phrase, "He's Mommy's little man."

THE HOSTILE PAIR.   In these instances, the emerging sexual desires of the oedipal age child are warded off by hostility. The mother mirrors these feelings by displacing hostility from the child's father onto the child (He's a "chip off the old block"); or the mother may see the child as an externalization of all she finds despicable in herself; or she may victimize the child in an attempt to master her own experience of victimization at the hands of the father. In these cases, the exchanges between mother and child are suffused with anger. For the male child, father's absence as an inhibitor of his desires for the mother often leaves the boy with no defense against the seductive potential of the mother except distance and/or anger. The female child, on the other hand, without a father to turn towards in her mastery of the oedipal dilemma, is left with the anger that is appropriate to this phase as well as her rage at the mother for depriving her of the father, and for getting rid of him. The strife between girls at this age and their mothers, in the absence of the father who might have moderated their dispute and competition, is striking, and the girls often feel doubly deprived.

THE FEARFUL PAIR.   In this type of interaction, the mother is overwhelmed by her own impulses, and the child identifies with the mother's anxiety. Her perception of her fate is informed by dread, fear, and hopelessness, and she sees herself and the child as set adrift, without direction, helpless and surrounded by danger. This perception of danger from *without*, reflects the mother's and child's fears of danger from *within*—with regard to the pull of internal impulses. Sometimes, children who experience the mother's terror will attempt to take over the role of parent to their own parent and assume a precociousness that can interfere with appropriate ego development. More often, the child shares mother's agitation and loss of functioning, and retreats from age-appropriate challenges.

CLINICAL INTERVENTION: THE RATIONALE

These clinical observations revealed the need for many of the families to participate in a process that would help mothers understand the special demands of their role as parents, the unique difficulties of approaching that role without a partner, and appropriate ways of resolving the special conflicts of oedipal development. The following propositions underlie the rationale for clinical intervention with mothers:

1. All actual (i.e., real) events in one's life are uniquely colored by the psychic structures of the mind.

2. These structures bear the individual stamp of character and the developmental limits of mind and memory.

3. There is a body of knowledge assembled by psychoanalytic Developmental Ego Psychology which, like any other body of knowledge, can and should be shared.

4. Most individuals are capable of responding to such knowledge in rational ways, and there are techniques relevant to parent guidance which can increase the capacity of the individual to make use of this knowledge.

It was not known which intervention model would best suit the needs of this population of single working mothers. The group structure seemed most satisfying for several reasons, primarily because it creates a sense of community, something that seemed strikingly absent in the lives of these young mothers. The group circle, it was hoped, could substitute for the family circle. Ekstein supports these thoughts in a paper describing his understanding of the meaning of the loss of the father in our society: "The lack of identity, the lack of family bonds, the aimlessness that we frequently face today, perhaps can be counteracted in work with and through groups...I would suggest that the helping professions...are now the powerful counterweights in a society which is in danger of becoming a society without the father" (1978, p. 442). Mothers in a group would have a safe haven for the open exchange of ideas, feelings, fears, and wishes. Their shared concerns would create bonds between them, and the group could provide a forum for considering changes. The group would also create an opportunity for multiple identifications; on the simplest level, the single mother would no longer have the sense that she stood alone but would realize her plight was shared by others. By forming therapeutic groups for these women, we hoped to create a facilitating environment (to borrow Winnicott's phrase) for the growth of both parent and child.

Still to be decided was what type of group would be most helpful to the mothers. Searching through recent literature on groups yielded no references to treatment models for single parents. Despite the fact that single mothers had become such a dominant social phenomenon, they were not treated as a special group in need of special therapeutic strategies, with a rationale separate from women's groups in general. Several parameters of the proposed group intervention treatment situation seemed clear:

1. The group could not be called a psychotherapy group because of the general reluctance of our population to commit themselves to anything that could be construed as "treatment." (They did not want to be seen as either "sick" or "crazy.")

2. Maintaining the boundaries of the traditional group setting in which the group members had no contact with each other outside of the group would be impossible since our mothers already knew each other from the day care center.

3. Strict confidentiality would be difficult to maintain within the day care center, and therefore personal revelations would have to be carefully monitored, regression discouraged, and transferential manifestations dealt with quickly.

4. The group had to fill not only an emotional need in our population, but a cognitive one as well. It had to provide a forum for the exploration of parent–child relations and offer mothers the benefit of professional guidance on these issues. Therefore, the group leader could be neither passive nor anonymous.

Two types of groups were created to meet the special needs of our single working mothers: the parent guidance group, an ongoing monthly discussion group, open to all parents at the center, which had an attendance rate between 10 and 30; and the mothers' groups, composed of 6 to 9 women, which had a fixed membership and met weekly. The larger parent guidance group was both a child development seminar and an individual parent guidance session. The mothers' groups embraced aspects of a woman's consciousness raising group and analytic group psychotherapy. Women were placed in the smaller groups according to specific variables including their level of education, language skills, capacity for self-reflection, and concerns. The mothers' groups offered them a chance to analyze experiences that might never have come to light in the larger, more public parent guidance group. Some of these shared vignettes captured the struggles of a single parent with peculiar vividness. One young woman, for instance, related an incident in which she was trying to force her stubborn 4-year-old to wear her sweater under her coat on a bitterly cold day. The battle between them took place in the elevator, in the presence of several other tenants. Finally, in a fury at the child's imperviousness to her reasonable pleas, the young mother said to the child, between clenched teeth, "You put that sweater on, or I'll hurt you!" Whereupon one of the men in the elevator turned to her and said, "You keep that up, and you'll destroy her!" The mother replied, "That may be, mister, but she's mine to destroy."

This particular incident characterizes the passion, problems, and possessiveness in being a single parent. The intense rage felt at being solely responsible for raising a young child, and at having no support when irritable or helpless, can be debilitating. This helplessness is often mitigated by the recognition that the mother is all powerful, and critical to the child's existence. The most primitive expression of this is child abuse; a more commonplace manifestation is inconsistency, i.e., overindulgence versus autocratic discipline.

Single mothers are aware of the potential destructiveness of the intense bond they have to their child. Mothers often come to the bittersweet realization that it is only with their child that they have found a love that is stable and enduring. Although this extreme emotional investment in the child can have dire consequences for the child's emerging identity, the bond between them, particularly in the absence of other loving relations, can be, as Christopher Lasch (1977) has put it, "a haven in a heartless world."

THE THERAPEUTIC ROLE OF THE GROUP LEADER

THE LEADER AS IDEALIZED PARENT. The role of the group leader was given careful consideration. We understood that the absence of a father in these women's family lives was likely to intensify their experiences with the group leader, investing the leader with some of the idealized aspects of the missing partner. Slavson (1958), for instance, has stated that all group therapies provide an opportunity for the therapist to symbolically acquire the authority of the father, while the group itself can be seen as a nurturant, protective, empathic mother. It was speculated that this symbolic situation might be further intensified in a group made up of mothers without husbands. An additional factor was the reality that many of the women in the project had experienced parental deprivation in their own childhoods— usually the loss of their fathers.

THE LEADER AS NEW OBJECT. Since many of the single mothers had received inadequate or interrupted parental care as children, a goal of parent guidance was to increase the mothers' potential to acquire new responses, in order to help them transcend the compulsion to repeat their own childhood pain. The group leader offered herself as an organizer and confirmer of new responses, and lent herself as an object available for imitation and identification. As the clinical work progressed, some of the mothers who participated in the program were found to be suffering from borderline, narcissistic, or impulse disorders which impaired their capacities to cope with both their own lives and those of their children. The group was able to offer them a holding environment by providing the ongoing support necessary to permit them to nurture their children with less strain. The group leader, then, functioned as an auxiliary ego for the borderline parent with inner feelings of panic and fragmentation. The group members with more structured egos often helped the less stable members. Group processes also encouraged the development of frustration tolerance among members. Through the leader's interventions, members evidenced a slow accumulation of knowledge, frustration tolerance, and insight. Mothers were able to bring this ego growth to bear upon their relations with their children.

THE LEADER AS EXPERT. In the parent guidance group, advice was imparted on the assumption that it could be given and received in a spirit of rational responsiveness, provided that the limitations of such advice-giving were also confronted and discussed.[1] Refusal to give any advice, on the basis that it would be subverted by the underlying power of the unconscious, did not seem pertinent to our group. If advice is to be meaningful, it should take into account the developmental level and potential of both parent and child. If carefully timed, as any effective intervention must be, it can parallel the topic being discussed. The group leader tried to resonate the parents' concerns and mirror them in such a way that the mothers could understand their implications in their own lives.

THE LEADER AS A LINK WITH THE PAST. One of the most vital ways that parents can be helped to identify and empathize with their children is by aiding them in recalling their own pasts. Therapists do this with individual patients. What makes a group different is that remembering is a shared experience. One reason why being the parent of an oedipal age child is so difficult is that the memories associated with this period of development are not available to most of us. Theoretically, they are the very memories most likely to be repressed. Consequently, parents of oedipal age children are more prone to acting out their oedipal age experiences with their children, rather than recalling them. When it is impossible to revive these memories, an attempt is made to construct a narrative from what we know about normative development that somehow resonates with the parents' own experiences. Here the skill of the group leader requires the ability to shift gracefully from an educative to a therapeutic role, sensitivity to individual variations in personality, the willingness to share aspects of her own experience in an unobtrusive fashion, and a capacity to create a forum for the safe exploration of conflict.[2]

Everything emphasized in the method and rationale converges with the ultimate goal for this entire therapeutic project, that is, to create and maintain a setting in which it is possible for the single working mother under stress to identify and scrutinize her conflicts, and to internalize stronger, more effective ego structures. This project at-

---

[1] In this attitude, we were guided by Anna Freud (1960), who emphasizes that mothers do not have to change their personalities in order to change their handling of their children.

[2] This author is greatly indebted to Ms. Carol Michaels, a valued staff member on the project, who has led the mothers' groups for several years. Her resourcefulness, sensitivity, and clinical talents have made the success of these groups possible.

tempts to expand the possibilities in these mothers' lives, to combat the pain of the past, and to restore their hopes for the future.

REFERENCES

Anthony, E. J. and Benedek, T., eds. (1970). *Parenthood: Its Psychology and Psychopathology*. Boston: Little, Brown.

Aries, P. (1962). *Centuries of Childhood: A Social History of Family Life*. New York: Knopf.

Blanck, R. and Blanck, G. (1974). *Ego Psychology: Theory and Practice*. New York: Columbia University Press.

Ekstein, R. (1978). The search and yearning for and rebellion against the father. *International Journal of Group Psychotherapy* 28(4): 435–44.

Foulkes, S. H. and Anthony, E. J. (1957). *Group Psychotherapy: The Psychoanalytic Approach*. Baltimore: Penguin Books.

Freud, A. (1969). The child guidance clinic as a center of prophylaxis and enlightenment. *The Writings of Anna Freud, Vol. 5: Research at The Hampstead Child Therapy Clinic and Other Papers*, pp. 281–300. New York: International Universities Press.

Freud, S. (1905). Three essays on the theory of sexuality. *Standard Edition* 8:207–30.

Greenson, R. R. The real relationship between the patient and the psychoanalyst. In *The Unconscious Today*, ed. M. Kanzer, pp. 213–32. New York: International Universities Press.

Hampton, P. J. (1962). Group work with parents. *American Journal of Orthopsychiatry* 32: 918–26.

Hartmann, H. (1958). *Ego Psychology and the Problem of Adaptation*. New York: International Universities Press.

Isaacs, S. (1945). Fatherless Children. In *Childhood and After*, pp. 186–207. New York: International Universities Press.

Kestenberg, J. S. (1975). *Children and Parents: Psychoanalytic Studies in Development*. New York: Jason Aronson.

Lasch, C. (1977). *Haven in a Heartless World: The Family Besieged*. New York: Basic Books.

Loewald, H. W. (1951). Ego and Reality, *International Journal of Psychoanalysis* 32:10–18.

Loewald, H. W. (1960). On the therapeutic action of psychoanalysis. *International Journal of Psychoanalysis* Vol. 4, pp. 16–33.

Neubauer, P. B. (1960). The one-parent child and his oedipal development. *Psychoanalytic Study of the Child* 15: 286–309.

Robbins, L. (1963). Parental recall of child development practices. *Journal of Abnormal and Social Psychology* 66: 261–270.

Rutter, M. (1974). *The Qualities of Mothering: Maternal Deprivation Reassessed*. New York: Jason Aronson.

Shapiro, T. (1977). Oedipal distorting in severe character pathologies: Developmental and theoretical considerations. *Psychoanalytic Quarterly* Vol. 46, 4: 559–579.

Slavson, S. R. (1958). *Child-Centered Group Guidance of Parents*. New York: International Universities Press.

Winnicott, D. W. (1969). *The Child, the Family and the Outside World*. Baltimore: Penguin Books.

Wolk, H. H. and Call, J. D. (1965). *A Guide to Preventive Psychiatry: The Art of Parenthood*. New York: McGraw Hill.

Yalom, I. D. (1970). *The Theory and Practice of Group Psychotherapy*. New York: Basic Books.

EDITORS' DISCUSSION

GROUP COMPOSITION. Dr. Siegler's project serves interracial, urban, employed, semiskilled, single mothers. The mothers are young, and their children are between 3 and 6 years old. Two types of groups were created to meet the special needs of this population. The parent guidance group was an open, ongoing, monthly discussion group—available to all mothers served in the project. Attendance ranged from 10 to 30 women per meeting. The mothers' groups were each composed of 6 to 9 women. Their membership was fixed, groups met weekly, and were selected on the basis of assessment. Specific criteria included educational level and ego strengths such as advanced conceptual and cognitive capacities. Participants in both parent guidance and mothers' groups presented a range of strengths and deficits. Diagnostically, many women presented various degrees of borderline deficits, impulse disorders, and narcissistic character structures. Such personality formation both interfered with and facilitated the members' ability to function under stressful life circumstances. Most of the women were subject to poor housing conditions, meager employment experience, severely limited financial resources, and varying degrees of social isolation.

SETTING AND PURPOSE. As Siegler notes, in New York City alone, more than 100,000 single working women are raising children under six years of age. This population is composed of relatively uneducated, unskilled women who have been divorced, separated, or abandoned, and who suffer financially because of poor salaries and the absence of consistent alimony or child support. Many receive public assistance and are in need of community subsidized day care for their children. The Early Intervention Program is a pilot project within a community subsidized day care center in Manhattan, whose goal, through outreach, education, guidance, and therapy, is to stave off pathological developments in the parent–child relationship. Its purpose is to undo harm early, and redirect and reeducate mothers, thereby enhancing their development as empathic parents who can better facilitate and support the age-appropriate, successful development of their children. Therapeutic input for the children occurs through work done with their mothers; the children are also provided with a consistent and predictable day care setting.

LEVEL OF INTERVENTION AND STANCE OF CLINICIAN.
Siegler's guidance groups aim for the same educational goals delineated in Weisberger's description of her mothers' group (this volume). By clarifying, enabling, facilitating, advising, and teaching mothers about child development and age-appropriate achievements, Siegler hoped to promote mothers' confidence and knowledge, and to provide peer group support for them.

Siegler's mothers' groups functioned more as therapy groups than discussion groups, though members were reluctant to consider themselves as sick, crazy, or in need of treatment. Traditional parameters of therapy, such as confidentiality, were not possible, given preexisting personal ties between the mothers in the day care center. Nevertheless, treatment goals, such as insight, clarification, and improved ego functioning, were attained through the sharing of experiences in the group setting.

The role of the leader is postulated at several levels, obviously pertaining to stages of group process, transference, and countertransference issues. We suggest that Siegler's depiction of the leader as idealized parent not be conceptualized in traditional transference terms. Since a number of the mothers served revealed considerable pathology and probably have not achieved object constancy, they do not relate to each other and/or the leader in a distinct self/other fashion. Therefore, the leader is seen as a potential gratifier of symbiotic subphase need (Blanck and Blanck 1979). Siegler suggests that the group provides an opportunity for new experience with a new object. We understand the object relations in these groups as a part object phenomenon, in which part of the self helps secure unattained earlier developmental achievements, like regulation of self-esteem and establishment of self-soothing mechanisms (Goldberg 1973). Siegler's description of the leader as expert we suggest be formulated, not in self/other terms but rather, in terms of idealization and/or merger transferences (my leader is the greatest). We again emphasize the work of Stone and Whitman: "when projection of primitive grandiosity onto others occurs, we see the idealizing transference with expectation of all powerful and all protecting caretaking by, e.g. the leader" (1977, p. 349).

We see in Dr. Siegler's encouragement of mothers to reexperience their past through her sharing of herself, a counterpart of Keith's (1968) building of the "pseudo-alliance" in child therapy. Previously, we formulated that adults whose ego boundaries are loosely structured may demonstrate a need, similar to a child's, to adopt the therapist's synthetic and observing ego. According to Kernberg's (1975) formulations on the development of normal narcissism, this process would help individuals to structure more cohesive self-representations. "Self-representations are affective-cognitive structures reflecting the person's perception of himself in *real* interactions with significant others and in *fantasized* interactions with internal representations of significant others..." (pp. 315–316, italics ours). Last, we view in Dr. Siegler's work a strong regard for her mothers. Her "kindly mood" was essential to establishing a consistent, empathic relationship with them.

GROUP PROCESS. Dr. Siegler's guidance groups allow mothers to learn appropriate modes of parenting behavior. Indirectly, mothers may sense their interrelatedness and experience feelings of mutuality, but interactions between members are deliberately not addressed in the group process. In the mothers' groups, the importance of identification with and imitation of other members is clearly noted, as is the mothers' need for narcissistic gratification. Individual members are depicted as learning through the therapeutic group experience—which is serving as a corrective family situation—to handle their "self" problems.

Siegler postulates oedipal period dilemmas inherent in the single parent home and pays particular attention to the mother who has a male child. It is suggested that the oedipal phase of development was not genuinely entered by the children in question, due to their earlier pre-genital arrests. Object relations theory would imply that their family composition and their mothers' pre-genital character structures would have an impact on the children's development. Pseudo-sexual and/or romantic manipulations are a result of inadequate repression, lack of individuation, and incomplete attainment of object constancy. In evaluating these families Siegler had to make a distinction between neurotic and "neurotic-like" symptoms and behaviors, distinctions also suggested by Tolpin (1979, 67).

GROUP DYNAMICS. Siegler incorporates an approach similar to what Tolpin (1978) outlines, in which direct interpretation of conflict is bypassed in order to avoid inadvertent repetition of childhood emotional assault. Discussions focus on the significance of group experiences, rather than on resistance. Moreover, the leader facilitates the mothers' development of a unique sense of self by emphasizing "group-as-a-whole" interpretations (Stone and Whitman 1977). Siegler seeks to establish aspects of a real relationship, but overall we see therapist and group members as a part of a self-object unit, by which we mean that group members enhance self-esteem and ego by incorporating parts of the leader and co-members. As Stone and Whitman (1977) have noted, "In group psychology, when this model is used, the leader and/or group is seen as a self-object which maintains the cohesion of the individual..." (p. 345).

Blanck, G. and Blanck, R. (1979). *Ego Psychology, II. Psychoanalytic Developmental Psychology*. New York: Columbia University Press.

Goldberg, A. (1973). Psychotherapy of narcissistic injuries. *Arch. General Psychiatry* 28: 722–726.

Keith, C. R. (1968). The therapeutic alliance in child psychotherapy. *Journal of Child Psychiatry* 7: 31–43.

Kernberg, O. (1975). *Borderline Conditions and Pathological Narcissism*. New York: Jason Aronson.

Stone, W. N. and Whitman, R. M. (1977). Contributions of the psychology of the self to group process and group therapy. *International Journal of Group Psychology* 27(3): 343–359.

Tolpin, M. (1979). Self-objects and oedipal objects: A crucial developmental distinction. *The Psychoanalytic Study of the Child* 33:167–184. New Haven: Yale University Press.

PART 3
Latency

Introduction: Group Intervention with Latency Age Children

Latency is a term coinced by Freud (1905) and subsequently widely applied by psychoanalysts to the middle years of childhood to suggest quiescence and repression of drives and oedipal longings. Some think the term an inaccurate description of the school age child (Thomas and Chess 1972). Others see the term applicable only to the absence of heterosexual attachments (Erikson 1950), given that everything else in the child's life at this time is overt rather than latent. What is agreed upon is that children at this age learn to submerge and contain feelings. Cognitive developmental milestones are rapid. These cognitive changes occur simultaneously with the formation of defensive mechanisms (Gardner 1978, Le Francis 1980, Vailiant 1977); it is at this time that sexual thoughts and aggressive strivings become part of unconscious processes:

Obviously to bring up "good" children is not without its
dangers. The repressions which are required to achieve this
result, the reaction-formations and the sublimations which
have to be built up, are paid for at a quite definite cost. The
originality of the child, together with a great deal of his energy
and his talents, are sacrificed to being "good." (Freud, A.
1935, p. 77)

Latency has traditionally been conceptualized as the time of childhood in which drive repression frees the child for cognitive growth, peer relationships, and diminished family ties. Erikson's (1959) description of the "age of industry" suggests competence, mastery, and acquisition of skills. More recently Sarnoff (1976) and others have questioned this formulation; they see in children from 6 to 12 years of age a lessened capacity for repression, overt sexual preoccupations, and more interference with ego development. Nagera's (1973) previously cited discussion on alteration/misapplication of benign permissiveness of parents may explain why there are fewer conflict-free spheres of ego development.

Despite societal, cultural, and social alterations of the meaning of parenting—some latency age children do resolve normal developmental issues via an attachment to the world of peers. "Sometimes by (laymen) behaviorist techniques, the latency group, often without adult intervention, aids its members in adaption to the social mores they have established on their own" (Berkovitz 1972, p. 2). Ordinarily, under "good enough" circumstances the latency-age child slowly develops a new self-image, a new ego ideal beyond his family membership. Social, academic, and athletic skills facilitate membership in the peer society. With this foundation, the child enters adolescence comfortably and securely and begins to prepare for a role in the adult social world.

Research by Mahler, Pine, and Bergman (1975) points to normal and typical achievement of separation and individuation, and attainment of emotional object constancy well before the kindergarten school years: before entry into latency. Nevertheless, even parents who could empathically support and let go of their differentiating child, struggle with the latency child's new allegiances and significant emotional attachments. Often parents, with humor and a touch of sadness, recount their first dethronement, when their child cites the authority, competence, and expertise of "the teacher" rather than the previously idealized parents. At this time parents must face the scrutiny and evaluation of their parent practices and their child during their first parent/teacher conference. The issues of parental self-esteem, anxiety, and uncertainty are frequently highlighted by the child's entry into latency and the public domain.

The above vicissitudes present their own developmental challenges for parents. Learning how to correct children without diminishing their desire to produce or making them feel inferior is difficult. It is a struggle for parents to let go, to allow their children freedom to explore the environment.

Psychopathology may be evident, on a continuum from mild reactive disorders to marked family suffering, as a result of developmental arrests, defects, and/or deviations. Schools and pediatricians commonly make referrals for evaluations and treatment intervention as the child enters that time of life when the refrain, "he or she will grow out of it" no longer suffices. Children at this age are prey to feelings of inferiority and unworthiness (Duval 1977). Parents are still the children's primary source of security and stability. Although children desire to achieve on their own, they still want parental approval. Children with learning handicaps usually have a damaging sense of inferiority. They are, for the most part, aware of their lack of competence. The need to establish groups for children with learning problems and for their parents is particularly strong during latency, given the psychological tasks for this developmental stage.

Criteria for determining indications for group treatment of latency age children are many and varied (Lubin, Reddy, Taylor, and Lubin 1978). A major obstacle to group work with the latency-age child is the manifestation of severe narcissistic pathology. Commonly, children with this problem are self-centered; they have a high degree of self-reference, suffer from poor peer relations, and are isolated. Traditional approaches have often catapulted such children into group therapy to supposedly improve their social functioning when, in fact, they may be too vulnerable to experience the group setting positively. Their withdrawal may be due to ill-timed or confrontative group therapy, which is experienced as a narcissistic assault. Self psychology demonstrates the need for an empathic therapist who will listen to the narcissistically disordered individual, if improved self-esteem is to result.

Fragile children may need one-to-one therapy prior to, or even in conjunction with, a group therapy experience. Trafimow and Pattak present in this section a description of work with a group of primitively fixated children, where the group, as symbiotic mother, and the therapist as auxiliary ego, provide a cushion of support and safety. It seems best not to include a schizophrenic youngster with more adequate children as rejection and scapegoating of the more damaged child may occur. With less severely impaired children, group therapy may ameliorate their problems where the natural peer group has failed.

We believe the modality of children's groups encourages the reduction of pathology and helps children work through developmental crises. Children integrated in a well-functioning group are more amenable to change among trusted and respected peers whom they wish to emulate. School and after school settings provide an accessible meeting place in which to establish groups.

REFERENCES

Berkovitz, I. H. (1972). *Adolescents Group in Groups—Experiences in Adolescent Group Psychotherapy*. New York: Brunner Mazel.

Duval, E. (1977). *Marriage and Family Development*, 5th ed. New York: J. B. Lippincott.

Erikson, E. (1950). *Childhood and Society*. New York: Norton.

——(1959). *Identity and the Life Cycle. Psychological Issues*.

Freud, A. (1935). *Psychoanalysis for Teachers and Parents*. Boston: Beacon Press.

Freud, S. (1905). Three essays on the theory of sexuality. *Standard Edition* 7:123–244.

Gardner, H. (1978). *Developmental Psychology—An Introduction*. Boston: Little Brown.

Le Francis, G. R. (1980). *On Children, An Introduction to Child Development*, 3rd ed. Belmont, Calif.: Wadsworth Publishing.

Lubin, B., Reddy, W. B., Taylor, A. and Lubin, A. W. (1978). The group psychotherapy literature, 1977. *International Journal of Group Psychotherapy* Vol. 22, No. 4: 518.

Mahler, B., Pine, F., and Bergman (1975). *The Psychological Birth of the Human Infant—Symbiosis and Individuation*. New York: Basic Books.

Nagera, H. (1973). Adolescence: Some diagnostic, prognostic and developmental considerations. In *Adolescent Psychiatry: Developmental and Clinical Studies* Vol. 2, pp. 44-55. New York: Basic Books.

Sarnoff, C. (1976). *Latency*. New York: Jason Aronson.

Thomas, A. and Chess, S. (1972). Development in middle childhood. In *The Process of Child Development*, ed. Peter Neubauer. New York: New American Library.

Vailiant, G. E. (1977). *Adaptation to Life: How the Best and Brightest Come of Age*. Boston: Little Brown.

CHAPTER 6

Learning Disabilities: A Trauma of Latency
MARY GIFFIN, M.D.

EDITORS' NOTES
Dr. Giffin presents the familiar diagnostic dilemma clinicians struggle with when confronted by hyperactive, distractible children with poor school performance. It should be stressed that the child with learning and perceptual handicaps does not simply have a school disability, but a total life disability. What interferes with the normal learning process (so often the precipitant for referral in the early latency period) also impinges on self-concept, self-image, self-esteem, peer relationships, family relationships, and social interactions. We include this particular chapter as there is a dearth of literature on specialized group treatment for this population, though, paradoxically, they have so much to gain socially from group work.

Each child with a learning disability presents a unique diagnostic problem. As the condition is manifest in a myriad of academic and behavioral symptoms, there is no set method of evaluation. The appropriate therapeutic spectrum is more enigmatic than dogmatic; for each child it should be intentionally idiosyncratic, based on multiple and complex diagnostic considerations.

Many children referred as psychiatric problems, in fact, have learning disabilities. The creative skills of clinicians are tested by the needs of individual children with uniquely different combinations of maturational and developmental disabilities, and emotional conflicts. It is hoped that the clinical material presented in this paper may stimulate other practitioners to recognize the importance of perceptual problems in the evaluation of children presented with psychiatric difficulties. Such considerations are crucial in planning an ongoing course of intervention.

In the field of study that focuses on learning disabilities much information has been accumulated; unfortunately, practical understanding has often lagged behind. Observations in the field of the perceptually handicapped prove that as classic as some of the patterns may appear, individual children have their own unique disability and add their own psychological reactions to it.

DEFINITION

For the purposes of this presentation, this author refers to perception rather simply, as "an activity of the mind intermediate between sensation and thought" (Strauss and Kephart 1955). In the course of maturation, most children move smoothly from awareness of diffuse, undifferentiated external perceptions to increasingly clear objective reality perceptions (Bender 1952). The perceptually handicapped child moves unevenly; often the child's disability permeates both the educational and the emotional life of the child.

It is possible to conceptualize six areas of brain activity: neuromuscular, inhibitory, cerebral sensory, peripheral sensory, perceptual, and intellectual. For most of us, fortunately, the inner workings, the interdigitation and imbrication of all these activities are meshed so perfectly that we rarely have to be made aware of them. Having mastered the necessary controls early in childhood, and having honed our associations in the crucible of daily life, we can proceed to other endeavors rather than having to continually focus upon what should be subconscious activity. In the neurophysiologically handicapped, a subtle uneasiness in gait, difficulty in alternating movements, or problems in the tracking of the eyes are often reflections of a neuromuscular dysfunction. More frequently noticeable is the lack of inhibition, or what Strauss and Kephart referred to as the "heightened interpersonal relations" that these children show. They quickly admit feelings, they verbalize their thoughts of a personal nature almost immediately, and their neuromuscular behavior often reveals an impulsive quality that catapults these children into clinics and social agencies as behavior problems. Because of these characteristics, more complicated intrapsychic problems are often overlooked. Similarly, brain activities—cerebral sensations, sensory appreciation, perception, and intellectual abilities—are characterized in these children by unpredictability and inconsistencies. In a tragically pervasive way, this child is a neuropsycho-physiologically handicapped person for life.

Some 320 characteristic symptoms of these children have been outlined; of the 10 most common characteristics, 3 are potentially psychiatric. These children typically show hyperactivity, perceptual motor difficulties, impulsivity, thinking disorders, specific learning problems, speech disorders, and equivocal neurological findings. Clearly the emotional lability, the impulsivity, and the thinking disorders cannot easily be attributed to organic or psychogenic causes. It must be kept clear that the children in this presentation are those for whom sights, sounds, and symbols are cacaphonous and confusing. A striking example of the predicament of such children was reflected in the comment of a child of 8 who had cooperated well through psychiatric and psychological testing evaluations. He had seemingly responded in an organized fashion through most of the testing; yet, when he was turned away from the examiner with only his ears for sensory input, he suddenly became panicky and noted, "My ears don't like it, my head doesn't like it, my whole being doesn't like it, and when it's like this I jump to *collusions* (sic)." This spontaneous and unusually perceptive comment about his own inner workings gives some indication of the Gordian knot of perceptual and associational difficulties confronting the child and psychiatric clinician.

In a busy practice oriented primarily to psychoanalytic evaluation and treatment, one is tempted to say that this kind of problem is really none of our business; we have arduously studied the unconscious, and after years of analyzing adult and child reconstructions, we find ourselves looking at the manner in which a child holds a pencil! However, the theoretical framework of this entire field represents an example of one of Freud's basic dicta; that all psychology is developed on a base of physiology. These children with neurophysiological problems, problems of visual-perceptual, visual-motor, auditory-perceptual, auditory-expressive, conceptual, translation, and speech difficulties suffer from handicaps which reflect the evolutionary hazard of moving from a simple reflex arc to that of a refined performance including abstract thinking. These are truly somatopsychic problems.

In some ways, perhaps the psychoanalytically trained clinician has the framework by which to conceptualize the psychoeducational, psychosocial, and intrapsychic problems more fully than others in this field.

ASKING THE RIGHT QUESTIONS

Adequate understanding of the perceptually handicapped child's personal, enigmatic problems is crucial for proper treatment. The importance of accurate diagnosis cannot be overemphasized since years of frustrating work may be poured into the psychotherapy of these children. Work of the highest order may unwittingly be sown on fields not yet fertilized by the maturation of factors which permit the integration of verbalized concepts, abstract interpretations, and psychodynamic correlations. Often the neuro-physiologically determined variability in sensorium or the scattered ability to "think" is misjudged as a sign of anxiety or defensive isolation, and the concrete tendencies of these children are often misperceived by psychiatrists as negativism or denial. These children will often say, "I can get the big words but I get lost on the little ones." Imagine what confusion develops if children must speak with continuing uncertainty as to whether they are using the word "was" or the word "saw," and in that confused state are subjected to the onslaughts of an ambitious therapist!

Perceptually handicapped children often act as interdisciplinary catalysts. They force cross-fertilization among the fields of education, neurology, psychology, and psychiatry; only by learning the answers offered by all of these fields can one learn how to ask the right questions in one's own personal interviews with these children. Only by learning to listen with a perceptive ear, to observe with a sensitive eye, and to order suitably refined and selected psychological tests, can one identify the handicapped child and clarify the dysfunction.

One diagnostic trap is the perceptually handicapped child's apparent humor reflected in what seem like puns. Unfortunately, this humor is not funny to the afflicted child. Recently a young girl asked if I had fun in my "adultery!" I could suppress a laugh only because my mentors had alerted me to the recognition that this was reflective of a word-finding problem, not a clever pun. The simple task of drawing a picture or a map may reveal the lack of spatial organization. Straightforward queries about dates and seasons will sometimes allow time sequential problems so characteristic of the perceptually handicapped to be detected. If, however, one does not ask the right questions, the diagnostician may remain locked within the emotional frame of reference.

If one routinely asks for drawings, the problem is "drawn out" in the diagnostic study. Similarly, in the area of abstract thought, one must be willing to consider fragmented thought and the inability to associate as reflective of organic problems in conception. Unless the clinician considers whether this be maturational or organic rather than emotional, the child does not have the opportunity to clarify his predicament.

Highlights of four cases emphasize the importance of asking the right question:

CASE 1.   An 8-year old boy had sucked his thumb and wet his bed nightly for 1½ years; his behavior had worsened in the preceding six months. He explained that "Kids pick on me at school." In attempting to define his problem and the reality factors of his school setting, he seemed almost totally lacking in self-observation. He was highly distractible; he salivated when he spoke; and he had a word finding problem. In addition, he had difficulty with temporal orientation and was unable to note the sequence of months or week days. Unable to find the name Thursday, he spoke of taking skating lessons the day before the last day of the school week and noted that Friday followed Tuesday in the week. On the basis of this initial observation it seemed that the presenting symptoms were a regressive defense against increasing educational predicaments.

Only adequate psychological testing can corroborate any diagnosis. The diagnostician must, however, learn to ask for the right psychological tests. Projective testing alone is often misleading. In this case, a complete battery of educational and maturational tests revealed a 19 point discrepancy between a higher verbal score on the WISC than the Performance, with an overall I.Q. of 103. The lowest subtest on the WISC was object assembly, in which, for example, he placed the lips at right angles to the nose. Subsequent testing revealed rotations of visually presented materials, evidence of forgetting, and dependence on tactile clues. In summary, the following psychological tests are recommended: Bender-Gestalt, House-Tree-Person, WISC-R, Wrat, Ravens Matrices, TAT, Rorschach. This battery can be increased, if specific auditory, memory, or sensory deficits are suspected.

Material from the parents indicated no major developmental problems, though both parents seemed somewhat overprotective of the boy, their oldest child. Both considered their son's difficulties to be primarily emotional and were surprised when the clinic diagnosed him as a perceptually handicapped child with secondary adaptational problems.

CASE 2.   In contrast, a 6½-year-old boy was referred by the pediatrician because of what he called "sibling rivalry." The pediatrician had recognized the jealousy of this child toward a new baby and thought that child guidance might prevent further problems. The mother presented her son as an unhappy child, one who burst into tears easily and constantly referred to himself as dumb and unlikeable. She also noted his unhappiness at school where his reading performance was not commensurate with his presumed intelligence.

In the psychiatric interview the boy seemed handsome, likeable, and verbal; he spoke warmly of his two younger brothers, and of the fact that everyone paid attention to the baby, but said that he himself preferred Tyrannosaurus Rex. He drew dinosaurs with alacrity and skill and noted that he wanted to come back to see the interviewer again.

Since the boy seemed obviously of "superior" intelligence, pyschological testing was mistakenly requested only in the area of projectives. These confirmed his "superior" intelligence and showed an expansive and aggressive child with considerable anxiety. During extended diagnostic contact, some of the boy's unhappiness was verbalized, and his adjustment improved. This took place in the summer. Unfortunately, as soon as school started, the clinic was alerted by the boy's teacher that his learning difficulties had increased and were compounded now by disciplinary problems. At this point we realized that we had not asked whether the reading difficulties that had occurred in the first grade were possibly of an organic nature? The answer was revealed in the intelligence testing. There was a 15 point discrepancy between the "superior" performance I.Q. and the "high normal" verbal score. His sight vocabulary was poor; he had difficulty distinguishing between "then" and "they," "look" and "took," "the" and "be," and "his" and "he." Reading was a laborious activity for him; content was well retained but often poorly understood; he had no ability to recall passages. In this instance, a boy of "superior" intelligence was handicapped by the unevenness of his learning abilities.

CASE 3.   Similarly, we did not ask the right questions in the case of a 4-year-old girl referred by her nursery school because of destructive behavior that fluctuated between intrusive affection and belligerence.

Psychiatric evaluation described her as a very energetic girl with a short attention span. No serious problems were noted. Interviews with the mother revealed her anxiety about the responsibility of rearing this adopted child; her panic centered around management problems. It was felt that assistance to the mother would be beneficial; casework therapy helped the mother in her anxiety. This child returned to the clinic 2½ years later. She claimed not to mind the fact that she was repeating the first grade. This denial was interesting in that she was able to tearfully comment that she could not learn in the same way as other children. By this time we had learned to ask more questions about learning.

The psychologist noted, "In her simplification of designs by lines and dashes instead of dots, her decrease in the number of circles, her difficulty with a diamond, her perseveration, her separation of the two parts of several designs and her expressed frustration over repeated failure," there was some suggestion of organic difficulty. By this time we were realizing, as Einstein noted years ago, "It is not so important to know the right answer as it is to ask the right question."

CASE 4.   Hopefully by now we do ask at least some of the right questions, as for example in the case of an 8-year-old boy who was referred, as he put it, because, "My mom and dad are after me," and because he fought constantly with his older brother and younger sister. He was in constant motion throughout the diagnostic session; his reactions were fast and his play, competitively challenging. It was of interest that he rotated his drawings by ninety degrees, and that his awareness of perspective was almost entirely lacking.

From the parents it was learned that he had been asked to withdraw from school because of his disturbing effect on the classroom; he yelled out, jumped up from his seat, crawled around on the desk on his stomach, and in general exhibited "nervous behavior." In addition, he had engaged in self-destructive activities such as crawling out of the window and had verbalized his dislike for himself and his feeling that no one else liked him either.

The psychologist was asked to determine whether the behavior could be organically based. In the psychological evaluation there was a 14 point disparity between the higher performance level and the lower verbal and again a full scale I.Q. well within the "normal" range. The patient was unable to copy a diamond or a parallelogram and showed a deficit in visual memory. In addition, there was definite evidence of auditory misperceptions in his consistently incorrect responses to auditory stimuli. It had been this child who spoke of his mind going so quickly, "I can't keep up and I jump to collusions (sic.)."

In most of the cases studied in our setting, clinical neurological evaluation reveals a few subtle, positive signs. These are usually in the area of parieto-temporal dysfunction and would not be considered pathological in degree. Characteristically the electro-encephalograms on these children are essentially normal, and there is seldom a history of obstetrical complications, encephalitis, or fevers of unknown etiology that might be related. It is not the intent of this paper to inquire into etiology, but the cases seen in a psychiatric clinic practice do raise genetic, chemical, neurophysiologic, and even somatopsychic questions concerning etiology.

THE TREATMENT SPECTRUM

The potential treatment spectrum for this group of children is broad. In general it has been our practice to undergird the total program with the best possible academic programming. In addition to educational programming, I would like to formulate a 6-step treatment spectrum necessary for children with learning disabilities. These include:

1. the therapeutic use of the completion interview
2. the therapeutic use of the testing data
3. the value of inquiring about genetic factors
4. the contribution of the educational family sessions
5. the usefulness of group and family therapy
6. the crucial nature of individual interpretive therapy in selected cases

Following the careful diagnostic assessment of the child and his parents, all invested family members should be a part of the completion interview. As with any medical ailment, all family members are affected when one member has a handicap or deficiency. The impact on each and all family members must be communicated to other family members.

In many cases ongoing family sessions for educational purposes may seem important even as the child may be treated in a number of other ways. Some school districts have special education teams in the schools that offer group therapy education for parents of the children in special education. Sometimes this form of service is provided by collaborative arrangements between school districts and adjacent mental health facilities.

Case three demonstrates the value of ongoing group education. Having initially asked the wrong diagnostic question, at the time of the second diagnostic evaluation we had to help the family come to a different understanding of the problems. In this instance the family elected to discuss the sense of failure that each of them felt. The discussions also focused on the pattern of denial used by the parents, the adopted child, and the 11-year-old natural daughter.

INFLUENCE ON PRACTICE

It must be remembered that perceptual handicaps are not a disease. As a clinic team becomes more sensitized to this handicapped group, the diagnostician expands the focus of his concern to include such behavior as unusual sleep disturbances, night wandering, patterns of unpredictable outbursts, and the ability to learn to ride a bike, contrasted with the difficulty in reading or in writing. Similarly, child diagnosticians are becoming more aware of neuromuscular coordination and insistent on being provided with drawings and evidence of academic abilities. It is startling to see the anthropoid quality of the pencil grasping even in an 8-year-old.

One becomes more aware of articulation and translation difficulties in speech and of the neologisms that break through even in the course of one interview. One becomes more sensitized to the possibility of hearing loss and learns early that youngsters with high tone deafness often have difficulty with the letters $d, k, n,$ and s. Games acquire a new dimension as they reflect not only problems with competition but also difficulties in spatial relations. As the subtleties of the problem become apparent, the diagnostician becomes more adept at asking the right questions. Similarly as the diagnostician's awareness of the need for total family understanding of the learning difficulties of the child increases, he or she is generally more willing to view the spectrum of treatment more broadly. Just as the special education staff has learned to program in depth for these children, clinicians must learn to offer treatment in depth, to include the therapeutic value of the testing material and to provide ongoing group and family sessions for both children and parents.

CONCLUDING REMARKS

Recent research on the social and emotional development of the learning disabled child suggests that the lack of certain social skills prevents these children from forming relationships. Recognition of social cues, taking an appropriate perspective, interpreting nonverbal signals, understanding nuances in emotional exchanges are all examples of skills that may be hampered by cognitive deficits. Small group experiences in which children begin to interact with others under the guidance of a leader alert to the subtleties of social exchanges offers the best opportunity for remediation and growth.

REFERENCES

Bender, M. B. (1952). *Disorders in Perception*. Springfield, Illinois: Charles C. Thomas.

Strauss, A. A. and Kephart, N. C. (1955). *Psychopathology and Education of the Brain Injured Child* Vol. 2. New York: Grune and Stratton.

EDITORS' DISCUSSION

"In the field of child psychiatry, as in other realms of psychiatry, the past 25 to 30 years has been marked by controversy between 'organic' and 'psychodynamic' modes of thinking and treatment. There has been much acrimony and little collaboration. Therapists seemed to require of their patients and themselves, a whole hearted and total commitment to the tenets of one faith or the other" (Laufer and Shelty 1979, p. 386). It is suggested that about 10 percent of most school-age children manifest academic difficulty. Some of these children's problems are reflective of mental retardation; the below-normal performance of others is due to emotional problems; those in the third group have learning disabilities that relate directly to how their nervous system performs. "As each aspect of the problems was studied, and as each professional group viewed these children within the context of their own discipline (medicine, education, or psychology), different descriptions and diagnostic labels were developed. Even now the multiple approaches to viewing these children and the many diagnostic labels in use pose major problems in reviewing the literature or in understanding the data or claims about different treatment efforts or follow-up studies" (Silver 1979, p. 416).

Special educational programs and appropriate, well-monitored medication must at times accompany the psychotherapeutic intervention. Silver notes that if "properly recognized, diagnosed and treated the child with this syndrome has the potential for a reasonably successful future.... The confusing feature of this syndrome is the multiple types of clinical pictures such children can present. All aspects of their minimal brain disfunction syndrome must be considered in understanding the child, planning a treatment program and advising the family and school" (p. 436).

It is assumed that even relatively minor defects involve a psychological process similar to that which is inferred by Niederland (1965). He states that "there often ensues from the time of recognition of any defectiveness ("recognition shock") a marked disequilibrium in the relations between mother and child—a disequilibrium which hardly ever fully subsides. Some mothers go into a prolonged...depression, often followed by renewed depressions or anxiety states. Others become oversolicitous, seductive or otherwise defective in their nurturing functions. The children are thus further traumatized through the unsatisfactory mother-child interaction...." (p. 533).

Anthony (1976) suggests that one of the major difficulties that results from a deformity or abnormality is the ensuing narcissistic development of both parent and child. Whether disturbances occur first in the mother's or father's narcissistic process depends on their specific vulnerabilities. Not uncommonly, injury to parental selves is severe and well out of proportion to the defect as assessed by others. Inevitably the injury to parental selves is transmitted to the child as part of his self's development. Anthony suggests that grandiosity is inevitable for the child who can injure the parents simply by existing. Thus the child who can make his or her parents feel impotent and helpless leads a grandiose self existence. The covertly grandiose self can be reached and constructively modified via family guidance, and group and individual therapy during childhood. Involvement of the latency child alone is not nearly as useful as supportive, psychoanalytically based work with parents and educators.

Anthony stresses the usefulness of the newer Self Psychology and understanding the part-self-object functions. He believes that educators and parents can greatly aid the dawning intellectual life of young children and possibly prevent the development of learning disabilities by serving as an auxiliary to the incomplete mental apparatus. The basis for this theory is the premise that each new substep in intellectual development recapitulates the sequence of differentiation described by Mahler (Mahler, Pine, and Bergman 1975) in the first years of life. The developmentally appropriate and necessary use of adults as part objects who perform some aspects of the tasks being mastered is emphasized. This is postulated as a prerequisite for lifelong learning since even in adult life some part-function must be performed by the teacher of adults until the task becomes autonomous. Thus, the importance of collaboration among clinicians, parents, and teachers can hardly be overemphasized. Furthermore, Dr. Giffin's recommendations for a range of interventions, including parent education groups and small group experiences for children, is particularly relevant to the social and emotional tasks of latency.

Anthony, James. The Self and Congenital Defects: Prevention of Emotional Disabilities. Association of Child and Adolescent Psychotherapists, Annual Meeting. Chicago, Ill., October, 1976.

Laufer, Maurice W., and Shelty, Taramath (1979). "Acute and chronic brain syndromes." In *Basic Handbook of Child Psychiatry*, ed. Joseph Noshpitz. New York: Basic Books.

Mahler, M. S., Pine, F., and Bergman, A. (1975). *The Psychological Birth of the Human Infant-Symbiosis and Individuation*. New York: Basic Books.

Niederland, William (1965). Narcissistic ego impairment in patients with early physical malformations. *The Psychoanalytic Study of the Child* Vol. 20. New York: International Universities Press.

Silver, Larry (1979). The minimal brain dysfunction syndrome. *Basic Handbook of Child Psychiatry*, ed., Joseph Noshpitz. New York: Basic Books.

CHAPTER 7

Activity Groups in a Special Education Setting
MARILYN WILSON, M.A.

EDITORS' NOTES
Ms. Wilson's paper vividly portrays the tone and commotion created by children with learning disabilities. While Dr. Giffin's paper focused on the difficulties of diagnosing children with learning disabilities, this paper documents the vicissitudes of the treatment process with regard to the hyperactive child who has difficulty with delay, abstract thinking, and appropriate social relatedness. These developmental lags, depicted in action terms, illustrate the lack of genuine latency level adjustment in these children.
Wilson's trial and error programming and her flexibility are firmly grounded in Ego Psychology. Her awareness of partialization, rapid gratification, and external structure demonstrates her recognition of the ego deficits of these children.

DEVELOPMENT OF THE GROUP

The children this paper describes were 5- and 6-year-olds with learning disabilities who were served by the early childhood center of a private school. In addition to academic difficulties, many of these youngsters appeared to have minimal social skills. Interaction with one another was of a physically aggressive nature—hitting, pushing, and kicking. Although direct verbal interaction occurred infrequently, when it did the tone was often angry and the decibel level always high. Classrooms from which group members were selected were quite noisy; however, the noise was not a result of children talking and playing with each other but rather, talking *at* one another, and to the teacher about one another ("Stop it!"..., "She punched me...," "He took my scissors...."). Given this situation, it seemed appropriate to organize a group whose purpose was to promote the social development of the participants.

As attendance at the school was irregular, group size was set at four to allow for the probability that one group member would be absent on any given day. Researchers agree on group size for younger children, particularly those with limited psychological and physical controls: Glass (1969) feels that group size for children with neurological impairments should be between two and four; Ginott (1961) recommends five as the maximum membership for a children's play/activity group and suggests that beginning group leaders limit group size to three. Thursday morning was chosen as the group meeting time. Monday and Friday were avoided for two reasons: the atmosphere in the school tends to be more chaotic prior to and after the weekend break. Furthermore, most absences occur on these days.

The format for the group evolved out of an initial conference with the teachers. Many of the children served in this setting have low frustration tolerance, poor impulse control, and short attention spans. Circle games and dances, for example, would not provide the structure necessary to facilitate optimal functioning in a new group situation. Projects with a structured nature would enable the children to direct their energies in a more socially appropriate manner. In addition, the participation of each group member was necessary. The structured setting would give group members the experience of working with others in order to reach a goal. In the planning stages activities such as making a collage or a mural were considered.

COMPOSITION OF THE GROUP

Ginott (1961) feels that there is a danger in placing friends and siblings in the same play/activity group as old patterns of behavior are perpetuated, and new ones are, therefore, less likely to emerge. Since the class sizes at the school are small (7 to 9), to form a group whose members were in close contact with one another five days a week was contraindicated. Additionally, the pain of exclusion would be somewhat lessened for those not participating in the group if two, rather than four, out of eight students were chosen. If all members of the group were from the same class, a subgroup might form that could interfere with the functioning of the class of eight as a group. While it is possible that such a subgroup might have a positive effect on the classroom group by serving as a model for the rest of the class, there was no way to ensure this. The disadvantages of taking all members of the activity group from the same class seemed to outweigh the advantages. Since the teachers of the 5- and 6-year-olds were enthusiastic about the activity group and often coordinated their schedules for joint activities, it seemed natural to select the group members from the two classes.

Ginott discusses the importance of selecting group members carefully so that the group experience will be a positive one for those participating; specifically, he feels that the "effectiveness of group play therapy depends on a harmonious combination . . . ." (1961, p. 29). The initial concern in this situation was to select children who would benefit from a group experience. In deciding which combination of four to choose for the group, the emphasis was on children whose respective strengths and weaknesses would complement one another. The group was racially mixed: three blacks and one white participated.

GROUP MEMBERSHIP

Although somewhat withdrawn and inactive, B, age 6, appeared to have more social skills than most of the children in his age group. His mode of interaction with both adults and peers, while infrequent, was more advanced developmentally than that of many of his classmates. Because B exhibited a good deal of impulse control and frustration tolerance and was generally able to conduct himself in a socially appropriate manner, it was postulated that he might serve as a model for the other group members. Ginott would call B the neutralizer—the child who exhibits socially acceptable behavior and will most likely disapprove of group anarchy. The group experience could be valuable for B, as it would provide him with the opportunity to engage in a special relationship with other children and, perhaps, encourage him to begin more spontaneous interactions and involvement with his peers.

E, also 6, was in many ways the opposite of B. Often friendly and outgoing, E was active in the classroom and appeared to be in a state of perpetual motion. He had difficulty controlling his impulses and was sometimes very aggressive. He could tolerate very little frustration and employed extreme physical measures in order to obtain the teacher's attention. Because E needed to learn to modulate his aggressive behavior and direct his energies toward tasks that would give him a sense of accomplishment, his participation in the activity group seemed appropriate.

S, age 5, also seemed a natural choice as she did not appear to be as far behind the others developmentally. Her verbal skills were adequate for the group situation, and she seemed most able to make contact with other children. S was overactive, however, and found it difficult to focus her attention on one task for any length of time.

K was very much the opposite of S. Her behavior was somewhat perseverative, as she was able to remain involved in one activity for an exceedingly long period of time. In the classroom her behavior was controlled, and she seemed to be isolated from the other children. K's language skills were considerably less well developed than those of the other group members. Her infrequent attempts to communicate were usually one word utterances.

PHYSICAL SETTING

The importance of the physical setting for a children's activity group is stressed by both Slavson and Schiffer (1975) and Ginott (1961). In order to facilitate the corrective purposes of an activity group the setting should evoke suitable responses that are eventually internalized, and thereby help strengthen the egos of the group members. Slavson (1964) discusses the importance of situational rather than direct restraint in activity group therapy, claiming that the former avoids the resentment, rebelliousness, and uncontrolled acting out that are often provoked by the latter. There were two rooms in which group sessions could be held. The first one, known as the resource room, had what appeared to be obvious disadvantages: it was necessary to pass through the room to get to the bathroom; the sink, stove, refrigerator, and supply closet were located in the room; the door connecting this room to another rather noisy classroom was often open; and a staircase led directly into the room. In all, the room was impractical because it was not far enough away from the other activities of the school and offered too many distractions.

The second possibility was a room located in a corner of the building that could be closed off completely from the rest of the school. It was separated from the nearest room by a short hallway, so noise would not be a problem. It had only two doors—one leading to the street and the other to the hallway. Additionally, the room contained a piano, desk, and gymnastics mat. It seemed the obvious choice because it was set apart from the rest of the school, and the group activity was not likely to be disturbed. The first two and one-quarter meetings were held in this room, and utter chaos was the result: the children climbed on the piano, jumped off, banged on it, jumped on the mat, turned the lights out and attempted to leave the building. Not exactly what was intended!

The group temperament changed markedly during the third meeting, and initially the change was attributed to the fact that a more structured activity had been planned. The meeting began in its regular location, but it began to disintegrate quickly; out of desperation, everyone was moved to the resource room. As soon as the group members were seated at the table with their trays and clay in front of them, an atmosphere of relative calm settled in. In a subsequent conversation with one of the teachers, it was discovered that the original room was known as the "gross motor room," a place where children went specifically to engage in physical activity. In addition, they were dismissed from this room at the end of each school day, and the conditions that prevail at dismissal time are such that associations to this time of day would not be of a calm, cooperative, socially appropriate nature. The behavior that occurred during the first two meetings was certainly partially due to the fact that we were meeting in the "gross motor room."

REVISION OF GOALS

The project for the first few meetings (construction of a work table) arose out of necessity. The plan was to have the group sand the table-top. This activity proved to be a complete failure as it resulted in total disruption of anything resembling group activity. The task was too amorphous and did not secure the attention of any one child for more than a minute or two at a time. With one exception, the group members could not grasp the idea that we were making a table for our use. The concept of the five of us as a group was too abstract for most of the members, and the connection between rubbing sandpaper on a piece of wood and a completed table was equally difficult for them to understand.

Before the first meeting, the goal had been to have the members work together on a single group project and through this experience learn social skills such as cooperation and sharing. After two fruitless attempts at getting the tabletop sanded, the goals for the group were quickly revised. The immediate goal now was to have individual members working on arts and crafts activities at the same table without too much disruption. The eventual goal was to have the group members sharing materials such as glue and scissors. These children needed to have more immediate gratification from their efforts. Basic ego deficits prevented their grasping the abstract goal of sanding the table.

GROUP PROCESS AND DYNAMICS

The concept of the group members and leader as a separate unit was not comprehended. *B* was the only group member who understood the implications of the five of us meeting every week to work on special projects together. During the first session he said, "Oh, you mean just these people will be meeting with you." During the fourth session *S* expressed some sense of the group as a closed unit, when she responded to an attempt by some boys from another class to join in our activity with, "No, this is only for us!" On the morning of the fifth meeting I found *E* waiting in the resource room. He helped set up the table and then told me who to pick up for the group. While he and *B* were always very eager to come to group, the other two were not. *K* was reluctant to leave the particular classroom activity in which she was engaged at the moment. However, when we went to pick her up for the sixth meeting she did respond to *B*'s urging to join us. The next time she came quite willingly and even asked, "What are we going to do?" *S* was not really a part of the growing cohesiveness of the group as she missed meetings five and six, which were followed by a three-week winter vacation.

The fourth meeting was a turning point in that, for the first time, we functioned successfully as a group with all members present. Much of the success of the session can be attributed to the nature of the task, and the structure that was provided from the beginning. The activity involved using cookie cutters to make different shapes out of play dough. The activity table was completely set up before the group arrived. Group members were able to begin immediately as little instruction/demonstration was necessary.

The next meeting went relatively smoothly for many of the same reasons. Putting miniature decorations on paper Christmas trees served as the week's activity. However, a new variable was introduced: *one* bottle of glue and *one* container of glitter. This meant that the group would have to share in a very new way for them. When E tried to grab the glue from K the leader intervened and, returning it to K said, "We are going to share the glue. Now it's K's turn, then it will be E's turn...." B and K were able to share more naturally than E, who needed to announce aloud whose turn it was next. As a whole, the group depended on the leader to monitor the turns. Aggressive physical exchanges were absent during this meeting as each child was very much involved in his or her project and showed little interest in what the other group members were doing. Group interaction was limited to the verbal exchanges pertaining to sharing the materials.

The importance of structure for these children was underlined once again during the sixth meeting when the format changed slightly, and as a result the situation did not run as smoothly as it had previously. Because B's fine motor coordination was more advanced than the other group members', he was usually the first to finish the project. Without anything to keep him occupied at the group table, he often ran around the room. If the leader was unable to bring him back, the group was totally disrupted. Alternative activities were brought to the sixth meeting. Rather than provide B with a second activity when it was needed, he was presented the different activities as choices for the entire group at the beginning. While he was able to make a choice and begin working, E and K became confused and tried to do everything at once.

An important event in the life of the group took place during the seventh meeting when for the first time concern and support was shown in an exchange between two members. Upon discovering that he had two Santa stickers B said, "Here, E, you can have a Santa," to which E responded, "Oh, thank you, B." Identification with the leader was also shown this week by B, who exclaimed, "You got your hair cut—so did I!"

After a three week Christmas break, we had our eighth meeting. The time that had elapsed since the previous meeting and the fact that, owing to an unforeseen schedule conflict, we had to meet in the gross motor room resulted in regression on all levels of group and individual functioning. The concepts of community ownership and sharing that had been gradually accepted and implemented by the group appeared to have been lost forever.

Slavson (1964) reminds us that when children enter the group session and exhibit hyperactivity, aggression, or destructiveness, it is most likely related to a preceding event and should be overlooked until it automatically dissipates. E and B brought the tension of their classroom to the group. The aggression and destructiveness exhibited by the boys could only be ignored at the expense of their own safety and that of the rest of the group. This did not seem feasible. B, who had recently returned from an annual Christmas visit to a father who lived out of state, seemed to have suffered the greatest setback. While E behaved much as he had during the early meetings, B regressed to levels that he had not previously exhibited in the group.

Slavson describes children's activity groups as alternating between states of disequilibrium (hyperactivity) and equilibrium (constructive work) and following a progression whereby the periods of disequilibrium shorten while those of equilibrium increase in length (Slavson and Schiffer 1975). Spontaneous recovery from the post-vacation regression did occur, and the next meeting went fairly smoothly.

Preparation for termination was begun by telling the group that they would meet two more times and that at the last meeting would have a party. This announcement was met with silence. The topic was brought up a few more times without success. The leader began to wonder if she had been understood. Finally, E was asked directly, "How many more times is the leader going to come here?" Without looking at the leader, he held up two fingers. The fact that S and K did not respond may be partially attributed to denial and partially to their limited understanding of what "two more times" meant.

B was present for the next meeting, which began in a state of heightened disequilibrium. After announcing his dislike for the activity that had been set up, B led the group in a run between the resource room and the gross motor room. After convincing the rest of the group to go to the table, attention was focused on calming B. Upon hearing that the next meeting would be our last, he responded angrily with, "You're not coming back?!" and ran to his classroom. The ending of the group was added to the list of painful separations and disruptive events in his life, and he had apparently reached the point of feeling totally overwhelmed. After B left, equilibrium was achieved once again.

The final group meeting was both touching and frustrating. The mechanisms of identification and empathy which Freud (1921) describes as basic to group formations were more visible during this meeting. While the group members had at different times expressed signs of identification with the leader, it was not until the last meeting that their identification with one another through the common tie to the leader was manifested. (Although somewhat tentative, empathy among group members was also expressed during the final meeting.) We had arranged to eat lunch together for the last meeting, with cupcakes as a special treat. S and K immediately inquired as to why this was the last time, after having ignored my attempts to talk about it during the past two sessions. The explanation was that the leader's school required her going to school on the day they used to meet. After the group was over S asked, "Why don't you go to school at night?" B greeted me with "It's the last time"; E seemed unusually subdued, yet made no mention of this as the last group. Throughout the luncheon, however, he asked if the leader was coming tomorrow...or next week. After saying good-bye he gave me his phone number and asked me to call his mother so she could invite me over.

For the first time in the life of the group, K made personal contact by offering the leader her apricot drink and asking that she wear a paper ring she had made. K was also able to extend herself to B by letting him have the last pink frosted cupcake. S offered some of her lunch to E. The group sang Happy Birthday, perhaps in response to the red party plates and cake. In any case, it qualified as a spontaneous, nonaggressive group activity—a milestone in the life of this group.

By the last meeting B and E appeared to have switched roles. Unable to sit at the table and eat lunch with the rest of the group, B ran in, out, and around the room. He pulled his pants down and tried to coax the others, especially E, to follow suit. The growth that E had made was evident in his ability to control himself and resist most of B's urging. At the same time it was discouraging to watch B, who had been so excited about the group in the first place, as his agitation culminated in an attempt to urinate on the group members and finally the floor. While the group seemed to have served the others well, it had somehow failed B.

The group situation is one that most readily facilitates the development of new social skills in many young children and is thus often the treatment chosen to modify the physically aggressive mode of interaction among group members. Ginott considers an activity group as a "...tangible social setting for discovering and experimenting with new and more satisfying modes of relating to peers" (1961, p. 11). Children can help each other to become aware of their responsibilities in interpersonal relations. Ginott feels that both inhibited and aggressive children can learn new ways of relating through the group setting. The inhibited child discovers that he receives more satisfaction by making his wants and needs known, and the aggressive child learns that there are instances in which waiting patiently will get him farther than acting impulsively.

E is an example of an aggressive child who made tremendous progress in the activity group setting. By the fifth meeting he was able to control this behavior by modeling the leader's verbalization, i.e., "Next is B's turn." With external cues E was able to delay gratification of his needs to some extent. At the seventh meeting E was able to ignore B's urging to turn out the lights and instead heed the leader's reminder that the lights stay on during group. At earlier sessions E was only too eager to comply with such suggestions. Gradually he was able to spend longer and longer periods of time at the table; in fact, he spent the entire eighth session involved in the activity. More than anyone else, E seemed to want physical contact with the other group members. He was able to move from somewhat aggressive bodily contact to painting on their projects, and eventually the latter behavior diminished, although it never ceased entirely. K learned to speak up for herself, as time and again S tried to help her with her projects. K much preferred to work on her own and soon discovered that the only way to maintain her privacy was to ask S to stop.

Dinkmeyer and Muro (1971) also discuss the group as a safe place for new reality testing to occur. The nonthreatening, accepting atmosphere of the group setting facilitates experimentation with new ways of relating and provides immediate feedback as well. The group makes certain demands that each member must meet to remain part of the group. S learned to respect K's desire to work by herself; E discovered that grabbing was not the most successful method for gaining access to group materials.

In addition, the activity group provides members with an experience of mutuality and acceptance that increases their self-esteem. The earliest stage of intimacy and trust was established in the group and was manifested in the last few meetings when group members reached out to one another. Hopefully, the mutual acceptance and empathy, as well as the opportunity for new reality testing provided by the group setting, will allow the participants to take on more constructive roles in other situations.

The developmental level of the group—dependency—did not change from beginning to end. However, there was a difference in the quality of the dependency by the latter sessions. Although the group still wanted the leader to fulfill its needs by making decisions and providing love and nurturance, it was not the chaotic dependency of the beginning.

REFERENCES

Dinkmeyer, D. C. and Muro, J. J. (1971). *Group Counseling: Theory and Practice*. Illinois: F. E. Peacock.

Freud, S. (1921). Group psychology and the analysis of the ego. *Standard Edition* 18:67–143.

Ginott, H. (1961). *Group Psychotherapy with Children*. New York: McGraw-Hill.

Glass, S. (1969). *The Practical Handbook of Group Counseling*. Baltimore: BSC Publishing.

Slavson, S. R. (1964). *A Textbook in Analytic Group Psychotherapy*. New York: International Universities Press.

Slavson, S. R. and Schiffer, M. (1975). *Group Psychotherapies for Children*. New York: International Universities Press.

EDITORS' DISCUSSION

COMPOSITION. Four developmentally impaired children were selected for this group. Three of the children were black, and one was white. All were from lower-middle and middle-class homes, attending a private inner city school for children with developmental lags and severe learning disabilities. Wilson noted that the children lack social skills as well as perceptual-motor and cognitive strengths. Frequently, children with the cognitive deficits associated with learning disabilities have parallel delays in emotional development, particularly with regard to attaining object constancy (Buchholz 1978). The children were chosen on the basis of their level of ego development and their anticipated potential to help each other improve social functioning and learn less egocentric behavior. Care was exercised to neither select nor exclude children from only one classroom. Thus they were chosen in consultation with the teachers. The group was deliberately kept small in light of the needs of these children and the beginner skills of the clinician.

SETTING AND PURPOSE. The pervasive influence of old associations is particularly significant to children who, for example, have difficulty distinguishing different uses of a room. Wilson was aware of this when she selected the meeting room. The group was hyperactive in the "gross motor room" and could not settle down for other types of activities.

The general goal set forth by Wilson was to improve the children's ego functioning through collective work on projects such as murals, collages, and refinishing a table. In addition, the author hoped to improve the children's socialization and work skills and to diminish hyperactivity and egocentricity. An additional goal must be noted, which was Wilson's need to fulfill her graduate school practicum requirement. Goals for the children were quickly revised as the author integrated theory and practice. Once aware of the real meaning of deficits and problematic behaviors of these impaired children, she shifted program planning, simplified activities, and offered even more structure and support while struggling with the realities of hyperactivity, impulsivity, lack of ego synthesis, and impaired object relations.

LEVEL OF INTERVENTION—CLINICAL TECHNIQUES.
Discovering that these children were still operating at a nursery school level, engaging in solitary or parallel play, rather than calm and controlled peer interaction, Wilson quickly assumed a more directive stance. She had to establish herself as the moderator of reality. As a parent does with the pre-schooler, she allowed feelings to be expressed and, at the same time, set limits. "While language is present for both the children and the adult, interpretation and the quest for insight play no part in the armamentarium of this method, though understanding is quite often a by-product" (Frank 1976, p. 103). As a teacher—teaching children to share, and to wait—the therapist is a representative of the object world (Blanck and Blanck 1979) and, consequently, a teacher of reality.

Wilson's presentation reflects many of the common vicissitudes and practice dilemmas that clinicians and patients face. Wilson did not have adequate time to be able to see her children integrate beginning gains so visible in just ten meetings. She could not continue for many reasons, not the least of which were internal problems that threatened the very existence of the school. Practicum requirements often satisfy training needs of students rather than the clinical needs of clients. Such disabled children (and adults) prove to be reachable and treatable, but gains from compressed or short-term interventions are not always sustained.

GROUP PROCESS. The designated goal was to develop a group process that embodied group cohesion, a sense of unity, commonality, and improved peer interaction. The leader had apparently hoped to enhance entry into latency, expecting that self and other interactions would improve cognitive capacities and mastery of age-appropriate tasks. We suggest that these children lacked self/other distinctions and a cohesive sense of self and object; and therefore a genuine group feeling never formed. In fact, the children underwent symbiotic merger with one another and with the leader. Boundaries between themselves and nonmembers were delineated somewhat. Given the organic and emotional limitation these children present, Brazelton's and Als' (1979) comments appear to be applicable: "The immature organism with its vulnerability to being overloaded must be in constant homeostatic regulation—the physiological and the psychological. Handling input becomes a major goal" (1979, p. 354)—and the presence of the therapist appeared absolutely crucial to these children. She responded intuitively to rapprochement manifestations that the children presented when termination was introduced. In view of their dependence on her, and the regression that occurred during the last meeting, Mahler's comments concerning the process of individuation are particularly apt: "As the toddler's awareness of separateness grows—he now seems to have an increased need and wish for his mother to share with him his every new acquisition of skill and experience" (Mahler 1972).

GROUP DYNAMICS. It should be noted that Wilson's interpretation of failure with *B* is open to question. For a child who has difficulty relating to people, he showed appropriate connections with group members and leader. His regressive behavior at the last sessions may well point to his sense of dismay with termination. In general, Wilson enhanced social performance in these children. Also, regression in subsequent group meetings is to be expected and does not necessarily imply that previous activities failed to stimulate growth among the children.

These children's resistance and relative non-alliance cannot be viewed in traditional terms applicable to neurotic, more intact children. Reluctant to engage from the start, they could be neither calmed nor contained, out of unmanageable fear and anxiety. They lack the internal structure to maintain an adequate defense system that would better bind in anxiety, impulsivity, or fear of new situations. Furthermore, their ego impairments prevented them from being able to grasp the abstract concept of why they were brought to activity group treatment. Gradually, mirror and merger identifications (not self/other transference manifestations) appeared. As noted earlier, the therapeutic alliance was that of symbiotic merger; gradually the children responded to others by mirroring the leader's behavior.

Brazelton, T. B., and Als, H. (1979). Four early stages in the development of mother-infant interaction. *Psychoanalytic Study of the Child* 34:349–369. New Haven: Yale University Press.

Buchholz, E. S. (1978). Emotional Development and Emotional Controls in Learning Disabled Children, PCR Report, New York University.

Frank, M. G. (1976). Modifications of activity group therapy: responses to ego-impoverished children. *Clinical Social Work Journal* 4:102–109.

Mahler, M. S. (1972). Rapprochement subphase of the separation-individuation process. In *The Selected Papers of Margaret S. Mahler* Vol. 2. New York: Jason Aronson.

CHAPTER 8

Modified Activity Group Therapy with Ego Impoverished Children
MARGARET G. FRANK, C.S.W.

EDITORS' NOTES
This paper demonstrates the natural curative factors within the group process. The leader underscores the necessity of protecting the crystallizing self of these children by accepting feelings and separating behavior from emotions. The severely limited "ego impoverished" child presented here might also be described as narcissistically injured; the treatment suggestions are consonant with Ego and Self Psychology. This paper appeared in *Clinical Social Work Journal*, Vol. 4, no. 2, 1976.

Classic activity group therapy, as developed by Slavson (1943) and others, is a method of treatment designed for latency-age children who, though emotionally disturbed, have relatively intact and available ego strengths. Clinical rosters are filled with young patients so deficient in ego equipment that they cannot utilize the traditional approach in its pure form. Therapeutic modifications have had to be devised to meet the developmental needs of these children. In this author's experience as a practitioner, supervisor, and teacher, the only modifications in the treatment of ego impoverished children that have seemed meaningful have had their roots deeply embedded in the theory of activity group therapy.

It is the intention of this chapter to view the theory and practice of this approach and to point to modifications that are applicable to the developmental needs of ego impoverished children.

ACTIVITY GROUP THERAPY'S ROLE AS PROGENITOR

At the risk of oversimplification, it is important to outline the configurations of classical activity group therapy to provide a common frame of reference with which to view the modifications. Classic Activity Group Therapy can be viewed as a treatment method that aims to bring about a high degree of restitution for emotionally damaged children. The setting, group membership, and the therapist's actions are designed to provide a corrective emotional experience. Geared to the developmental language of the latency child, action and interaction with materials and people are the media through which the children reveal their needs and play out their conflicts. Similarly, the therapist treats through action, reaction, and interaction. While language is present for both the children and the adult, interpretation and the quest for insight play no part in the armamentarium of this method.

The selection of children for any given activity group is based on a number of principles; one is the provision, within the fabric of group membership, of resources for ego learning. This can be expressed, in a somewhat oversimplified way, by saying that the child who expresses aggression too freely provides a model for the passive child, and vice versa. The fearful child who clings to the therapist demonstrates to the member who needs to keep his or her distance that adults can be approached. The weave of the membership is composed of a range of differing disorders, modes of coping, and ego capacities which, under the handling and responses of the therapist, can become models for learning. Obviously, this range cannot be productive if the extremes that the children present to each other are threatening to the ego. Another major principle that guides the selection of children for activity therapy groups is the importance within the membership of a setting or stage; this enables the therapist to act as a curative force. If the members can act as checks and balances on each other, then the therapist is free to be an accepting and relatively noninterventive figure.

Activity groups were originally established to provide long-term treatment for children with character disorders. The process of the group was intended to let children experience initially an atmosphere of acceptance with a nonretaliatory, nurturing adult. This atmosphere is created in order to bring about regression in the service of the ego. As needs and conflicts unfold and, most important, are experienced as *acceptable*, the ego is free to search for more appropriate ways of coping with impulses and conflicts.

Within these groups, the burden of "badness" has been, to a great extent, removed. The world outside focuses on the *behavior* of the children, supporting that which is deemed "good" and condemning that which is deemed "bad." When adults tell children not to fight or scream and insist that they share, they may intend only to influence unacceptable behavior. Too often, however, children hear the message not simply in terms of behavior being unacceptable but of the underlying feelings being bad. Since they cannot rid themselves of anger and jealousy, they must conclude that *they* are bad. It is only when feelings are found to be acceptable and are separated from behavior that there is the freedom and the energy to try new behavior.

Activity group therapy provides an acceptance of feelings, a chance to separate feelings from behavior, and, finally, an atmosphere with resources for ego learning. After nearly twenty years of practice and teaching of activity group therapy, the success of this approach in its classic form, though an "expensive" method of treatment, is remarkable.

It is expensive on a number of levels. For example, with respect to duration of treatment, we are aware that it is not feasible for many settings concerned with the emotional well-being of children (schools, hospitals) to offer a method of treatment that takes years. Either the patient population is not available for that length of time, or the clinical setting has to cope with the ongoing pressures of serving large numbers of clients.

The selection criteria often becomes another "economic" stumbling block. Those who are experienced in group formation and the concept of group balance know that often 25 profiles of children are reviewed before the final selection of 7 or 8 who, in combination with each other and the setting, suggest a good prognosis. Still within the context of criteria for selection, we have to acknowledge that there are many settings which, by the nature of their service, have no proper range of disorders from which to choose.

Concerned about duration of treatment and availability of a range of suitable children for groups, clinicians have been led to seek modifications of the traditional form of activity group therapy. The need for change is apparent when one takes a closer look at the kinds of children selected for the traditional groups. They are, despite their emotional disturbances, equipped with a considerable range of ego strengths. Picture the child who is about to fight able to experience the preventative actions of the therapist as calming and protective gestures. This is a child with a refined degree of ego perception. Or, envision a group of children who can be told that the extra food on the table is theirs to deal with as they may. The above, relatively intact children, though made anxious by this message, have the ego equipment to evolve eventual solutions for situations involving need and/or rivalry.

Too many of the children who come to our attention today are ego blind, that is, they do not have the equipment to experience subtle maneuvers as protective. They are inundated by longings and rages, because their own devices are so pathetically inadequate. The severity of ego impoverishment in a large proportion of the children who come to us for treatment, combined with the variety of treatment settings available, have forced clinicians to seek new approaches for disturbed latency children. Unfortunately, these pressures have too often given rise to chaos—for example, children are placed in groups that focus on behavior changes where the therapist replicates, albeit with kinder intentions, the scolding, demanding, angry adult world; or, "trampoline groups," created to vent physical energy; or groups that demand discussion and insight, where the children lack the equipment for such activities. These groups share a sense of desperation and panic. Commonly, they lack philosophical foundation for treatment that is related to the development of the children. Classic activity group therapy, on the other hand, teaches us that the therapist, the group, and the setting must first provide safety, acceptance, and nourishment.

GROUP FORMATION

Extending these concepts to the more ego impoverished children, some immediate implications for group formation are apparent. The more bereft a child is of ego equipment, the more vulnerable he or she is to different disorders. Many therapists are motivated by the nature of their clinical settings to place children of similar dynamic disorders together in groups; this is desirable, not merely expedient. Most residential settings, for example, would not place a fearful, withdrawn child into a group of acting-out children, knowing that each would terrify the other. There is a comfort, even a safety, in being with children with similar problems.

Some years ago, this author helped form a group for infantile acting-out girls. They had little tolerance for anxiety, and their longings were as great as their rages. They lacked the emotional knowledge of sublimation; feelings were translated quickly into action. This group of seemingly similar children was found to have a wide range of ego equipment. For example, there was the "clown," whose humor had a degree of self-observation, a quality singularly lacking in most of the girls. Another child's conversations displayed an emerging awareness of cause and effect in social interactions. This element of perception was also rare among most members. A third child displayed an inordinate attraction to soap operas and the feelings of sadness and loss they evoked—feelings generally denied by the other members.

Classic activity group therapy has taught us to look closely at ego functions. The concepts of group formation which too often are used strictly as a recipe *imply* that if the group cannot provide the resources for ego learning and safety, then the burden falls to the therapist and the setting and atmosphere created.

SETTING LIMITS: PROTECTION, NOT PUNISHMENT

The theory of activity group therapy teaches us to enter into the children's disruptive behavior only when their egos appear to be threatened. Such actions are motivated by the need to protect, not the desire to punish. Punishment generally stems from the anxiety felt by the threatened adult ego.

In the girls' group, for example, the therapist anticipated the need for setting protective limits from the beginning. Specific personnel in the setting were alerted to be ready to direct the children back to the room if they "bolted" from the group. In doing this, the therapist was relieved from the burden of having to chase the children and was enabled to be accepting of their need to "bolt," while another member of the staff represented reality. As the social hungers of the children grew, and their desire to belong increased, the therapist capitalized on these changes and eventually became a representative of the real world for these children. The therapist frequently commented to the children as they colluded in destructive behavior which they were unable to control: "I worry about your doing this because I want us to be able to meet together as a group."

THE THERAPIST AS A TEACHER OF EGO CAPACITIES

It is clear that children who do not have the equipment to curb or sublimate their impulsive behavior need not only the safety of protective limits, but, *simultaneously*, active tutoring in ego capacities. If the group members cannot carry the main role of "teacher," then the therapist must initially, and often, for a period of time.

A vignette from an early session of the girls' group centers around a fight over some scissors. There were not enough for all who were involved in cutting some fabric. They were kicking each other, spitting, pulling hair, and cursing. The therapist stepped in, physically separated them, and then began to talk: "Let me tell you what some girls would do if they all wanted the pairs of scissors." She then suggested several possible resolutions: drawing turns from numbered pieces of paper to decide who would go first; working together in pairs; discussing the problem. What is important in this vignette is that the therapist accepted the fighting and the rivalry, and in no way expressed disapproval. Rather, the girls were rescued by demonstrating what stronger children might do. In the beginning months of treatment this approach was used repeatedly. The therapist tried to suggest approaches that represented higher levels of ego functioning such as "talking it over."

At first the children tended to select the most structured resolutions. These were numbering systems that listed whose turn it was by drawing straws. This tendency bears a faint resemblance to the obsessive-compulsive rituals of the young child who is coping with early issues of control. In time they took a step forward and finally reached for suggestions that implied talking things over. When looking at the uses of discussion in latency groups, it is important to distinguish between the use of discussion to bind the therapist's anxiety about action and acting-out in the group and the teaching of the use of talk as an ego capacity to children who lack this skill.

The children in the group demonstrated patterns of action and acting-out. Feelings and impulses were accepted at the same time that the therapist was providing possible options for handling these feelings. What was clear was that the girls had no concept of how to communicate, except by hurling insults at each other. (In the leader's struggles with yelling children, it was useful to remember that verbal insults are developmentally higher than kicking and biting.) The group members lacked self-awareness, an understanding of the relationship between feelings and behavior, and any sense of the effect their actions might have on the feelings of others.

The therapist chose to teach some of the rudiments of ego perception through the device of role-playing, feeling that "play-acting" would provide some relief from the intensity of interaction within the group. Usually role-playing is utilized to show interaction—cause and effect—but this seemed too advanced a level of ego perception. The technique was used initially to teach that behavior often contradicts or hides deeper feelings. Anecdotes that the girls brought in involving trouble with school authorities were used for the script.

At first the therapist played the alter-ego—the voice of the feelings—while two girls played the infuriated, nasty, aggressive student and the punitive teacher. Focus was mainly on the student. The teacher's role was just a dramatic prop, and cause and effect was initially ignored. The therapist suggested fear, a longing to be liked, and the desire for approval when playing the alter-ego to the aggressive student. The girls at first booed—"not one of them felt that way." Some time later the therapist devised a role-playing situation to show them how fearful they were to acknowledge and experience their own fears. The girls were "hooked." The role-playing provided them with distance, action, and the opportunity to learn about themselves. That it was successful was evident in their increased capacity to take on the alter-ego role and express feelings underlying their behavior. Eventually they could understand the teacher's feelings and, finally, the interaction between student and teacher. During the final months of group therapy, it was evident that with nurture, acceptance, and active ego teaching, the girls had developed numerous ego capacities; they had the resources to return to doing things, being together, and planning together, like a rather well-equipped social group.

The vignettes from this group are intended to demonstrate that the concepts of group balance and formation provide us with awareness—a capacity to "read" the elements of disorder and strengths that are in groups. This reading in turn implies the role the therapist will have to play and the kind of atmosphere and setting that has to be created. These qualities of safety, acceptance, and nurturance are universal requisites for the beginning of any treatment. How they will be demonstrated will depend on the needs of the members. The group conditions that would provide safety for a neurotic child would, for a child with severe ego deficits, be like participating in a sensory deprivation experiment. Inevitably, the impaired child would be inundated by impulses and fantasies.

In contrast to classic activity group therapy, where the ego learning occurs from the group membership as well as from the therapist and follows a period of planned regression, groups with ego impoverished children depend on the therapist to provide immediate ego teaching, while, simultaneously, working to create an atmosphere of safety and emotional acceptance.

Encouraging the development of ego equipment highlights the importance of a developmental approach. The anecdotes involving the role-playing are presented in light of their therapeutic usefulness, and to show that there are stages in the development of ego capacities with which therapists must be familiar if they are to assist ego deficient children. Therapeutic tools are valuable only if they emanate from an overall treatment philosophy and are related to the developmental needs of the children being treated.

The theory of activity group therapy in depth suggests a model for developing effective treatment for latency-age children. While the techniques are appropriate to the needs of children with a relatively high level of ego functioning, the theory must be translated and modified to serve children with severe ego deficiencies. Finally, when one assumes the responsibility of providing a method of treatment where the major therapeutic forces reside in the corrective experiences, one becomes aware of how much emanates from knowledge of "good parenting."

REFERENCES

Slavson, S. R. (1943). *Introduction to Group Therapy*. New York: The Commonwealth Fund.

EDITORS' DISCUSSION

GROUP COMPOSITION OR POPULATION. Frank's group was composed of latency-age, infantile, acting-out girls. She describes them as ego impoverished and specifically mentions their minimal tolerance for anxiety. The author notes that ego blindness is a result of the lack of inner structure and psychological equipment to provide adequate defenses or appropriate protective subtle maneuvers. The inability to defend—sublimate—results in feelings that are quickly translated into action and impulsivity. The specific number of children and their exact ages is not provided.

SETTING AND PURPOSE. Similarly, setting is not specified, but the format and approach seem appropriate for children served in a multitude of facilities. A setting such as a public school would seemingly not fit into the author's format, given her presentation of relatively long-term, uninterrupted work with an ongoing clinician. Schools' academic schedules create interruption and discontinuities. Very short-term treatment models would be contraindicated with such damaged children. An experienced clinician, however, might well overcome such obstacles in a school setting. The beginner practitioner would need the guaranteed continuity, from one academic year to the next, of contact with the children.

Ego growth, stimulated by the leader, is the stated purpose of the group. Specific focus is the improvement of object relations, i.e., self and other distinctions, improved tolerance for frustration, delineation of the distinction between feelings and behavior, and an understanding of the impact of actions on others. Ego perceptions, modulation of drive expression, and development of age-appropriate defenses, are the goals of the described treatment.

LEVEL OF INTERVENTION—CLINICAL TECHNIQUE. The author reviews classic activity group therapy which aims to create an atmosphere that will cause regression in the service of the ego. The clinician's stance is that of a benign agent who treats through action, reaction, and interaction. All conflictual material is received as acceptable in order to free the child to search for better ways of handling conflicts. In the proposed modified approach, benign, nonactive, neutral acceptance is not recommended. In fact, in view of the author's attention to developmental psychology, it would be contraindicated. The damaged child population presented needs more active intervention by the therapist, who must set limits and represent reality. This is done via techniques such as role-playing, the assumption of alter-ego roles by the therapist, active teaching, modeling, acceptance of feelings but not necessarily actions, and intervention. In short, the therapist takes on the role and tasks of the firm, nonpermissive mother.

GROUP PROCESS. Implicit in the author's presentation is an initial emphasis on child/worker interaction, rather than peer exchange. Later, gradual group cohesiveness develops and in such play activities as presentations of realistic dramas, the children take over the leader's roles. Children who have been nurtured and accepted respond to active ego teaching and mirror the leader's stance. The length of time together suggests that after early mirroring and merger with the therapist, affects, controls, and improved functioning are genuinely introjected and internalized. This implies a differential use of self by the leader; in response to the children's growth and demonstrated ability to take on more responsibility of group process and group interactions, her own assertiveness diminishes.

Frank emphasizes that for ego impoverished children, traditional, permissive approaches in which the therapist chooses to remain inactive, are experienced as a frightening deprivation. The impaired child in a permissive environment is then prey to his or her own unneutralized, overwhelming drive and fantasy material.

GROUP DYNAMICS. Given the author's focus on less than neurotic, apparently atypical and borderline children, we emphasize that symbiotic merger and narcissisistic, mirror transferences, rather than self/other transference and displacement, occurs. The clinician is conceived of as symbiotic need gratifier (Blanck and Blanck 1979). The primitive levels of functioning, cause children to project onto the therapist their own primitive superegos. Such projective identifications are what Keith (1968) warned therapists to avoid, i.e., "unholy alliances." Incapable of forming a true alliance that embodies the split of observing and experiencing ego, this population may instead manifest a pseudo-alliance (Zetzel 1956). The child's lack of attainment of object constancy causes self and object to remain split into good and bad. Frank responds to this developmental arrest by initially being the "good mother" and having another staff member assume the role of the "bad mother" who sets limits. An example of this is when a child who has bolted from the session must be controlled. The leader does not engage in the chase; instead, this is handled by the adjunct staff person. Ultimately the author suggests a fusion of good and bad mother. Finally, the therapist can assume controls, dispense with adjunct staff, and be regarded with ambivalence and affection. In the terms of Mahler, Pine, and Bergman (1975) the child is on the way to object constancy.

Frank does not directly refer to resistances, but they are implied in the inherent difficulties such impoverished children present when engaged in a treatment program. Problems such as a lack of trust, fear of objects, and impulsivity must be contended with in the initial phase. Stubbornness must not be viewed pejoratively but rather as an attempt at self-definition, acted out by children whose development has been arrested at pre-genital levels (Blanck and Blanck 1979). Opposition may well safeguard against merger and envelopment. Aggressivity is also postulated as a binding force. Jacobson (1964) suggests that aggression and resistance can represent strivings for separation and individuation, steps in identity formation.

COUNTERTRANSFERENCE. Frank makes no direct reference to potential countertransference dilemmas. The standard dilemmas created by such taxing children are cited by Proctor (1959), Stierlin

(1975), and Stone and Whitman (1977). With regard to the therapist's handling of anxiety, Frank urges caution. The use of discussion, and clarity, should not be aimed at relieving the clinician's struggles for control of the group, but instead toward effective teaching and the transmission of problem-solving skills to the children. It can be speculated that the author's continued reference to the ego impoverishment of the group members reflects diagnostic acuity and empathy, which can aid clinicians in containing counterreactive and/or negative responses. In our view, this is exemplified by the author's indirect reference to protecting the ego rather than punishing out-of-control children.

Blanck, G. and Blanck, R. (1979). *Ego Psychology II–Psychoanalytic Developmental Psychology*. New York: Columbia University Press.

Jacobson, E. (1964). *The Self and The Object World*. New York: International Universities Press.

Keith, C. R. (1968). The therapeutic alliance in child psychotherapy. *Journal of Child Psychiatry*, 7:31–43.

Mahler, M., Pine, F., and Bergman, A. (1975). *The Psychological Birth of The Human Infant–Symbiosis and Individuation*. New York: Basic Books.

Proctor, J. T. (1959). Countertransference phenomena in the treatment of severe character disorders of children and adolescents. In *Dynamics of Psychopathology in Childhood*, pp. 293–309 eds. L. Jessner and E. Pavenstedt. New York: Grune and Stratton.

Stierlin, H. (1975). Countertransference in family therapy with adolescents. In *The Adolescent in Group and Family Therapy*, pp. 161–177, ed. M. Sugar. New York: Brunner/Mazel.

Stone, W. N. and Whitman, R. M. (1977). Contributions of the psychology of the self to group process and group therapy. *International Journal of Group Psychology*, 27(3):343–359.

Zetzel, E. R. (1956). The concept of transference. In *The Capacity for Emotional Growth: Theoretical and Clinical Contributions to Psychoanalysis, 1943-1969*, pp. 168–181. New York: International Universities Press, 1970.

CHAPTER 9

Group Psychotherapy with Primitively Fixated Children

EILEEN TRAFIMOW, PH.D.
SANDRA I. PATTAK, M.A.

EDITORS' NOTES
This chapter is based on clinical work with groups at a children's psychiatric facility with out-patient, in-patient, and day-hospital programs. To arrive at a conceptual framework, principles of individual development were applied to group processes. It is postulated that children serve as multiple or alternative objects for one another, creating and maintaining a loose but strong network of shifting psychological connections. The therapist team acts as auxiliary ego to ensure the maintenance of group equilibrium and to allow the children to benefit from their own objectal array. Another therapeutic variable, the group as symbiotic mother, provides a cushion of support and safety that reveals itself only in implicit and subtle ways. An earlier version of the paper was presented at the Annual Conference of the American Group Psychotherapy Association, 1979.

Psychotherapy groups for children have traditionally been reserved for intact out-patient populations (Ginott 1961, Slavson and Schiffer 1975). Only a few experimental groups have reported using very disturbed child populations (Speers and Lansing 1965, Coffey and Weiner 1967, Lifton and Smolen 1966, Ganter, Yeakel, and Polansky 1967). In an attempt to explore the potential of groups for more disturbed populations, experimental psychotherapy groups for in-patient, day hospital and out-patient children were established at the Pritzker Children's Unit, Michael Reese Hospital, Chicago, Illinois, several years ago (Trafimow and Shapiro 1974). Children in this project had received a range of diagnostic labels, though all exhibited serious ego deficits, developmental delays, and primitive personality structure.

The following is a description of the theoretical structure developed to conceptualize the group's dynamics. The notion of developmental lines, the object line in particular, will be used as a framework for understanding interactional processes, therapeutic techniques, and the impact of the group experience on each child's development.

THEORETICAL FRAMEWORK

Observations of highly disturbed young children lead one to ask whether such children have psychological meaning or existence for one another. At times they seem totally unresponsive to others—at times, exquisitely responsive. Similarly, sometimes they seem to differentiate adults from children; sometimes they do not.

In examining this question, our attention has become focused on the objectal and narcissistic lines of development. That is to say, we have tried to understand what internal representations of self and others the children bring with them to any group situation and to determine whether a formal treatment group can influence those representations in therapeutic ways.

REVIEW OF OBJECT DEVELOPMENT. Briefly, the object line of development can be divided into three stages; namely, the pre-object, the early object, and the true object. The pre-objectal stage (Spitz 1965) is also known as the stage of need satisfaction (Freud, A. 1965) or normal symbiosis (Mahler 1965). It ensues when the infant becomes aware that gratification is somehow dependent on another person. The primary narcissism of the earlier, autistic stage begins to give way to a partial, functional awareness of another. This early level of relatedness includes, of course, massive dependency, with great attendant anxiety and intermittent rage at moments of deprivation. It is still a highly delusional, hallucinatory stage marked by the persistence of extreme grandiosity and a lack of differentiation between self and the other. The universe consists only of these two; together they form a total sustaining unit, a whole. Presumably, this stage of development occurs normally from about 2 to 6 months of age.

What we are calling the early object stage follows and is characterized by the slow disintegration of the delusion of symbiotic union (Mahler 1975). Increasing experience, memory, perceptual ability, motor development, and maturation combine to promote awareness of separateness from the symbiotic partner. The good mother, that is, the one who gratifies, is distinguished from the bad mother, the one who does not gratify. Primitive feelings of impotence alternate with delusions of grandeur, and aggressive feelings alternate with positive feelings of great strength. It is presumed that this stage normally occurs from about 6 months to 2½ years of age.

The third, or true, object stage begins with the attainment of a lasting maternal introject that combines heretofore contradictory elements of both the good and bad mother (Hoffer 1955). As part of this process, the child achieves a relatively comfortable, age-appropriate level of self-esteem or secondary narcissism. With the appearance of object constancy, the development of a rudimentary sense of self, and the accretion of cognitive/perceptual experience, a capacity for true object relations evolves.

REVIEW OF NARCISSISTIC DEVELOPMENT. A different, though related, series of insights concerning development can be obtained through understanding narcissism as a developmental line. Development, from this point of view, deals with others as part of self rather than as separate objects. The narcissistic line, if assumed to exist from the beginning of life in parallel fashion to the object line (Kohut 1971), begins with the autoeroticism of primary narcissism. This equilibrious position is inevitably disturbed by frustration, as the undifferentiated caretaker fails to provide perfect gratification or attention. To recapture the bliss of primary narcissism, the infant establishes a grandiose exhibitionistic image of self. This "grandiose self" appears in three different forms, representing three different developmental levels. The earliest, most archaic form is referred to as merger through the extension of the grandiose self. During this stage of development the object is absorbed by the self. Later, the other is experienced as a separate person, who only has significance as an admiring mirror, affirming the child's existence and value.

The other strategy employed by very young children who have lost the bliss of the earliest experience of primary narcissism involves transmission of that wish to a newly acknowledged, admired, omnipotent other.

Transmuting internalization is the mechanism by which the developmental progression just described can unfold. That is, when a tolerable, phase-appropriate loss of some discrete maternal function is experienced, the young child depersonalizes that function, separates the function from residence in the caretaking object. The narcissistic object cathexis is then withdrawn, and the function is preserved as part of inner psychological structures. Theoretically, then, it is through the process of transmuting internalization that several early developmental achievements are accomplished. The self-object becomes first the need-satisfying object and, finally, a separate being as the child's own workings gradually replace the mother as an instrument for maintaining narcissistic homeostasis.

Parenthetically, it should be noted that object relatedness and narcissism are inseparably entwined at these early levels. Whether or not they are in fact separate developmental lines (Kohut 1971, Freud 1914) is of lesser significance here. It is important to state, however, that children, especially during the early object phase, require a great deal of mirroring, attention, affirmation, and exclusivity. Their ability to acknowledge or tolerate others, much less to "play," is inextricably related to the status of their narcissistic balance at that moment in time. It should be clarified that we are not referring to play in any classic sense. Rather, we use that term to designate those periods of relative contact among the children that have an imaginative or symbolic component.

EXTRAPOLATION TO THE GROUP SETTING

Having described the objectal and narcissistic lines of development as they occur within a given child the question arises of whether a group process independent of any other treatment modality available to the child, can be utilized as a therapeutic tool to enhance objectal development and psychic growth in general. We hypothesize that at least three aspects of the group process are indeed growth inducing.

The first is the presence of the other children. This is crucial because other children provide an array of objectal alternatives. Each post-symbiotic group member, carrying with him a rather limited, primitive notion of "other," is able to choose selectively among the other children, relating to those aspects of the others that are most compatible with a given need. For example, the child may seek a symbiotic connection with another group member. Again, the child may model after a peer who uses some different type of coping strategy or assume a caretaking role with a child in need of nurturance.

A second advantage of "child others" is based on the fact that even the most primitive, post-symbiotic children have learned some elementary role differentiations. They are aware of the differences between adults and children; because they perceive other children as more similar to themselves, the processes of identification and imitation are facilitated.

Finally, some children, even at an early developmental level, have adapted by withdrawing from adults, evading them. Such children are especially likely to relate more comfortably to other children.

The second aspect of the group situation that induces growth is the work of a therapy team. In principle, two therapists function as auxiliary group egos. They intervene, sometimes specifically and immediately, to provide whatever necessary aspect of ego functioning is missing in the group at that time. Always, however, their goal is to return the group to the children: to enhance or support the workings of the group, to reinstate sufficient equilibrium to allow the group members to take over again. That is, the goal is to return the group to the point where individuals can again share some variety of ego skills, and benefit from the objectal array.

The third variable that is embedded in successful group treatment seems to transcend the specific efforts of children or therapists. This variable reveals itself in the consistently positive valence with which group members have approached sessions. This remains constant despite the fluctuations within individual children, the difficulties engendered by their interactions, shifting membership, and therapist absences. We relate this phenomenon to the recent concepts of "Mother-Group" (Scheidlinger 1974), or the group as transitional object (Kauff 1977).

Scheidlinger in particular has developed this concept as a result of his work with unstructured, adult psychotherapy groups. He has defined a process in which the members identify with the group-as-a-whole in an unconscious effort to recreate the blissful experience of the symbiotic attachment to mother. Thus, the image of the group-as-a-whole, the "mother-group," allows an unconscious return to the need-gratifying (symbiotic) level of object development. The group-as-a-whole may substitute for the therapist by serving the maternal function and defining the self, just as the inanimate object may represent self and mother for the developing infant (Winnicott 1948).

These concepts are especially relevant for our group in the sense that most of our children are functioning at the post-symbiotic or early object level. Thus, the group-as-a-whole contributes to the necessary gratification by providing the protection, or "cushion," needed for further experimentation and progressive development. It offers the opportunity for testing and confronting the split "bad-mother" image, as projected onto others, within the safety and security of the protective maternal image. As children can identify with this symbol of exclusive union with mother, they can more freely tolerate "others" and even use them to further growth and development.

CLINICAL ILLUSTRATIONS

To illustrate these ideas, vignettes of three children's initial presentations and treatments are offered.

BRAD.   The case of Brad, a 7-year-old boy, highlights the importance of the availability of "child others." Brad was initially seen by an individual diagnostician for a period of two months. During these sessions he was largely unresponsive. At the time of his diagnostic staffing, recommendations included placement in the day hospital program and transfer to the children's group. He was then seen exclusively in group therapy for nine months. Upon admission to the group he avoided making eye contact, and had bizarre mannerisms that included licking his fingertips and pulling out his hair and eyelashes. During meetings, he frequently and emphatically shunned contact with adults. While he did not actively avoid his peers, his interactions were marked by vagueness, emptiness, and even absence. His vocabulary was meager; his articulation and syntax, poor.

During Brad's first month in the group, he remained a shadowy, evasive figure. Therapist interventions during this period of time were, consequently, minimal. With the admission to group of another nonverbal, though less disturbed boy, Brad's behavior changed dramatically. Suddenly, his presence became more apparent via his interaction with this other child. Together they giggled and wrestled and played, always nonverbally. It was not that Brad, per se, became suddenly more apparent, but rather that he borrowed substance from the other, more intact child.

Brad's exclusive attachment to the other boy continued for some time. If the other child withdrew from symbiotic contact, Brad would court him frantically until the union was reestablished. If the other child was, in fact, absent, Brad returned to his initial regressed stance. Many months later, we began to notice clear indications of Brad's increasing separation-individuation from the other child. He attempted to form relationships with other peers, seemed more energetic, and evidenced greater initiative in play. In addition, Brad began relating to the therapists more affectively. He spoke to us more and seemed to be struggling to achieve higher levels of cognitive mastery. He increasingly wanted to demonstrate emerging skills such as spelling, writing, and memorization. During this time we worked especially closely with his teacher, well aware of the need to capitalize on his new emotional readiness to learn.

We understand Brad's development in group as follows: initially, he was a withdrawn, emotionally impoverished child who shunned contact with (adult) others and relied almost exclusively on self-stimulating behaviors. When introduced to another nonverbal, though better structured, child, Brad was able to form a symbiotic attachment from which he could extract emotional supplies and continue his self-development. After repeated experiences with this "child other," Brad slowly began to explore additional relationships. His increasing sense of self allowed for a dramatic developmental leap in cognitive functioning—most notably, speech and language. This acquisition, then, further enhanced his opportunities and ability to relate to others. The availability of the "child other" appeared to be the primary factor that facilitated Brad's movement from a post-symbiotic, borderline adaptation toward greater separation-individuation and expanded ego functioning.

CARL. Like Brad, Carl was a 9-year-old boy who had been seen individually for diagnostic evaluation and was subsequently referred to the group because the transference and countertransference issues raised by his disorder seemed more manageable in a group setting. He was seen as an outpatient exclusively in group therapy for almost one year.

When first admitted he was unable to stop talking—about himself. He went on and on about his achievements, trophies, and brilliance. He literally did not talk to anyone, but rather, kept up a continuous stream of chatter whether or not anyone else was listening. In play he was outrageously demanding and exquisitely sensitive to any competition from the others. He usually chose to play out acrobatics, something he could do very well, but he would not draw, something he could not do well. Mostly he made continuous demands for praise and attention. Neither therapist found him gratifying, nor felt he differentiated the members of the audience.

Early therapist interventions consisted of pointing out very gently that no one seemed to be listening; or that Carl needed to tell us so many times how superior he was. We were informed in no uncertain terms when these comments were too painful, by tantrums that consisted of falling to the floor, kicking, screaming, fuming, and throwing toys. At these times the therapists benignly commented on how terribly criticized and hurt he must be feeling. Despite the fact that he was generally not very gratifying, therapists capitalized on any warm, genuine interaction that arose. We looked for excuses to smile, make eye contact, or touch his shoulder, in short to demonstrate regard for the boy rather than the victor. Simultaneously the other children began to have considerable effect and impact on him in their own way. They might demand that Carl wait his turn, or ask him to keep quiet. Soon another very bright child entered the group and began to compete successfully in the academic contests Carl arranged. It was truly a corrective experience for him to see how matter-of-factly this other child accepted intellectual triumph.

At a later stage in treatment it was clear how much he valued group membership, or indeed any stable connections. He spoke warmly of his teams, his clubs, his schools. He spoke of boys who had left the hospital. The importance of group membership was especially striking in light of the fact that his relationships with individuals were still undifferentiated and relatively poor. His tolerance for his own imperfection also increased. He reacted less violently to being one of the group and accepted comments about his worries and fears with growing curiosity. Slowly he began to complain in a more focused fashion about the unavailability of his parents, and his profound loneliness. Finally, one day he talked of wanting all the money in the world. He then began to sing, "money, money, money you've got love in your tummy." He spoke of food and his mother, and the wish to be close to her. On another day he didn't feel well and the group spent one entire session with Carl lying on the table, surrounded by everyone else sitting in their chairs. Another child picked at the curls in his hair while a therapist rubbed his ankle and everyone talked.

Our assessment of Carl's progress in group might be stated as follows: in the beginning, he was almost totally narcissistically involved. He seemed unrelated to others and could not even accept praise when it was forthcoming. He was painfully unhappy and felt extremely pressured to perform. Despite all his efforts, however, he failed to be engaging or appealing. The adults began pointing out his great sensitivity which resulted in a loss of self-esteem. They were particularly accepting and supportive at those rare moments of genuineness or vulnerability. Carl began gradually to demonstrate that group membership was important to him, by making it clear that he wanted to be there. He began to play with the other children to some extent. He tolerated empathic comments with increasing comfort. Toward the end of his stay in the group, he was sending clearer and clearer messages in asking for closeness and nurturance. In short, he moved from an attitude of fear and agitated courting vis-à-vis others, to a position of greater mutuality and trust.

KIRK. Kirk was a 10½-year-old boy who had been an in-patient for over a year before he was referred for group psychotherapy. Referral was initiated because staff felt he needed an opportunity to counterbalance the regressive pull stimulated by daily individual psychotherapy sessions. In addition, the presence of several extremely primitive, autistic children in his dormitory precluded the possibility of optimal peer experiences in that setting.

Upon admission to the group he was a pale and fragile looking boy who made little eye contact. His verbalizations were often either bizarre, incomprehensible, or loosely related. He frequently carried such items as sticks, folded paper, or drawings with him and imbued them with life and feelings. His initial response to being in the group was to explore the room in great detail, as if in a panic. He asked many questions and walked about in an agitated fashion. Over the next several sessions his wish/fear of being a part of the play was apparent, as he continued to dart about physically on the fringes of the play. He asked questions about the games, joining in tangentially and briefly when he could, but otherwise remained absorbed with his own fantasies.

Initially, the therapists made no attempts to suppress Kirk's psychotic productions. Rather, they chose to encourage as much interaction as possible around them. For example, during a play activity when the other boys were making up silly stories, Kirk was invited to add his own idiosyncratic elaborations. To do so, however, he needed to track the plot as others embellished the tale, wait his turn, and conclude his part upon the request of others. The boys usually enjoyed

Kirk's silliness and thus cooperated in this initial treatment attempt to foster recognition and differentiation of others.

Months later, as Kirk's beginning sense of self and other became more firmly established, he used group sessions to actively learn new skills and practice more adaptive styles of relating. To accomplish this he turned more to the other children and relied less on the adults. The other boys would interrupt their active play to show Kirk how to jump on and off boxes. Kirk would then practice this, frequently asking as he did it, "Am I tough?" As the adults supported these actions by mirroring his newly discovered strength, Kirk was able to use these skills to participate in a group game. Often he became frightened by his sense of power and needed physical restraint and verbal reassurance that it was safe for a boy to grow strong. When the other boys were absent from the group, Kirk would continue to practice the games he had learned, though his affect was notably dampened.

A parallel process was noted during this phase of treatment by child care workers who observed Kirk's accelerated attempts to achieve motor mastery. We helped them understand the meaning of this new behavior, so they would support Kirk through the inevitable periods of regression and heightened anxiety.

It should be noted that Kirk's psychological stance also provided an impetus for learning in the others. Because his fears of loss of body integrity and his intense affective states were so frequently expressed, these issues became important topics of discussion. The other boys, who were much less able or inclined to identify and verbalize similar worries, were offered a kind of permission by Kirk's behavior to deal with these issues too.

In summary, we note that the group experience with its multiple variables had a therapeutic impact on Kirk's psychological development. The therapist team devised an initial treatment strategy based on their understanding of Kirk's objectal status. They offered permission for him to maintain his psychotic defenses but encouraged him to be interactive as well. They carefully structured his integration into the group until Kirk and the other children were able to sustain interaction more autonomously. After this was accomplished the therapist team shifted its function to provide intermittent, auxiliary support in those instances when the other children could not do so for Kirk. Of equal importance, the other children began to have fun and form alliances. They gradually came to understand and comment on Kirk's maneuvers. They invited Kirk's participation and over time expected it to assume more age-appropriate forms. Lastly, in conjunction with his individual treatment, the group-as-a-whole provided the safety, cushioning, and structure necessary to support Kirk's exploration of others.

Thus, the group provided a safe, but seductive setting that in some ways forced Kirk to shift his psychological position. The combination of the therapist team, the children, and the mother-group promoted Kirk's development from an exclusive post-symbiotic, psychotic orientation, to one that was more differentiated, separate, and interactional.

TRANSLATING THEORY INTO PRACTICE

In the following discussion, an attempt will be made to translate theoretical material into some of the more practical, day-to-day issues of group treatment with severely disturbed young children. The specific goal will be to demonstrate how technical practice follows directly from a sturdy theoretical base.

The aspects of clinical practice that shall be considered include (1) patient selection; (2) physical arrangements and equipment; (3) frequency and duration of sessions; and (4) structure of sessions. In discussing these technical issues, two points of view will be interwoven: the concept of developmental lines and the impact of the three group curative factors mentioned above.

PATIENT SELECTION. Children who evidence what has been globally referred to as severe "pre-oedipal" difficulties have traditionally been considered inappropriate for group treatment. However, recent theoretical advances have yielded a better appreciation for the complexity and diversity of the developmental and characterological pathologies that make up the pre-oedipal disturbances. Specifically, the notion of uneven growth along various developmental lines can be used to revise the guidelines for patient selection and group composition. Instead of diagnostic categories or superficial symptoms, the focus is placed on the total developmental organization of each child with regard to his or her potential for a therapeutic group combination. Children are selected and grouped to form a balanced network of functional capacities and defensive styles, with a combination of coping strategies and a variety of developmental deviations that maximize the range of the objectal array.

The primary requirement for a potential group member is some (significant) development beyond the symbiotic level. Within the group, post-symbiotic, part-object styles of relating should vary so children can learn from each other and offer new opportunities for obtaining gratification. Given this "webbing," the group can successfully support a variety of profound developmental weaknesses. This certainly means that schizophrenic children are viable group candidates, as are children diagnosed as borderline characters, as having severe behavior disorders, or as being developmentally delayed.

Within this framework, the specific contraindications for group membership are few. In proper combination with others, any child can probably be managed, though poorer candidates might include autistic children functioning at a pre-symbiotic stage of primary narcissism with very poor potential for relating to others, symbiotic psychotics who are fixated at the symbiotic level with very little capacity to view others as separate from self, and severe character disorders with extreme sociopathic, sadistic, or narcissistic tendencies. Again, the major determinant in all cases rests not on the specific disturbance or behavior pattern, but rather on the "fit" among the children.

PHYSICAL ARRANGEMENTS AND EQUIPMENT. The physical environment provided for group therapy is not a trivial matter. Indeed, principles of individual development and group process should be reflected in the selection and use of surroundings. Thoughtful manipulation of the external environment can enhance the internal functioning of each child and facilitate the emergence of the three group curative factors.

On an individual basis, post-symbiotic children require external boundaries to compensate for the fluidity that exists between self and world. By carefully utilizing the environment, the therapist can provide a relatively safe atmosphere which allows children to explore new relationships with others. Optimal physical conditions also simplify the therapist's job.

To illustrate the importance of physical arrangements, the issue of room size can be considered from the perspective of both individual development and group process. The room should be small enough so that individual children do not feel lost or overwhelmed. In addition, the room should permit the therapist to stay close to the children and protect them more effectively. In the small room children are able to remain closer to one another, which enhances the opportunity for interaction. On the other hand, a room that is too small may evoke intense panic reactions related to fears of merger and reengulfment.

Equipment should also be considered carefully. Too many toys are overwhelming to disorganized children. Also, toys with regressive potential such as water colors or finger paint may be frightening. Toys more appropriate to the children's developmental levels and more conducive to group interaction might include large heavy wooden boxes with a single open side. Children can climb into these boxes together or alone, but they need to engage others to move them about. Again, cardboard bricks might be a useful group toy to encourage sharing. Such simple materials do not stimulate regression but provide ample opportunity for creative fantasy play. Occasionally, chalk for the blackboard, or crayons and paper can be used, though these materials are more often used to provide a calming atmosphere than to facilitate group interaction.

Though preparing food is commonly employed as a form of activity in group work with children, the present theoretical orientation precludes this. More specifically, the use of the other children as a primary therapeutic force, in order to downplay the role of the therapist as the exclusive major object, is the basic goal.

FREQUENCY AND DURATION OF SESSIONS. In working with borderline or other primitively fixated children, one always notes deviant object relations characterized by limited and distorted internal representations of self and other, and marked affective fluctuations. Anxieties about the degree of intimacy or isolation vis-à-vis others are prominent. Therefore, the time span within and between group sessions must be planned to balance these opposing internal pressures: frequent prolonged contact to ensure psychological connections must be tempered by sufficient distance in order to avoid panic or further regression.

Very disturbed children are unable to retain mental representations of one another if contact is limited to one session per week. The fragile process of rebuilding trust and networks of relating is made much more difficult if so many days intervene that newly acquired ego functions are not nurtured.

At the other extreme, too frequent or too prolonged contact among primitive children risks excessive contagion, merger, or overstimulation. It puts stress on the therapist's capacities to maintain auxiliary support, and it may overstimulate and overgratify wishes for symbiotic union with the mother-group. Therefore, daily sessions or sessions beyond a standard therapeutic hour are usually contraindicated.

STRUCTURE OF SESSIONS. The structure of sessions, as with every other aspect of the group, should follow from the individual personality structure of each child as well as the impact of the group variables. From an individual viewpoint, typical group members are just barely post-symbiotic. With little internal capacity for self-regulation, they are highly dependent on external cues and structure. Such functions as awareness of body boundaries, and memory modulation of affect and impulse control may be irregular and poorly developed. Each child's internal structural weaknesses require external supports that are clearly defined and consistently applied.

From a group dynamics viewpoint, one can expect the power of the objectal array to be weakened by the periods between sessions. To reestablish the objectal network, affirmation of the symbiotic substratum (as embodied in the mother-group) and the potent presence of the auxiliary ego functions of the therapists are needed. Once the network has been reestablished, each child becomes a potential support system for the others. Object relations are facilitated. Children can often relate to common themes in a kind of "parallel talk" fashion and may even be able to respond to one another with empathy and true differentiation.

These factors suggest that external structure should be most evident at the beginning and end of sessions when each child's fix on the world is necessarily in flux. One way to increase the structure at those times might include gathering the children at a small round table to talk for a bit. The firm, unchangeable nature of table and chairs strengthens the child's physical boundaries and helps define physical limits. Eye contact also encourages and promotes at least cognitive recognition of the others present.

During the course of each group session less external structure is required as children are able to support one another. They can leave the security of the round table and make use of the available toys. During this period a kind of pre-play or courting may be seen as a series of objectal matches are made. This middle part of the session may peak in a period of relative contact among the children.

SUMMARY

In exploring the meaning that children with primitive ego structures have for one another, we conceptualized group interaction based on the developmental lines of object relations and narcissism.

We theorize that our psychotic or near-psychotic patients are functioning post-symbiotically, at early, tenuous levels of relatedness.

While learning to separate from mother and move toward others, they are also working on early narcissistic issues. These fixations are manifest in group activities through regression to symbiotic positions alternating with interest and participation in the other-than-mother world. The impetus and support for growth stems from the permanence of the group-as-a-whole, the auxiliary ego provided by the therapist, and the opportunities for relating offered by the other children. Group members are increasingly free to explore each other, comfortably aware that more exclusive "refueling" (Mahler 1975) is possible as needed. In principle, then, the group fosters growth by offering an array of objectal alternatives that encourage participation in an increasingly gratifying post-symbiotic world.

REFERENCES

Coffey, H. and Weiner, L. (1967). *Group Treatment of Autistic Children*. Englewood Cliffs, New Jersey: Prentice-Hall.

Freud, A. (1966). *Normality and Pathology in Childhood: Assessments of Development*. (Writings of Anna Freud: Vol. 6). New York: International Universities Press.

Freud, S. (1914). On narcissism: an introduction. *Standard Edition* 14:67–71.

Ganter, G., Yeakel, M. and Polansky, N. (1967). Retrieval from limbo: The intermediary group treatment of inaccessible children. New York: Child Welfare League of America.

Ginott, H. (1961). *Group Psychotherapy With Children*. New York: McGraw Hill.

Hoffer, W. (1955). *Psychoanalysis: Practical and Research Aspects*. Baltimore: Williams and Wilkins.

Kauff, P. (1977). The termination process: Its relationship to the separation-individuation phase of development. *The Journal* 27:3–18.

Kohut, H. (1971). *The Analysis of the Self*. New York: International Universities Press.

Lifton, N. and Smolen, E. (1966). Group psychotherapy with schizophrenic children. *International Journal of Group Psychotherapy* 16:23–41.

Mahler, M. (1965). On the significance of the normal separation-individuation phase. In *Drives, Affects, Behavior*, ed. M. Schur, pp. 161–169. New York: International Universities Press.

—— (1975). *The Psychological Birth of the Human Infant*. New York: Basic Books.

Scheidlinger, S. (1974). On the concept of the mother-group. *International Journal for Group Psychotherapy* 24:417–428.

Slavson, S. and Schiffer, M. (1975). *Group Psychotherapies for Children*. New York: International Universities Press.

Speers, R. and Lansing, C. (1965). *Group Therapy in Childhood Psychoses*. Chapel Hill, N.C.: University of North Carolina Press.

Spitz, R. (1965). *The First Year of Life: A Psychoanalytic Study of Normal and Deviant Development of Object Relations*. New York: International Universities Press.

Trafimow, E. and Shapiro, B. (1974). Paper presented at 12th Annual Conference, Illinois Group Psychotherapy Society, Chicago, Illinois.

Trafimow, E. and Pattak, S. (1980). Group psychotherapy and objectal development in children. *International Journal of Group Psychotherapy*.

Winnicott, D. (1948). Pediatrics and psychiatry. In *Collected Papers: Through Pediatrics to Psycho-Analysis*, pp. 157–173. New York: Basic Books, 1958.

EDITORS' DISCUSSION

GROUP COMPOSITION.   The authors state that change is largely influenced by group population. Descriptions of the ego functioning of participants are clearly stated, as are classifications of children who would not be appropriate to these groups. The number of children that constitute a group is not delineated, but fluctuation in group membership is alluded to. The children's importance to one another is stressed. As peers encourage each other's emotional development in nonpathological communities, group members offer a corrective experience through their interactions. Without careful selection of group members it may be assumed that these benefits would not occur.

SETTING AND PURPOSE.   Careful preparation of the therapeutic environment reduces the need for therapists to constantly impose verbal restrictions. Perhaps the presence of two authority figures automatically helps children realize the existence of external boundaries and controls. Through the therapist's understanding of the ongoing pathology, the external world is sculpted to fit the needs of these primitively fixated children. According to Kohutian theory, these children have grown up in the absence of an empathic environment. Group treatment allows them the opportunity to gradually incorporate the responses of others like them. This enables the children to learn to tolerate frustration and to adjust to their own inner reactions.

LEVEL OF INTERVENTION. The ego state of the group and group members determines the level of intervention necessary. Co-therapists act as a team, analyzing the procedures and individual behaviors in terms of ego functioning.

The purpose of the group is to allow children to function as autonomously as possible, enhancing feelings of industry and competency. Leaders intervene as necessary: directly, immediately, and specifically. Thus, therapists, as aids to faltering egos, provide a corrective emotional environment by offering themselves as models for growth.

GROUP PROCESS. Interactions between members are of primary importance and considered to be a particularly significant curative feature within groups. Group interaction is one of three aspects of process that is of therapeutic importance. The other procedures are the use of the co-therapy team to reinstate harmony and the establishment of a comfortable and nurturing group climate. This latter factor also influences the group in a dynamic way; so that to the unconscious, group-as-a-whole is the need-gratifying symbiotic mother. All three components of group process provide alternatives for the children's relationships and attachments. The peers serve as alternative objects; the co-therapists are ego-aids; and the group-as-a-whole offers a symbiotic tie.

GROUP DYNAMICS. Many of the children selected for this group treatment are described as having transference problems in individual settings, or as posing countertransference problems for therapists. Interestingly, as complex as group therapy is, with these children it seems to sufficiently alleviate or delete transference difficulties. The very fact that children are with other children relieves the tension the child faces in being alone with adults who may be seen as threatening or unavailable. Children provide selective identifications and mirroring for one another in a way that adults do not. When children need a benevolent, accepting adult the co-therapists are capable of corrective empathy. The therapists freely admit to their own countertransference problems. At times they have to search hard for genuineness and vulnerability in children. The presence of two therapists might lessen countertransference interference as each therapist can rely on the other as a sounding board for feelings that have not been worked through.

An important dynamic is the function of group as a mother substitute. As a whole, the group is a positive object. Therefore, it is a safe place to try out negative feelings; the children need not fear being overwhelmed by rage and anger. Some of these emotionally hampered children are frequently prone to intense reactions of frustration and fury. The group seems to facilitate expression without reprisal and thus can contain much of the regressed behavior, while simultaneously motivating healthy progress.

PART 4
Adolescents and Their Parents

Introduction: Adolescents and Their Parents in Group Therapy

Current thinking defines the period of adolescence as extending beyond the teens and recognizes it as a major developmental stage. Societal changes in this century are particularly apparent in today's adolescents. Their parents experience tension and anxiety dealing with adolescent issues as they have not traveled the same developmental pathway. "The gap currently has reached such proportions that parents are out of empathy if not sympathy with adolescents... and have almost abrogated their parental rights" (Anthony 1970). Adolescence has been referred to as a moratorium (Erikson 1950), a crisis (Scherz 1967), a second separation-individuation (Blos 1967, Furman 1973), and a period of mourning and depression (Laufer 1966), a time when the child makes a final separation from parents and bids farewell to childhood. Until the recent studies of Offer, Sabshin, and Morris (New York Times, July 7, 1981), most authors and researchers agreed that in this phase both parents and children reflect regression. Parents are narcissistically vulnerable, subject to their own dethronement and constant bombardment by the fluctuating ego states of their children. The adolescent's super ego and ego become shaky and impoverished in response to the upsurge of hormonal change and heightened instinctual strivings. Family ties are lessened and there is a growth in the importance of, and attachment to, the peer group.

Recent research has been concerned with a less studied period, that of early adolescence (Hamburg 1974) and notes that even for the model individual, early adolescence is intrinsically a time of great stress when coping skills are most impoverished. Owing to inadequate ego functioning, the defenses are shaky; secondary interference in autonomous functions—learning, reality testing, regulation of sexual and aggressive drives—may result; and the synthetic, integrating, and organizing functions may decline. The better functioning adolescent whose defenses are stable will demonstrate capacity for sublimation and intellectualization. Creative outcomes can include energetic productions of poetry, painting, and intellectual or physical activity. Children from 12 to 15 are the most emotionally vulnerable as this is when the child is in a heightened state of adolescent narcissism.

The period of early adolescence is a time of critical development that involves the negotiation of unique biological, psychological, and social demands, the adaptive challenge of which has been underestimated. Magnified awareness of body image, concerns about adequacy and attractiveness, and resultant mood and affect swings (Jacobson 1961) characterize this stage. Greater academic expectations, the new role status, the repudiation of parental values, and the resultant resurgence of the grandiosity and omnipotence of toddlerhood create the bewildering and disquieting child. This is threatening to the parent. "Object removal" describes this process in which the child replaces old objects.

In contrast, the period of late adolescence, from 17 through the mid-20s, marks the beginning of reconsolidation of the personality. The ego and super ego are no longer at the mercy of the id, and the stance of total narcissism is surrendered. Empathy reappears, and parents and family regain significance and importance. Parents no longer loom as threatening incestuous objects. Peers are no longer all-important, and solid gender identity is established. Clarification regarding educational and occupational goals is generally noted.

Anna Freud (1958) states that the adolescent upset is inevitable, welcome, and beneficial. She notes that the character structure at the end of latency represents the outcome of long drawn out conflicts between the id and ego, and that the balance achieved is precarious and insufficiently developed to allow for either quantitative increases in drive activity or changes of drive quality—both of which are inseparable from puberty. Consequently, this preliminary balance must be abandoned in order to integrate adult sexuality into the individual personality. She notes that so-called adolescent upheavals are no more than an external indication that such internal adjustments are in progress. Teenagers showing no outer evidence of inner unrest are described as remaining as in latency. Their considerate, often submissive, behavior signifies a delay of normal development, and should be regarded as a danger sign. Freud suggests that when fixations to the parents have been exceptionally strong and maintained throughout latency, with strong fixations to the mother, not only during the oedipal phase, but due to preoedipal attachment as well, the adolescent phase will be predictably difficult.

Pathology in adolescence is difficult to delineate, as it is difficult to draw the line between normality and pathology; in addition, adolescent symptomatology is similar to symptoms shown by neurotics, psychotics, and those with antisocial disorders. Masterson (1967, 1968), however, disagrees. His data suggest that symptoms other than mild anxiety or depression are uncommon and not normal in healthy adolescents. Symptoms in relatively healthy adolescents tend to be mild and episodic in duration. He suggests that initial diagnosis of disturbed adolescents is difficult, but that the difficulty is not in distinguishing between adolescent upheaval and severe illness, but in correctly diagnosing the precise illness. He further notes that it is erroneous to assume that the stage of post- or late-adolescence will normally evolve in adolescents who shed their symptomatic difficulties.

Some researchers believe the most dangerous characteristics of adolescence are located in the id impulses and fantasies. Additionally, danger is experienced in the very existence of the love objects of the past—thus the anxiety to break with parents and removal of these all-important objects via displacement, and sudden and intense attachments to friends, teachers, the gang or peer group. Parents are treated with indifference and contempt; generally, as a defense, the adolescent overemphasizes all new attachments. Projection is common, and the adolescent's aggression is ascribed to the parents. If libido cannot be displaced from the parents, reversal of affect is often evident. Emotions are often inverted: love becomes hate, respect becomes contempt.

Those researchers that have recently suggested that the extreme upset of adolescents is not universal say that the personality upheaval of this phase of life can be reflected primarily by manageable, nondebilitating rebellion and depression. It has also been suggested that normative teenagers experience little if any of the inner turbulence or acting-out behavior ascribed to them in the earlier literature (Douvan and Adelson 1966). Other writers suggest that rebellion occurs over minor matters of music and dress, and that adolescents continue to share with parents a core of stable common values. Offer (1969) and Offer, Sabshin, and Marcus' findings (1965) describe rebellious behavior as occurring only during early adolescence, over matters of dress, household chores, and curfew. Delinquent acts or great emotional upheaval are not universally evident. Transient feelings of anxiety, depression, guilt, and shame, but no debilitating forms of anxiety or depression, were reported. Their studies reveal that adolescents normatively maintain psychic equilibrium while struggling with developmental tasks and remain able to demonstrate successful social and family adjustment. Depression and anxiety exist in mild forms, and disagreements with authority figures are minor. Rutter, Graham, Chadwick, and Yule (1976) examine rural youth aged 14 and 15 and find disagreement only on minor matters.

Oldham suggests a number of factors that perpetuate what he terms the mythology surrounding adolescent turmoil. "These factors seem to be professional, cultural, and personal in nature....Our culture persists in its expectations that adolescents can be marked by anything except stability and relatively peaceful growth. Teenagers are frequently typecast as brooding idealists or impulsive delinquents and inherent in both roles is alienation from the adult community" (1978, p. 277). Oldham cautions against the power of the self-fulfilling prophecy and recommends that mental health professionals base their expectations of adolescents as much as possible on available data.

We do not suggest any compromise or reconciliation between the presented conflicting views. We do note, however, that much of the recent research was conducted on middle- and upper-middle-class, white, intact suburban families or rural adolescents. The majority of adolescents studied were college bound (Offer 1969). While this is not a complete sample of contemporary adolescents, it does represent a significant portion of the population, and, indeed, raises questions about the "storm and stress" tradition.

Considerable research by others, past and present, suggests that adolescence is by nature an interruption of peaceful growth, and that equilibrium during this period is abnormal. Thus the "normal" adolescent presents inconsistency, unpredictability, simultaneous feelings of love and hate for parents, desires for freedom and dependence, wanting the prerogative of adulthood while being taken care of, selfishness, altruism and generosity, and role experimentation. Few parental situations are so difficult to bear, even in light of the knowledge that their child's rebelliousness is an adaptive response to reawakened sexual feelings and early dependency longings.

Parents struggle to work through their own unresolved earlier conflicts and/or reactivated conflicts. Additionally, they struggle with the "disparity between the actual self-representations and ego-ideal and super-ego. Earlier regulation and fusion of drives are assaulted; regressive problems of separation reappear; all the parental longings and unachieved hopes which were fused with idealized object representations of the child are disrupted. The parents whose realistic personal achievements and gratifications are more commensurate with their idealized self images are able to endure the tensions between ego-ideal and super-ego" (Cohen and Balikov 1974, p. 221). Cohen and Balikov emphasize the need for idealized objects that persist through adolescence, though they warn that the needed object is not necessarily what the adolescent states is wanted. The adolescent does not expect to be taken literally and is likely to react with confusion to parental helplessness and parents' diminished self-esteem.

These authors suggest that the phenomenon of parental assertiveness has not been sufficiently valued as a positive and binding force. Schafer (1960) notes the relationship between limit-setting roles and non-abandonment. He emphasizes that parental reproaches signify protection and caring. Problems of narcissistic imbalances are frequently followed by maladaptions to hostile impulses with unstable ego-ideal and super-ego structures. Parental capitulation, distancing, overindulgence, and commands to children "to be happy" in order to preserve parental narcissism are frequent outcomes of faulty separation-individuation.

Kohut (1966) notes the need for parents to show empathy, humor, and wisdom. "The importance of the vicissitudes of the transformation of narcissism for the internalization of stable structures is of particular relevance for understanding the adolescent process.... In cases of defects in the original consolidation of the self in early childhood the loosening of structure implicit in these adolescent changes, i.e., the final separation from the parents as archaic self objects—may threaten the cohesiveness of the personality as a whole" (Wolf, Gedo, and Terman 1972). Kohut (1972) notes that frequent oscillations in self-esteem are often caused by alternating fusions with archaic ideal images, and accompanied by hypomanic excitement and disappointments: this may lead to depressive affects and narcissistic rage. Adolescents rely on friends and peers to maintain a narcissistic balance, as archaic idealized parental images are deidealized and replaced by newly internalized idealizations in the form of new self objects. As the peer group is the adolescent's bridge away from parental ties, group therapy is often a successful modality for adolescents.

Our discussion regarding work with parents of these adolescents assumes that parental attitudes constitute part of the formation of the self. Kohut (1972) emphasizes that "... the side-by-side existence of separate developmental lines in the narcissistic and in the object-instinctual realms in the child (are) entwined with the parents' attitude toward the child, i.e., that they relate at times to the child in empathic narcissistic merger and look upon the psychic organization of the child as part of their own, while at other times they respond to the child as to an independent center of his own initiative, i.e., they invest him with object libido" (p. 363). Therapy for parents of disturbed adolescents is viewed as essential and integral to ongoing direct therapy with the troubled adolescent.

REFERENCES

Anthony, J. (1970). The reaction of parents to adolescents and to their behavior. In *Parenthood, Its Psychology and Psychopathology*, pp. 307–324, eds. J. Anthony and T. Benedek. Boston: Little, Brown.

Blos, P. (1967). The second individuation process of adolescence. *Psychoanalytic Study of the Child* 22: 162–186. New York: International Universities Press.

Cohen, R. and Balikov, H. (1974). On the impact of the child's adolescence upon parents. In *Adolescent Psychiatry Vol. 3– Development and Clinical Studies*, eds. Feinstein and Giovacchini. New York: Basic Books.

Douvan, E. and Adelson, J. (1966). *The Adolescent Experience*. New York: Wiley.

Erikson, E. (1950). *Childhood and Society*. New York: Norton.

Freud, A. (1958). Adolescence. *The Psychoanalytic Study of the Child*, Vol. 13. New York: International Universities Press.

Furman, E. (1973). A contribution to assessing the role of infantile separation-individuation in adolescent development. *The Psychoanalytic Study of the Child*, 193–207. New Haven: Yale University Press.

Hamburg, B. A. (1974). Early adolescence: A specific and stressful stage of the life cycle. *Coping and Adaptation*, eds. Coelho, Hamburg, and Adams, pp. 101–124. New York: Basic Books.

Jacobson, E. (1961). Adolescent moods and the remolding of psychic structure in adolescence. *The Psychoanalytic Study of the Child* 16: 164–183. New York: International Universities Press.

Kohut, H. (1966). Forms and transformations of narcissism. *Journal of the American Psychoanalytic Association* 14: 243–272.

———(1972). Thoughts on narcissism and narcissistic rage. *The Psychoanalytic Study of the Child* 27:260–400. New York: Quadrangle Press-New York Times Company.

Laufer, M. (1966). Object loss and mourning during adolescence. *The Psychoanalytic Study of the Child* 21:269–293. New York: International Universities Press.

Masterson, J. (1967a). *The Psychiatric Dilemma of Adolescence*. Boston: Little, Brown.

———(1967b). The symptomatic adolescent five years later: He didn't grow out of it. *American Journal of Psychiatry* 123:1338–1345.

———(1968). The psychiatric significance of adolescent turmoil. *American Journal of Psychiatry* 124:1549–1554.

Offer, D. (1969). *The Psychological World of the Teen Agers*. New York: Basic Books.

———, Sabshin, M. and Marcus, D. (1965). Clinical evaluation of normal adolescents. *American Journal of Psychiatry* 121:864–872.

Oldham, D. (1978). Adolescent turmoil—A myth revisited. In *Adolescent Psychiatry 6*, pp. 267–279, eds. S. Feinstein and P. Giovacchini. Chicago: University of Chicago Press.

Rutter, M., Graham, P., Chadwick, O., and Yule, W. (1976). Adolescent turmoil: Fact or fiction. *Journal of Child Psychology and Psychiatry and Allied Disciplines* 17:35–56.

Schafer, R. (1960). The loving and beloved superego in Freud's structural theory. *The Psychoanalytic Study of the Child* 15:163–190. New York: International Universities Press.

Scherz, F. (1967). The crisis of adolescence in family life. *Social Casework* 48:209–215.

Wolf, E., Gedo, J. and Terman, D. (1972). On the adolescent process as a transformation of the self. *Journal of Youth and Adolescence* 1:257–272.

CHAPTER 10

A Group Approach to Depressed Girls in Foster Care

JUDITH A. LEE, D.S.W.
DANIELLE N. PARK, M.S.

EDITORS' NOTES
Mutual aid groups that promote improved ego functioning of adolescent girls in foster care are described in this paper. Growth in self-esteem through help in handling depression and the application of newly learned coping strategies served to lessen rage reactions and encouraged positive feelings. This paper appeared in its original form in the American Journal of Orthopsychiatry *48 (3), July, 1978.*

Depression is a salient characteristic of a broad range of adolescent girls, especially those in foster care. The behavioral manifestations of depression color the critical developmental task of self-discovery. Intervention aimed at helping the foster adolescent girl with her struggle for identity (Erikson 1950) must also be addressed to relieving the burden of depression. This can free the girl to use her strengths to develop better coping mechanisms, which is not possible when she is caught in the "Cinderella syndrome," at the stage where she uses the fact that she is a foster child to avoid taking self-responsibility. The Cinderella syndrome—or "woe is me, I am a foster child" and "don't expect anything of me"—is manifested by a range of adolescents and later abandoned for myriad reasons.

The depressive reaction is understandable when losses have been severe. The turmoil of adolescence is heightened by the internal stress and external pressures that exist in the world of the foster child and all "abandoned" children. Although some seem to escape manifest depression, all too familiar is the foster adolescent who moves aimlessly into self-defeating situations. This chapter, which is addressed to the pervasive problem of depression in foster adolescents and to the nature of a foster care agency's interventive help, offers a useful approach for group work with a range of children suffering critical object loss. A description of work going on in a "typical" group (Lee 1976, Peterson and Sturgies 1971), the kind of group approach used, and the history of establishing adolescent groups in the New York City Division of Foster Home Care (Schwartz 1971) can be found elsewhere. Although this chapter focuses on work with girls in a group setting, the authors believe that there is significant carry-over to work with foster children in a one-to-one relationship as well as with other populations of depressed adolescents. The role of the worker in helping the adolescents—relating to depressive feelings, dealing with anger and feelings of worthlessness, encouraging coping, and promoting a climate conducive to genuine mutual aid—will be demonstrated through excerpts from actual records.

PSYCHODYNAMICS OF THE FOSTER CHILD'S DEPRESSION

Reference to the "Cinderella" story is frequent in work with adolescents in foster care. One adolescent, Cherise, described her situation at length. She tearfully elaborated on her conviction that her foster mother loved her own daughter so much more and treated her like a slave. When Cherise finished, the group sat in silence until Pat said, "It is just like Cinderella, and that's the way it is!" The foster child strongly identifies with the Cinderella story. Psychodynamic explanations of such stories as described by Masterson (1972) are useful for our understanding: "These stories portray in dramatic form abandonment and the defenses against it: object splitting, denial, projection of hostility and rescue fantasies. On the narrative level these are stories of a girl's conflict with a hostile stepmother. On the psychodynamic level they are stories of the girl's defense of object splitting to deal with her hostile feelings toward her depriving mother" (p. 25). (The difficult task of the foster mother is implicit.)

Further defenses may include identification with, and often introjection of, the hated lost love object (Bibring 1953). When the rage and aggression felt toward this ambivalent and sometimes idealized loved object are turned toward the self, serious depression may result. According to Freud (1917), there is also, in reaction to the loss by death or desertion, "...an extraordinary fall in his [the bereaved person's] self-esteem, an impoverishment of the ego on a grand scale...he represents his ego to us as worthless, incapable of any effort and morally despicable; he reproaches himself, vilifies himself and expects to be cast out and chastised" (p. 155). There could hardly be a better description of the feelings of any abandoned child.

The realities of the specific population worked with—black, female, usually poverty level adolescents—must be considered. The anger felt by blacks in this society, so well described by Grier and Cobbs (1968), combined with being both female and poor, augments feelings of helplessness and despair. As the black poetess Ntozake Shange said:

i cdnt stand bein sorry & colored at the same time, it's so
redundant in the modern world...but bein alive & bein a
woman & bein colored is a metaphysical dilemma/ i havent
conquered yet.

Jacobson (1971) pointed out the range of depression from "simple sadness" to pathology. The foster child qualifies all along this continuum.

MANIFESTATIONS OF DEPRESSION IN THE ECOLOGICAL FIELD

While depression entails great personal suffering, its resonance in the living area of the depressed individual may cause greater suffering (Auerswald 1969). The obvious sadness of some foster children is only the tip of the iceberg. The more frequent sign of this depression is destructive behavior in the foster families, schools, or personal lives of these adolescents. Bright youngsters fail, are truant, and fight in school. They may reject the love offered by the foster homes, they may run away or they may act so provocatively that they are ejected from the foster home. They may take the route of finding someone to care for them by becoming pregnant and having a baby, or become pregnant and then abort. The appearance of apathy and hostility, pretended indifference that hides the hurt inside, and a myriad of other defenses are marshalled against the pain of loss.

In addition, the undermining aspects of the environment are also legion (Germain 1973): the chaos in the urban school system; the racist dominant culture; the lack of concensus as to what constitutes the child's best interests (Freud, A., Goldstein, and Solnit 1973); the realities, negative and positive, of foster home experiences; the erratic behavior of natural parents; the pressures of the ghetto neighborhood only begin to describe the milieu of these children. So-called "maladjustment" in the school, home, or community can be seen both as a manifestation of chronic or acute depression combined with adolescent turmoil, and as part of a vicious cycle of interaction, action, and reaction.

Help is, of course, most effective when it is aimed at both internal and external sources of stress. The appeal of an ecological perspective (Auerswald 1969, Germain and Gitterman 1975) lies in the fact that it calls for active mediation (Schwartz 1971) in family, school, agency system, and even political spheres, while simultaneously helping the client attain sufficient self-understanding to negotiate her world with greater ease—in this case, to help dispel the pervasiveness and power of her depression.

A description of our intervention on all fronts is beyond the scope of this chapter. But it must be understood, as we describe our work within the group, that concurrent efforts to alleviate stress are being made from all sides.

GROUP FORMATION

Girls were invited to the group on the basis of a caseworker's recommendation. All were in foster care and between 15½ and 18 years old. Referral forms were used, and selective screening interviews were held in questionable situations. Any available diagnostic material was shared. Often, however, this material was not available, so that in-depth profiles were more frequently an outgrowth of group participation than a prerequisite. Girls already involved in psychotherapy on an individual basis were invited only when referred by their therapists. Occasionally, initial group meetings would reveal that a girl was unable to benefit from the experience due to immaturity or pathology; in such cases, referrals to individual therapy were suggested. Although a variety of serious problems were represented, the majority of youngsters fell within the range of "normal" adolescents, all of whom were struggling to varying degrees with depression. Since the group was voluntary, members not ready for the group experience were able to screen themselves out by not returning after the initial meeting. Twenty girls might have to be recruited to get a group of 10 to 12 members. Ultimately, a cross section of youngsters was generally represented, and the groups were usually balanced in terms of degree of "adjustment" and other factors. If this approach did not yield such a balance, additional "balancing" factors were added, such as another well-functioning youngster.

Groups usually met once a week from September to June. Some groups decided to continue with the same nucleus into another school year. In our experience, attendance was good; the average number at each group meeting was eight. One of the groups discussed in this paper met in this way for three years before mutually agreeing to terminate. Others met for a year or less.

BEGINNING PHASE

As in all work with clients, the worker's ability to establish a mutual contract early on (Schwartz 1971) is critical. In our case, it was particularly important to deal directly with issues of foster care and to relate to anger openly as it emerged. This allows depression to surface and be acknowledged, and encourages the expression of anger, perhaps initially projected onto social workers or the agency. That the acceptance of these angry feelings is the first step in helping the process is illustrated by this excerpt from a first meeting:

I recognized Leticia's scowl, and said that I knew some of the girls felt forced to come today and weren't too happy about that. Leticia heartily agreed, as did most others. Cherise, who had been in a younger group last year, said they would really like it now that they'd come. Pat asked, "What do we do here anyway?" I said the group was offered so they could discuss things that bother them as teenagers and as foster children. Cherise added that mainly you talk about problems and things on your mind. I reinforced what Cherise said and asked how that sounded to them. Pat said angrily, "I don't like that foster children part—neither the foster nor the children." I said,

"Good, tell us more!" She did, and the girls went into their reactions to the word *foster*—"it means being on welfare and being unwanted—we're not on welfare and we're wanted"... Glenda said thoughtfully, "being foster is like being some kind of new and strange race— nobody knows what to do with it." Serious nods. "Except to hide it," I said. Yeah, relieved laughter. I said, "Here you don't have to hide it and you can share what makes you mad about it." "Right on," Kenya said....

In response to this invitation, the girls quickly shared more of their own experiences with foster and natural parents. This established an atmosphere of commonality and helped the girls determine whether they could trust the worker and the group with feelings that were "secret" but surprisingly close to the surface. In addition to testing the worker at this stage (Garland, Jones, and Kolodny 1968) the group may tend to "depress itself" with the sadness of its lot. The worker can help by handling her own anxiety arising from the emergence of these painful feelings and by recognizing the foster child's anger. The worker must be careful to allow members full expression, to show understanding, and to help the girls establish perspective on the work of the group by offering a vision of what might be achieved (Schwartz 1971). This excerpt from a third meeting is illustrative:

After some talk on boyfriends, there was a silence. I waited. Pat then wanted to know why social workers care, and why they come around anyway? I sat silently, then said, "It is rough when you don't live with your natural parents. You often have to go through a lot of changes." Cherise said sadly that she doesn't think that anyone loves you like your natural mother who "birthed" you. Some of the others agreed and each shared her fantasy around how easy and beautiful life would be with her natural mother....Cherise added, "Social workers are all alike; they say, oh how sad, how can I help you? But they can't do anything unless they can bring my mother back!" Silence. Then Pat said to me, "Well, what do you think of that?" I had trouble answering, so I asked what they thought, but Cherise asked me again. I then said, "No one can bring a mother or father back and I can hear you are all angry about that. You are also wondering about what life would have been like with your parents. You hope it would be better than you have now." Nods and comments in agreement. I said, "It is rough, but perhaps this group can help to make things better for you by helping you to deal with the things on your mind and the way things are for you now." We shared a thoughtful silence, and they began to clean up the room.

The worker's initial response to why workers care brought Cherise's angry and depressed feelings to the surface. The worker was able to respond to this and offer understanding, which allowed Cherise to express her sense of rage and hopelessness—"All you can do for me is bring my [dead] mother back." At any given moment, there are a number of helpful responses to make. The worker does not probe or explore fantasies about "what could have been" but sensitively recognizes what the girls are feeling and gently offers some hope for change. This faith in the expression of feelings for the sake of better coping is repeated throughout the beginning phase.

WORK PHASE

As the group engages in working on the contract, it moves solidly into its agreed upon task. The leader must be able to explore depression, help the group to work, and maintain a balance in the level of the group's work. A poignant excerpt, from a midphase meeting, indicates the extent of the psychic damage felt by some foster children:

Cherise said, with feeling, "I hate social workers, they are a constant reminder that you are a foster child. Suppose you had an operation and they cut off your left breast. You came home and your husband said, 'ho, ho, ho, you have no breast'. How would you feel? That's what a social worker does, constantly reminding you that you are a foster child." I said I could see how much pain she was in. I then asked for the others to add their reactions. They said, "It hurt so much you wanted to forget it but you couldn't. Inside you knew, with or without reminders." I offered that perhaps social workers could also help with all that hurt. Cherise looked me in the eyes, said "maybe", and looked away . . . .

Her analogy could not have been more profound. The child's words are both a plea for help and a warning to tread carefully. It is here that the worker is faced most openly with the twin pitfalls of avoiding such pain completely or of wallowing in it. When the route of avoidance is chosen, the worker and group subtly find many ingenious ways of entering into complicity. The easiest is for them to change the contract to "let's forget all this sad stuff and have some fun." Fun can be excellent for this group, but not for the sake of avoiding its task. The worker may choose to adopt a "topics" approach, in which the group is encouraged to discuss such "interesting" topics as dating, race, poverty, and appearance. Another way for the worker to deal with avoidance is to repeatedly express empathy for feelings expressed by group members. But, though a first step, this soon tends to immobilize the group and may become another form of avoiding next steps in the work.

The group itself is likely to avoid dwelling on pain through the use of a variety of mechanisms, from scapegoating one of its members, to vandalism and other forms of acting up, to turning on the worker, who "deserves it for making us sad." The worker, rather than either avoiding or dwelling on pain, must steer a middle course, as in the following excerpt:

After the work on sex there was a silence. After waiting, I asked what everyone was thinking about. Shrugs. Rhonda then said she was wondering about her natural family. I asked if that was something everyone wonders about sometime. Rhonda wondered if the others ever thought about who their fathers were. She said it was easier to think about your father leaving you than your mother. I said I thought that might be so, and wondered what the others felt. Each shared what she felt about not knowing her father. Charlene: "I don't really care"; Cherise: "Well, mine owns a yacht somewhere and he probably could take care of me but I don't get nothing from him and he's good for nothing to me"; Rhonda: "I'd like to know who he is"; Belinda: "Me too, especially what he looks like cause I'm so much lighter than my mother"; Pat: "I'd call mine an SOB and spit in his face!"

With each, I commented on the sadness, curiosity, search for identity, and anger they were expressing. They continued in the same vein. I said I knew it was tough not to know who your father was. Cherise said it was worse not to know your mother. Charlene left for the bathroom. Pat then recited how she felt about her mother—coldly and, she thought, without giving away her feelings. Cherise was about to continue on mothers when Pat and Belinda got up to leave for the bathroom. I said, "Wait girls, sit down. I think all of this going to the bathroom is trying to tell everyone something. This talk about natural parents makes everyone sad and kind of nervous. Fathers are enough for one day, we don't have to continue talking about mothers today if you don't want to" Pat said, "Good." Rhonda asked if it would be hard to feel that your parents didn't care about you. Everyone reacted to her. "She's so stupid", etc. I said, "I think it's hard for everyone to think about that right now." Pat said, "Yeah, can't we think about pleasant things?" I said, "Sure." Rhonda said she could think about the unpleasant things—they were a fact of life. Belinda said, "Yeah, but you don't have to think of them all the time." After the group scapegoated Rhonda, I moved the work into a neutral area and the girls unwound for some forty minutes....

The worker uses herself as a delicate instrument, detecting when work is real, when it is not, when it is too hard and defenses need bolstering, and when gentle confrontation can be used. In the following excerpt, the worker helps the girls direct their anger where it belongs. In contrast to the preceding episode, the worker's assessment is that the girls are ready to work in this way. The techniques she uses in the process are labeled in parentheses.

Leticia rushed in and angrily shared an article from a local newspaper. It was about the removal of three children from a foster home. I asked what happened and everyone joined in telling the story. They directed their strong anger at the director of our agency for causing this removal. After some exploration as to their own worries around removal, which met with denial, the anger at the director escalated (exploration, and reaching for their fears). I then wondered if they were really angry at the director or at something else. "What's making you so angry?" I asked (staying with the anger, asking for them to work on it, challenging the projection). Leticia then shared that she talked with her worker, who made her mad by comparing her to her own child: "She said I should keep my mind off other people's business, and study and go to college like her own child. I told her that I'm a foster child; we can't be compared." I asked, "Why not?" (challenging the position). She said, "We're just different." I asked if the others would accept that they are different from other children (asking for other views on the position). Pat said, "No, I'm treated very well in my foster home, I don't feel any different." Agreement except for Cherise, who said, "No, we're different, we're not real children, we're phony children." I said, "That feeling hurts," and asked how they are different (recognizing the feeling, empathizing but asking for more work on it). Cherise said the foster parents love their own kids more and told of not getting pretty clothes like the foster mother's own child did—and of wearing her hand-me-downs. Kenya said quietly that she felt loved and got nice clothes. I reflected what the two "sides" were feeling and wondered if "real" kids didn't wear shabby clothes and feel unloved. Cherise said she did know of one "real" child who was treated worse than she.

I promised to look into her clothing situation and the others went on to tell other stories of "real" kids with problems.... Leticia then showed the group an unflattering caricature of the director and they all laughed. I said, quietly again, "I don't think you're really angry at the director" (challenging the projection). Cherise said, "No, we're angry because we are foster." Leticia added, "and because our foster mothers didn't give birth to us no matter how they love us." Silence. I waited (waiting the silence). She added slowly, "I hate my natural mother sometimes, that damn whore!" "Yeah," was the echo. I said, "I think that's it" ... and stories of their placements followed....

The worker feels the expression of anger is productive and presses to focus it. She helps the group members look at what they are feeling about themselves and universalizes that "real" kids also feel as they do. She helps them to listen to each other, so both positive and pessimistic views are heard. She accepts their hurt but not their projections, and they are thus able to move to the source of the depression. A further step may have been to reassure them of their "realness" and to highlight that they are also saying that most do have mothers who love them, regardless of the labels "real" and "foster."

In subsequent meetings help was given in building these positive defenses. But Cherise was a girl whose depression was so great that even the positive aspects of her situation were negated. She had been in therapy as a youngster and was referred again while in the group. She continued in the group, since it meant so much to her, but the worker paid special attention to her depression. Again, in the following excerpt, the interventive techniques are indicated parenthetically:

After a round of work, prompted by Pat's home visit, on accepting natural mothers for what they were and on allowing foster mothers to be the good mother, Cherise said her foster mother was old and didn't care much about her. She felt she had no family to talk about here. Her natural mother is dead, they don't know where her natural father is, she's never met her brother, and on top of all that, she doesn't feel she belongs in her natural family. The girls were overwhelmed by this and saddened. They looked at me. I said, "Cherise feels that everything has gone wrong for her. Let's help her take it one part at a time" (helping them to partialize with her). The girls asked different questions about what she had said. After she told her story, I said, "I think she feels particularly upset today because each of you except Cherise has a living mother to talk about. She feels left out" (interpreting and pinpointing the immediate provocation for her depression). Cherise nodded in agreement. The girls were very supportive but Leticia added, "Yeah, but with or without mothers, dead or alive, we all wound up in the same boat anyway—foster care and none of us got fathers." They all laughed, including Cherise. The work continued on a new level about foster families, and Cherise was attentive.

With help from the worker, particularly in terms of the level of her intervention, the mutual aid of the girls was helpful to Cherise. In this phase of the work, depressive feelings are surfaced, understood, and challenged. The building of new positive defenses and coping mechanisms is encouraged (Freud, A. 1958, Hersko 1968). Feelings of worthlessness are examined. The worker, restraining her own fear of opening a "Pandora's box," encourages the girls to verbalize the painful, negative things they think of themselves, as well as what they believe society thinks of them. They easily discuss how they are treated by doctors and merchants who take paying customers first and remind them of how long it takes to be paid by the city. There is no doubt that, in addition to their personal losses, they suffer from being stereotyped as people on "the city bill." Only their justified anger at such treatment keeps them from greater internalization of such an image. Yet each story must be examined to help them separate genuinely despicable treatment from their own pessimistic feelings.

The connection between angry feelings and feelings of worthlessness becomes increasingly apparent to the girls as their self-awareness develops. The following excerpt demonstrates how the worker helps clarify this connection:

Leticia explained, "Some fights are caused by someone making a remark about my mother. The kid would be joking and not know that I'm in foster care." I said, "It must hurt, and no one really knows why you are fighting." She went on about how she's always having to fight. Carin then asked, in exasperation, "What's all this fighting about?" I said, "I wonder what Leticia is trying to tell us, perhaps we can figure it out together. It sounds like maybe Leticia feels she has to prove something." Carin said, "You're just trying to prove that you're as good as them." Leticia was silent. Carin said, "Don't you know you're as good as anybody else—don't you know who you are?" I said, "This is part of what we're here for, to help figure out who we are. Maybe Leticia is fighting because she doesn't like who she is—a foster kid." She replied, "It makes me feel small." Carin suggested that she just walk away. I said, "The feelings are rough and it isn't that easy for everyone." Silence. Millie then quietly said, "Being foster is like being a piece of garbage. You're just something somebody tossed out...."

Each girl deals differently with this feeling of worthlessness. Leticia fights and carries a chip on her shoulder, expecting the world to repay her for its gross injustice. Carin, who is bright, searching, and a high achiever, expresses it in another way, as another meeting shows:

Carin, who had been reading, lifted her head, put her hands flat on the table, and said, "I got one for the group—what would you do if you thought you were going crazy?" There was a silence and the members looked at one another. I asked Carin if she was talking about herself. She said yes, and the girls appeared to freeze. I asked if she could tell us what this going crazy feeling feels like. After thinking, she said seriously, "It feels like nothing matters to me anymore." Kenya asked her what about school, and as she unfolded her story we all helped her to decide to go to a therapist. I let them know that it wasn't so crazy to feel that way with a life like Carin's has been, and that foster is a hard cross to bear. It was agreed that you need all the help you can get....

Although each girl handles her feelings differently, the group and the worker are able to offer each girl help. As feelings that interfere with the ability to cope are understood and dealt with, the focus can shift to behavior that helps each to "make it" in everyday life.

"MAKING IT" AND MUTUAL AID

As depression is slowly dispelled, the individual ego strengths of each girl become more apparent. The problem-solving work within the group pools these individual ego strengths to create a stronger "group ego." Where certain members lack coping ability, another member is able to give direction. Mutual ego identification takes place (Redl 1955). A "group superego" also emerges, with various "leaders" who embody it (Freud, S. 1922). A new set of norms and values develop. Just as negative norms influence behavior in the adolescent gang (Cohen 1955), positive values emerge in this group and are reinforced by the worker. For example, acting out in school and in the foster home is viewed in a negative light; value is placed on achievement, higher education, and career plans. Early pregnancy is frowned upon, and self-responsibility in all areas is a norm. Stability is valued, self-pity and impulsivity are questioned. The weaker sister is offered a great deal of nonjudgmental, familial love and is encouraged to grow (Scheidlinger 1952):

Pat began to tell of her foster home, where she was the baby and generally given all she wanted. Despite this, she ran away a month ago to her natural mother who said she wanted Pat to live with her. She added that her mother is living with a Puerto Rican man who hates blacks. Kenya asked, "Isn't your mother black?" Pat said, "Yeah, and he beats her up all the time!" The girls gave long meaningful looks to Pat and each other. Pat replied, "Yeah, I guess she's a crazy lady. I wanted to see if I

could live with her but I couldn't. My mother doesn't care
what that man does to her, or to me. I'm leaving, I can't make
it there."

The other girls agreed, but wondered where she was going,
and what she was going to do. She said she wasn't sure, but
she'd really like to go back home (to her foster home). Millie
asked her if Mrs. X would let her come back, and would she
rub it in? Pat said she thought Mrs. X understood, but maybe
she'd go live with her 22-year-old sister who was in town from
Ohio. Carin said, "Look, your sister isn't much older than
you, she has a baby, no husband, and is on welfare. How
could she take care of you? How would you eat and live?" Pat
said she'd go on welfare. "Great," said everyone in unison. Pat
looked down.

I said, "Pat seems to be in a rush about something and it's
hard for her to think as clearly as you right now." Pat said
angrily, "I am eighteen this week and I wanted to get out of
foster care by the time I was eighteen! I wanted to get back
with my natural family, but it isn't working." I said, "Those
were very heavy decisions to make in one week, and I think
you were hurt by what you found at your mother's." She
elaborated and we related to her disillusion and letdown. I
then refocused on what she was going to do now. She brought
up Ohio again. Millie asked, "What about school and all your
plans?" She looked down and said she got kicked out of school
while she was at her mother's. The girls were shocked. But
Carin said, "You can't escape by going to Ohio." I reminded
Pat that she said she would really like to go home to Mrs. X.
Pat said sheepishly that Mrs. X didn't know she had been
kicked out of school. I said maybe she felt like the prodigal son
returning home, sort of licked and embarrassed. Pat smiled
and agreed and everyone laughed gently. Kenya said, "Look,
you're Mrs. X's baby, she loves you." The girls went on to help
her strategize how she would return to Mrs. X, what they
might say to each other, etc.

The group gave Pat a chance to share her pain and think out loud as the members shared their evaluations with her (Bellak 1973). They provided her with a place where she could be at loose ends and tried to help her tie those loose ends together. As the girls learn to cope better in situations where they previously felt hopeless, life becomes more manageable, less confusing and depressing. A sense of competence and hopefulness is born of the group experience.

ENDINGS AND TRANSITIONS

At the end of the year, when the girls decide whether to finish or to meet again in the fall, they work on defining what the group has meant to them. It may be a time of saying good-bye. It is a time of consolidating gains and of looking forward. The girls speak for themselves in the following excerpt from a final meeting:

The mood was quiet, thoughtful, and very close. Leticia said with pride and determination, "This group helped me to be different. I'm the only one in my family not pregnant, and I'm the only one going to college." Kenya said, "Yeah, me too. I never thought I'd even make it out of high school. I guess I never cared either. I used to run around and mess with dope and everything. But I did those things when I had nothing better to do, now I'm gonna give college a try." Carin said softly, "Life matters more now, not always, but more. When I become a doctor I'm gonna help a lot of people." Kenya said, "I'll be your first patient"—and everyone laughed. Millie, who steadily plugged away at school, said, "No one at home thinks I can make it, but I know now that I don't have to show them. Millie is going to make it for Millie!" Glenda said, "Right on!" and added, "I love college and I think I may even become a social worker. Life is great, my foster mother loves and trusts me now more than ever!" Her only complaint was that her younger sisters were in trouble and driving the family crazy. The agency ought to start a group for 11- and 12-year-olds! Everyone agreed with her suggestion, saying they could have used it too. Cherise spoke of nursing school and of moving south with her foster family. Then she added quietly, "I wish I could stay here with the group. I've changed in the group. I've grown from hate into kindness...."

Self-hate, rage, and depression are replaced by ability to love and to enjoy life; this, at least, is the hoped-for outcome of our work. Carin is doing well as a pre-med student, and many of the others are completing college. But not all have achieved in this way. Kenya was in some serious trouble before marrying and having a child. Pat lives with her foster mother, has a child, and is training to become a nurse's aide. We have lost track of Cherise. But her nonquantifiable growth "into kindness" is the kind of gain we aspire to for all group members.

CONCLUSION

It has long been established that groups are an excellent way of reaching foster adolescents (Hersko 1968, Schwartz 1968). What our experiences have demonstrated is that the emphasis on depression and coping behavior is useful, integrative, and necessary. As depression is dealt with, the ability to cope increases. As coping skills become more effective, depression is further dispelled. This is a circular relationship. Work with depressed members demands the most from even the seasoned practitioner.

The group process itself is a significant part of the healing process. The group's role in ego identification and development is a key factor. One cannot underestimate either the group's importance or the worker's role in facilitating mutual aid and influencing the development of norms within the group. But perhaps it is the group's resemblance to a family that means the most to the girls when all is said and done (Scheidlinger 1952). In this family, help is given regardless of whether members "deserved it" or not. They were loved and valued unconditionally. The worker represented a nurturant and structured mother figure, and group members alternately took on this role. In the group that lasted three years, several defined roles emerged (Hare, Borgatta, and Bales 1955). Two girls were consistent big sisters and role models; another personified the "street girl" who was making it despite the pulls of the ghetto; of the several "more average" members, one was looked up to not for her brains but for her compassionate response to the others, her persistence and her common sense. Each of these girls was seen as a leader in her own area of strength (Redl 1955). Another member, who was needy and immature, was affectionately seen as the baby and given advice accordingly. The group offered a place to share feelings, to think out loud, test that thinking, and get direction from those with different ego strengths. But most of all it became a place to say, "Hey look at me, Ma, I can make it!"

Overall, this was an effective approach in dealing with depression related to "being foster" and in enhancing coping skills and ego development in the girls. Since this was a central but not exclusive focus, we wonder whether further progress could be made if depression and coping were the exclusive foci of the group. We sought to address as broad a range of foster girls as possible, and in a natural way—that is, while working on normal developmental tasks. The danger is that the central focus can at times become obscured, given so much that requires attention. It is necessary to order one's priorities. We also agree with Glenda about the need for groups for younger children. But in terms of ego identification and growth, a more homogeneous group of girls like Cherise would not be particularly workable. Although such an exclusively focused group would lack significantly different available strengths, it may be a useful treatment option for the more severely depressed foster adolescent.

For the broad range of youngsters in foster care, depression will continue to be widespread unless it is tackled directly. We favor this emphasis on depression and coping in the context of the developmentally oriented mutual aid group.

REFERENCES

Auerswald, E. (1969). A systems dilemma. *Family Process* 8 (2):211–234.

Bellak, L. (1973). *Ego Functions in Schizophrenics, Neurotics and Normals*. New York: John Wiley.

Bibring, E. (1953). The mechanism of depression. In *Affective Disorders*, pp. 13–48, ed. P. Greenacre. New York: International Universities Press.

Cohen, A. (1955). *Delinquent Boys: The Culture of the Gang*. Glencoe, Ill.: Free Press.

Erikson, E. (1950). *Childhood and Society*. New York: Norton.

Freud, A. (1958). Adolescence. *Psychoanalytic Study of the Child* 13:358–373.

———, Goldstein, J., and Solnit, A. (1973). *Beyond the Best Interests of the Child*. Glencoe, Ill.: Free Press.

Freud, S. (1917). Mourning and melancholia. *Standard Edition* 14:237–258.

——— (1921). Group psychology and the analysis of the ego. *Standard Edition* 18:67–144.

Garland, J., Jones, H., and Kolodny, R. (1968). A model of stages of development in social work groups. In *Explorations in Group Work*, ed. S. Bernstein. Boston: Boston University Press.

Germain, C. (1973). An ecological perspective in casework practice. *Social Casework*. 54:323–330.

—— and Gitterman, A. (1975). Social work practice: An integrated approach. Invitational Paper #46, annual program meeting, Council on Social Work Education.

Grier, W. and Cobbs, P. (1968). *Black Rage*. New York: Basic Books.

Hare, P., Borgotta, E., and Bales, R., eds. (1955). *Small Groups*. New York: Knopf.

Hersko, M. (1968). Group psychotherapy with delinquent adolescent girls. In *Differential Diagnosis and Treatment in Social Work*, ed. F. Turner. Glencoe, Ill.: Free Press.

Jacobson, E. (1971). *Depression: Comparative Studies of Normal, Neurotic and Psychotic Conditions*. New York: International Universities Press.

Kraft, I. (1961). Some special considerations in adolescent group psychotherapy, *International Journal of Group Psychotherapy*. 2:196–203.

Lee, J. (1976). Group work with mentally retarded foster adolescents. *Social Casework* 58:164–173.

Masterson, J. (1972). *Treatment of the Borderline Adolescent: A Developmental Approach*. New York: John Wiley.

Peterson, J., and Sturgies, C. (1971). Group work with adolescents in a public foster care agency. In *The Practice of Group Work*, eds. W. Schwartz and S. Zalba. New York: Columbia University Press.

Redl, F. (1955). Group emotion and leadership. In *Small Groups: Studies in Social Interaction*, pp. 71–86, eds. P. Hare, E. Borgotta, and R. Bales. New York: Knopf.

Scheidlinger, S. (1952). *Psychoanalysis and Group Behavior: A Study in Freudian Group Psychology*. New York: Norton.

Schwartz, W. (1968). Group work in public welfare. *Public Welfare* 20–26.

—— (1971). Introduction. In *The Practice of Group Work*, eds. W. Schwartz and S. Zalba. New York: Columbia University Press.

—— (1971). Social group work: The interactionist approach. *Encyclopedia of Social Work* 16th ed., 2:1258–1262. New York: NASW.

Shange, N. (1975). *For Colored Girls Who Have Considered Suicide When the Rainbow is Enuf*. New York: Macmillan.

EDITORS' DISCUSSION

GROUP COMPOSITION. Under the auspices of the New York City Division of Foster Home Care, adolescent girls were invited to join in therapy groups on the basis of their caseworkers' recommendations. Some of the girls were involved in individual psychotherapy and were referred by their therapists. All participants were female adolescents between 15½ and 18 years of age who had been placed in foster care. Referral forms were requested, and selective screening interviews were held in questionable situations. Diagnostic material was used when available. In-depth diagnostic understanding of the girls was an outgrowth of group participation. Participation in the group was voluntary and members not ready for the group modality screened themselves out by not returning after their initial meeting. As many as 20 girls might be recruited to obtain an ongoing group of 10 to 12 members who participated consistently.

SETTING AND PURPOSE. The groups usually met once a week from September to June. Some groups chose to continue into another year, and in fact, the group presented in this chapter met for a three-year period before mutually agreeing to terminate. The majority of groups met for a year or less. The setting was the New York City Division of Foster Home Care, a public agency.

The purpose of the groups was to assist adolescents in foster care, primarily those contending with depression over object loss of their natural parents. Clinicians were to relate to depressive feelings—feelings of anger and worthlessness that had resulted from having been "given away"—and to encourage coping skills and ego development in the participants. The goal was to help adolescents work on normal developmental tasks in addition to helping them confront the stigma of being cared for by the child welfare system. The rebellion and resistance many of these girls presented in their foster homes received a significant amount of group attention.

LEVEL OF INTERVENTION—CLINICAL TECHNIQUES. The overall therapeutic approach with the groups was supportive, rather than uncovering or reaching for rage, fantasies, etc. Mutuality, the creation of a benign, accepting environment, catharsis, and ventilation were encouraged. Clarification and ego supportive techniques were used to enhance frustration tolerance, reality testing, and drive modulation. In addition, group leaders involved themselves in active mediation and advocacy with family, school, and the child welfare system, in order to help the participants negotiate their imperfect worlds and to dispel the pervasive power of their sense of helplessness. Attention and intervention were directed to both internal and external sources of stress. Relying on an ecological perspective, the social workers sought to intervene in the systems that impinge on black, poverty level adolescent girls. Techniques employed were concurrently addressing intrapsychic, interpersonal, intrafamilial, educational, and social welfare systems.

GROUP PROCESS. The group was intended to provide a forum for reality testing, and certain types of gentle clarification (confrontation) were offered to facilitate reflective consideration among participants. The authors tried to deal directly with issues of foster care and to accept, even encourage, angry and rageful feelings. Sharing experiences with foster and natural parents established an atmosphere of commonality (Blanck and Blanck 1979). Identification with peers and the leaders who could be perceived as role models and parental figures allowed members to react nondefensively to painful material. Splitting—good and bad parents—was a universal defense in the ongoing group process; it was handled via encouragement of the "joining-in" experience. Additionally, the group process included acceptance, universalization, partialization, altruism, and ventilation.

GROUP DYNAMICS. Resistance to painful material was accepted by the leaders; yet, as some group members made a symbiotic merger or pseudo-alliance with the leader (good maternal object) and their peers (siblings), such resistance was eventually worked through. The social workers consistently, gently, and benignly imposed their own secondary process and rational behavior onto the treatment situation. Structural deficits and borderline conditions were recognized by the social workers and therefore no attempt at genetic reconstruction and interpretations of conflict was made, which would have led to regressive transferences (Tolpin 1978). Faulty self-esteem, anxiety, and depression caused some members to use the leaders and other members as self-object transference objects. The authors emphasize the group's role in ego identification as well as in providing mutual aid and understanding among members. Further delineation would consider the transference relationship that develops between members and the social worker as the pre-oedipal mother. This relationship is of decisive importance in groups of adolescents as the central conflict of adolescence takes place "between the need for dependency and the drive for individuation and identity" (Grotjahn 1972, p. 173). The group leaders become real to the adolescent girls though in a circumscribed way, not as themselves, but, rather, as representatives of the object world, catalysts to facilitate selective identification.

The potential for clinicians to react with anxiety, depression and helplessness when confronted with these emotions in others was noted by the authors. The warning to "tread carefully in the helping process" is explicit. Leaders are cautioned against program planning for fun, and against encouraging members to wallow in dysfunctional self-pity.

Many of the themes shared by the foster children parallel issues presented by children who have experienced parental loss. The stigma attached to being different chracterizes various adolescent groups and subgroups. The long-term supportive work described by Lee and Park is clearly applicable to a population greater than the foster children presented. The group's continuity is a critical variable. Long-term group work—with a closed and fixed membership—ultimately provides a familial, accepting atmosphere that tolerates anger, regression, and similar negative feelings to a greater extent than natural, step, single, or foster parents can.

Blanck, G. and Blanck, R. (1979). *Ego Psychology II–Psychoanalytic Developmental Psychology*. New York: Columbia University Press.

Grotjahn, M. (1972). The transference dynamics of the therapeutic group experience. In *Adolescents Grow in Groups: Experiences in Adolescent Group Therapy*, ed. I. H. Berkovitz, M.D. New York: Brunner/Mazel.

Tolpin, M. (1978). Self-objects and oedipal objects: A crucial developmental distinction. *Psychoanalytic Study of the Child* 33:167–184. New Haven: Yale University Press.

CHAPTER 11

Multiple Family Group Therapy with Adolescent Drug Addicts and Their Parents

CRAIG PODELL, M.S.W.

EDITORS' NOTES
This chapter presents an innovative treatment plan for changing relationships between adolescent addicts and their parents. The success for this therapy relies on the leaders' empathic recognition of the narcissistic wounds experienced by parents and children alike. Watching other families interact inspires group members to consider change without catastrophic anxiety.

Multiple Family Group Therapy (MFGT) is an approach to family treatment that effectively brings about change within families. This chapter will examine the theory, rationale, process, and dynamics of MFGT as it is used in the rehabilitation of adolescent drug addicts and their parents within the milieu of a therapeutic community. Attention will be given to the approaches, mechanisms, and interventions employed in the family group process. The purpose of MFTG is to help family members to uncover family secrets, multi-generational conflicts, and faulty communication patterns. In addition, some of the variables and obstacles that affect the process of the family group are identified. How co-therapists determine group interaction is explicated. Because of financial cuts in the budget of a large municipal hospital in New York City, the rehabilitation program for adolescent addicts did not have the counselors and social workers available to provide individual sessions to every family. Therefore, families were brought together into a group for treatment.

The setting for the MFGT is a 30-bed therapeutic community in a large municipal hospital in New York City. All of the patients in the therapeutic community were males between the ages of 14 and 27 years old. While a majority of the patients are addicted to heroin, recent trends have found an increasing number of individuals with multi-drug abuses; where barbiturates, alcohol, and mehaqualone (Quaaludes) were prevalent. Most of the addicts manifest character or personality disorders. Individuals who presented psychotic disorders or had other illnesses involving severe ego deficits were not treated within the therapeutic community and were referred to a more appropriate facility. Referrals to the therapeutic community came from the courts, methadone clinics, community health clinics, and the inpatient detoxification service connected to the hospital's adolescent drug treatment program.

REVIEW OF THEORETICAL CONSIDERATIONS

Most of the literature on MFGT consists of summaries of impressions made by leaders after leading MFGT groups in a variety of settings. Brief descriptions of the development and mechanisms of change within such groups are given. Little information has been reported on the variables that effect MFGT. Practically no efforts to examine family and/or group process have been attempted. Aside from the interest of one major theorist, Peter Laqueur, MFGT is noted as the "overlooked" treatment (Nevin 1974).

In Laqueur's early work (1972) in a state hospital, he discovered that treating families of schizophrenic patients in a group caused significant changes in harmful patterns of intrafamilial interaction within a shorter period of time than did treatment of the individual families. By using some of the family participants in the group in specific co-therapeutic roles, Laqueur observed that the modification of pathological behavior among the members was expedited. The uniqueness of MFGT, in contrast to all other approaches, was characterized by the patients' positive ego functioning, high motivation, interest in the group, and desire to interact and communicate within this setting. Unlike MFGT, the traditional peer group tended to produce a great deal of narcissistic soliloquy and was marked by patients' overall disinterest in the group and a lack of meaningful relationships among group members.

Individual family therapy, in contrast to MFGT, triggered anxiety and resulted in maladaptive defenses. The individual family approach often mobilizes denial, avoidance, and rationalization, and tends to increase intellectualization by all members of the family. Bringing separate families and addicts together into the treatment setting, lessens anxiety and diminishes defenses; this, in turn, motivates patients to become actively involved in working through developmental conflicts. In his MFGT work with schizophrenic patients, Laqueur observed that, "the presence of other families and hospitalized patients in the treatment setting seems to stimulate the patients to engage actively in the struggle toward increasing self-differentiation and independence" (p. 403).

Within the milieu of a psychiatric day care center, Davies, Ellison, and Young (1966) have reported that the MFGT allowed patients and families to more easily identify unresolved oedipal problems, including the feeling that the survival of the parents' marriage depended on the patients remaining in the home. Patients further feared that mature sexual behavior and marriage would be expected of them if they separated from their parents. The revelation of such core conflicts in MFGT is achieved by a process wherein patients and parents reproduce those primitive and chronic patterns in the family group that have created pathological family interactions. Learning occurs through analogy; as conflicts are identified, other patients and parents in the group identify with members of another family. They apply the revelations that occur in other families to their own case. Such identification of conflicts is accomplished in MFGT with far less anxiety than is usually found in individual family treatment.

Further differences in the influences between individual family treatment and that of MFGT have been recognized by Handlon and Parloff (1962) who observed that MFGT allows for support and acceptance of the patient by developing an accepting atmosphere, in contrast to the patient in the individual family session who often feels isolated and unique; it provides a nonthreatening atmosphere for reality testing, whereas within individual family sessions members share and support distortions; and it promotes transference distortions in the group that are often therapeutically useful. Within the traditional family approach such distortions support unhealthy family mythology. Additional support for these observations is reported by

Lewis and Glasser (1965). They recognize that MFGT breaks the family's taboos on family interactions as they are maintained by the family myths. Among a group of equals within a nonthreatening atmosphere, interactions can be explored and discussed. The presence of co-therapists who guide and mediate the group's discussion stimulates a situation whereby the hierarchy of power within each family is minimized; all members are given a chance to interact.

The structure of MFGT has been reported to help the parents of addicts recreate early family conflicts that have arisen out of their own familial history. Such sharing of familial history among the parents in the group evokes multi-generational conflicts that are often accompanied by an outpouring of rage, guilt, and fear which have been locked up in family members for many years. Bowen (1976), in his work on MFGT, found that the families within the group setting were allowed the opportunity to observe their emotional systems in what he calls the "family ego mass" with more ease than in individual family therapy. Bowen recognized that the participants within MFGT were reassured to find that other people have the same kinds of problems as themselves. Having participants in MFGT share their problems and experiences while supporting one another is what gives this form of treatment the power to effect changes in family systems.

Kimbro, Taschman, Wylie, and MacLennan (1967), in their MFGT work with families of adolescents, also recognized the efficacy of the sharing experience. In their opinion, the group experience allows families to share in the exploration of common problems, to view such problems objectively by hearing them verbalized by others who have similar problems, to participate as co-therapists, and to establish a milieu where peers challenge, support, desensitize, and educate one another. Kimbro emphasized that MFGT provided the opportunity for peer support and interfamilial adult adolescent relations and allowed therapists to avoid taking sides, which so often sabotages the therapeutic process within individual family therapy.

THE SETTING

As a result of the above observations and program developments, MFGT was initiated. Male adolescent addicts in the therapeutic community have been meeting regularly in two groups with their parents once a week for two 1½ hour sessions, led by clinical social workers who act in co-therapist roles. The group's size varied from four to six families. The open-ended structure of the group allowed individual families to participate in the MFGT anywhere from six to twelve months. While the family's involvement in MFGT was not a mandatory part of the treatment in the residential therapeutic community, parents were usually willing to enter the group because it afforded them the opportunity to see their sons more often. The MFGT sessions are held in a meeting room separate from the therapeutic community. In examining the particular behavioral characteristics of the patients and the family members who were represented in the group, it was noted that the addict's ego functioning was but an offshoot of the family's thinking and expressive styles. The patient's ego combines inner feelings with internalized representations of the family's experience. Pathological character traits and their symptoms (i.e., drug addition) were found to be affected by the pathological interaction and development within the family system itself. These patients and their parents were found to display such ego deficits as low frustration tolerance, inability to cope with pain and anxiety, a constant need to turn a "low" into a "high," low self-esteem, infantile feelings of omnipotence, difficulty in working effectively, superficial relations with secondary objects, impulsivity, and unsatisfactory sexual relations.

Most of the addicts in the group actively expressed their ambivalent feelings toward their parents; most lived at home but could not communicate with their parents. In general, they felt that their parents did not understand them, yet they were unable to change their behavior. The parents, more often than not, were both overly demanding and indulgent. Both of these traits were simultaneously present in a characteristic pattern of rejection and excessive support. The addicts were similarly ambivalent, desiring to separate from parents and yet unable to relinquish dependency ties to primary object relations. Frosch (1970) notes that drugs are often used as a means of gratifying pregenital drives and that such substances are "most often in the service of withdrawal from painful reality and in the fulfillment of unconscious fantasies. A fantasy object relationship is substituted for a real one. Incorporation of the addictive substance is a means of introjecting the fantasied object or some magical power represented by the substance relieves narcissistic injury by creating a sense of new or unique physical or mental power" (p. 210).

Additionally, oedipal conflicts are prominent in the adolescent addict. The relationship to the parents that prevailed during the period from 4 to 6 years old is reactivated. For many of the addicts in the family group, rejection by the father and strong attachment to the mother was a prominent theme. The typical family's background included an overprotective, seductive mother and an authoritarian father who is distant and punitive. Often the father had a history of heavy alcohol use. Thorpe (1956) views this as an unresolved oedipal situation in which the addict desires to win the mother from the father. This disastrous solution is avoided through drug addiction. "They could maintain their narcissistic dreams of monopolizing mother, and yet in reality father would have her" (p. 56). With a better understanding of the pregential and oedipal conflicts that affect addicts and parents pathologically, one can perceive how MFGT provides a unique modality with which to treat adolescent developmental struggles and drug addiction.

THERAPISTS' ROLES

The principle goal for which MFGT was designed was to improve communication between family members. All efforts in the group are based on the conviction that the client's drug addiction, delinquency, and aggression is precipitated—and perpetuated—by the family members. The process of increasing awareness of the interaction and communication within the family is facilitated by the mediation of the co-therapists. They try to provide a group milieu that allows families to develop introspective attitudes toward one another. In a sense, the therapists elicit the help of families in MFGT by directing them to cooperate in uncovering conflicts within particular families. This process is reinforced by the fact that all of the families in the group have a common problem: one of their family members has been identified as "disturbed." Within this frame of reference, it is observed that the addicts within the MFGT often identify with the communication blocks in another family and often confront both parents and their fellow peers with regard to these. Similar activities have been reported by Lecker, Hendricks, and Turanski (1973), whose work with adolescents in MFGT sought to utilize their patients' natural peer-group orientation to deal with family and individual issues. In that case the purpose was to clarify communication lines among the family members in the group.

In addition, therapists attempt to develop increased introspection and self-examination in the family, a goal that parallels the insight of individual therapy. Such introspection will hopefully be triggered by the efforts of the co-therapists to provide an appropriate group milieu for such introspective attitudes.

In the adolescent addiction groups, the co-therapists allowed group members to help other families examine conflicts and communication barriers through confrontation and identification, though it often became necessary for the co-therapists to assume a leading role. This proved necessary when the group began to become introspective and focus on core conflicts such as separation, multi-generational problems, or sexual issues. As the group became introspective and affective material began to be explored, family members attempted to mask their conflicts through intellectualization, rationalization, and various forms of manipulation. At home they sometimes aggressively acted out both verbally and physically. The group members themselves were hardly skilled enough to handle the exploration of each others' core conflicts. Parents would often use both their own children and other adolescents in the group as scapegoats. Fathers were even observed to challenge other fathers or the therapists to physical fights. At such times it was the responsibility of the co-therapists to remind the group that no physical fighting was allowed.

Once a group has begun to explore highly emotional conflicts, the importance of the co-therapists' ability to make use of the technique of "indirect interpretation" becomes critical. Many fathers began to express their rage toward their own fathers. It was discovered that in the majority of cases the fathers' punitive and ineffectual relationships to their sons were but projections and displacements of their relationships to their own fathers. Instead of telling members that they were unable to relate to their sons because their conflicts with their own fathers were unresolved, the co-therapists took a more universalized, educative approach. They noted that there appeared to be individuals whose relationships to their children were blocked as a result of conflicts and struggles with their own parents. As Laqueur observes, the direct personal interpretation causes clients to agree with sophisticated insights while they build inner defenses against what are actually unacceptable ideas. This requires many months of therapy to overcome. Indirect interpretation, on the other hand, allows the patient and family to learn by self-examination based on their observations of other family's problems. This eliminates the need to create defenses to ward off more confrontational exchanges (Laqueur, La Burt, and Morong 1964, p. 152).

To the extent that individual members or families develop trust, transference occurrences are unleashed by the members. Usually one of the co-therapists, or even another parent in the group, becomes the most likely recipient. Commonly, parents relate to the co-therapists and, to a degree, the other parents, as they related to their own parents. As these transference occurrences arise, the therapists must provide a corrective emotional experience, through the use of indirect interpretation, in order to diffuse and highlight the reaction while simultaneously attempting to stimulate other reflections and revelations.

An example of this occurred when a father in the group accused one of the therapists of fostering his son's aggression toward his peers. The therapist was criticized for being too strict in setting limits in the therapeutic community. The other therapist intervened to explore with the father and the group their views on limits and structure. Such exploration led the father to reveal his anger toward his employer and, eventually, difficulties he had had with the punitive limits set by his authoritarian father. Such intervention by the other therapist lessened the father's anger toward the first therapist while providing him with insight into his own transference reaction. Such revelation fostered identification among other fathers in the group who began to share their own experiences and conflicts with authority figures and parents.

Differences in the personalities and styles of intervention of the co-therapists in the group effects the process of MFGT. It has been recognized that most therapists who engage in family therapy are either "dominators" or "interactors." In our MFGT work with addicts and their parents it became clear that this author took on the role of the "interactor" while the other therapist assumed the position of "dominator" (Ackerman 1966). Recognizing that the differences in roles and personalities of the leaders of the group was impeding the group's development, the co-therapists worked out a more unified form of intervention in the group. It was decided that instead of taking an interacting or dominating role, the co-therapists would establish themselves in an enabling role that respected the equality and self-determination of the members. Instead of assuming the roles that belonged to the family members, the co-therapists took a much more flexible approach. This allowed the group members to make their own goals and interventions. Leaders only intervened when members began to act out aggressively, or when members were unable to handle certain affectual, anxiety-producing material or defensive maneuvers.

In addition to obstacles imposed by the particular composition of personalities in MFGT, the open-ended structure can obstruct the group process. Patients and their parents in our group participated in MFGT from 6 to 12 months; members entered and left the group randomly depending on the patients' progress. Consequently, the entry of new members into the group after families had begun to establish a rapport and intimacy with one another was upsetting to the established members of the group. This setup prevented the group as a whole from maintaining feelings of intimacy, as the continuous cycle of building was repeatedly interrupted. Additionally, the normal approach/avoidance anxieties demonstrated by the new members took time to work through, delaying the group process that much more.

To handle obstacles presented by the open-ended structure, the co-therapists made an effort to integrate the new members. Initially, the therapists introduced the parents into the family group, delaying the adolescent addict's entrance approximately four to six weeks until the parents felt secure in the group. Additionally the therapists set up a situation where they created a subgroup of new families who had common anxieties relevant to starting treatment. The co-therapists then sought to have the established families tell the new members about their own experiences as new members.

As the parents became more comfortable in the group setting, and their sons were allowed to enter the group, the issue of power and control became a central focus as family members presented their complaints about one another. Typically, parents supported other parents against the co-therapists, and the patients supported one another against the parents. An illustration of this development is seen in the following case.

David, a 16-year-old boy, entered the therapeutic community detoxified from a multiple addiction to barbiturates and other hypnotic sedatives. Before admission he was having problems with friends at school and while intelligent, his academic performance had declined markedly over the previous two years. When asked a question in school, David would often swear uncontrollably at his teachers. Prior to entering the therapeutic community, he had been under psychiatric observation as an inpatient at a local hospital. Reports from the examining psychiatrist revealed that David was admitted by his parents for observation after running away from home and overdosing on barbiturates. He maintained an extreme fear of authority with paranoid ideation. He believed he was being "spied on" by reporters. Diagnostically David was seen as a borderline personality. Continued individual psychotherapy was recommended to prevent further regression. Several unsuccessful attempts with individual therapy had been made. In each instance, David aggressively acted out against the therapist and withdrew. With the support of his social worker during his detoxification, David was able to enter the therapeutic community.

After his admission, David's parents entered the MFGT; they seemed to be a well-dressed, intelligent, middle-aged couple who were quick to adjust to the group and to assume leadership roles in the parent organization. The father was a very successful businessman who worked under his own father in a retail firm. The father presented himself as domineering and ineffectual. He responded to his son's acting out through impulsive and aggressive verbal and physical rebukes. The father reported that when David threatened to take some pills at home, he wrestled with his son, trying to take the drugs away from him. Additionally, the father had threatened David that he was going to "bug" his private telephone. The mother was an attractive, intelligent, and concerned woman who felt helpless and unable to intervene in what she saw as a "competitive" struggle between her son and husband. The parents' relationship was marked by hostility and criticism toward one another.

During the fifth week of the parents' involvement in MFGT, David entered the group. Sitting on the opposite side of the group from his parents and appearing flushed in the face, David was asked by the therapists to try to put what he was feeling into words. Bursting into tears, David began to angrily swear at his father for having ignored, beaten, and threatened him in the past. As he expressed his rage, David began to verbalize his fears of being further beaten and threatened. The father appeared overwhelmed by his son's expression. He responded by stating that he found it difficult to have a relationship with a son who was an addict. At this point, two of the other fathers in the group supported David's father, saying that they also found it difficult to be close to their sons whom they also saw as "druggies." The two other fathers then condemned the therapists for allowing David to express his anger for as long as he did. Drawing from this support, David's father looked at the therapist and said that he would offer his boxing gloves to anyone who disagreed with him. The therapists reminded David's father of the rule regarding physical fighting. They asked if anyone else in the group had thoughts about the problem between David and his father.

It was significant that another addict, who had previously remained quiet and constricted in the group, spoke out to support David's anger while identifying his own rage toward his controlling father. The father of this second youngster related his own belief that fathers and sons were always angry with one another. Then he described his own conflictual relationship with his harsh father. As this revelation focused the group's attention on another family's conflicts, the therapists had the opportunity to remove themselves from the power struggle and to point out to the fathers how conflict and anger are transmitted from one generation to the next.

Peer support and the therapist's indirect interpretation enabled David to express his resentment as he told how his own father often complained about his grandfather's domineering behavior. With the support offered by the other father in the group, who shared similar multi-generational conflicts, David's father was able to admit that he had projected and displaced his underlying rage toward his own father onto his son. This intervention created a great deal of pain in David's family, yet it allowed father and son to begin exploring the close emotional ties they sought from one another.

The above illustrates that during the stresses and emotions generated during the "power and control" phase of the group's development, the therapists did not seek to either mobilize further anxiety or confront individuals on their feelings and/or defenses. This would have intensified the power struggle. Rather, therapists relied on group members to offer their support and reveal their own conflicts while the therapists offered indirect interpretations to help family members work through their fears, rage, defensive maneuvers, and struggles for control. A similar process in MFGT has been reported by Donner and Gamson (1968) who found that "when support is given to the self-confessing group member, there is more self-expression of difficulties." "The group can develop a 'revivalist' atmosphere with bursts of emotion-grief, shame-frustration until the family emerges as the focal point of discussion."

While power and control in the group helped recapitulate autonomy issues for the families, intimacy in MFGT often exposes conflicts and blocks that parents have in developing and maintaining close emotional bonds both with their sons and in their marital relationship. For the families that were able to reach intimacy in the family group it was often the case that the spouses' specific relationship with their own parents had had a strong negative influence on their marriage and their children.

It was during the 16th session of their participation in the group that one of the other fathers related how his dependency on his controlling and manipulating mother interfered with the closeness he and his wife desired from one another. Identifying with this revelation, David's father remarked that his own mother had spoken out against his marriage from the day he was engaged to his wife. He related how close he had been with his mother during childhood and adolescence and told how confused he had become when his mother intruded in his family by focusing his attention on his wife's and son's weaknesses. With the support and empathy of his wife and the other parents over this confusion and conflict, David's father was able to recognize that his mother was turning him against his wife and son because of her own jealousy and dependency. Peer support allowed David's father to become introspective and examine how his mother's dependency needs and his hidden feelings of guilt over his separation from her had indeed prevented his intimacy with his wife and son.

While David's family was able to work through their own familial conflicts to achieve a greater degree of intimacy, the group as a whole found it difficult to progress toward more intimate interfamilial relations. Although many individuals within each family built stronger and healthier ties with their own parents or sons, it was difficult for most of the members to establish intimate relationships with secondary figures in the group. The open-ended structure of the group, whereby individual families stopped participating at different times, was partly responsible for this. Nevertheless, this obstacle did not detract from the ability of the members to differentiate their own family conflicts from those of others and to help each other by identifying conflicts, communication patterns, strengths, and weaknesses in each family.

Such assistance allowed many of the families to progress through the "differentiation stage," whereby parents began to accept the uniqueness of their sons' developing identity and to respect their aspirations for separation. Typically, discussions among families who have reached this stage of development focus on the patient's vocational or academic interests, peer relationships, plans for living, and housing accommodations after release from the hospital. Heterosexual and homosexual relationships of the patients were not brought up in the family group, as they were usually discussed in individual treatment.

In general, the family's termination from the group is determined by the patient's planned release from the therapeutic community. Typical outcomes of MFGT included a decrease in the patient's pathological symptoms and an accompanying progressive development in ego functioning. Many of the behaviors associated with termination, such as regression and withdrawal, were missing from the group. The members' lack of fully developed object constancy limited their ability to mourn.

After the family's termination from the family group, the patient enters the "community involvement" phase of the treatment program.

To further support the patient and his family during this Phase, a special family group is available that assists with the problems encountered in reentry and transition to the community and home environment. Some families continue to use the supports offered by this special family group long after the patient's final release.

CONCLUSION

MFGT can significantly effect the successful outcome of the treatment process of the adolescent drug abuser and his or her family. The mutual help and aid that the families lend to each other in MFGT, combined with the efforts of the co-therapists to offer a group experience that supports the exploration of communication patterns, uncovering of multi-generational conflicts, and sharing of feelings among family members contributes to the success of this form of treatment.

As the families in the MFGT gain an increased understanding of the significance of their communication patterns, they progress from viewing the client's behavior as a symptom, to seeing it in light of the overall interaction between all family members. Increased verbalization and self-examination among family members produces a healthier degree of ego functioning.

REFERENCES

Ackerman, N. (1966). *Treating the Troubled Family*. New York: Basic Books.

Bowen, M. (1972). Principles and techniques of multiple family therapy. In *Systems Therapy*, J. O. Bradt and C. J. Moynihan. eds. Washington, D.C., privately printed.

———(1976). Multiple family therapy. In *Family Therapy: Theory and Practice*, ed. P. Guerin. New York: Gardner Press.

Davies, I. J., Ellison, G., and Young, R. (1966). Therapy with a group of families in a psychiatric day center. *American Journal of Orthopsychiatry* 36:134–46.

Donner, J., and Gamson, A. (1968). Experience with multifamily, time limited, outpatient groups at a community psychiatric clinic. *Psychiatry* 31:126–137.

Frosch, W. A. (1970). Psychoanalytic evolution of addiction and habituation. *American Psychoanalytic Association* 18:209–218.

Handlon, J. H., and Parloff, M. B. (1962). The treatment of patient and family as a group: Is it group psychotherapy? *International Journal of Group Psychotherapy* 12:132–141.

Kimbro, E., Taschman, H., Wylie, H., and MacLennan, B. (1967). A multiple family group approach to some problems of adolescence. *International Journal of Group Psychotherapy* 1967, 17:18–24.

Laqueur, H. P. (1972). Mechanisms of change in multiple family therapy. In *Progress in Group and Family Therapy*, pp. 400–415, eds. C. J. Sager and H. S. Kaplan. New York: Brunner/Mazel.

———, LaBurt, H. A., and Morong, E. (1964) Multiple family therapy. *Current Psychiatric Therapies* 4:140–154.

Lecker, S., Henricks, L., and Turanski, J. (1973). New dimensions in adolescent psychotherapy: A therapeutic system approach. *Pediatric Clinics of North America* 1973, 20:883–900.

Lewis, J. C., and Glasser, N. (1965). Evolution of a treatment approach to families: Group family therapy. *International Journal of Group Psychotherapy* 15:505–15.

Nevin, D. (1974). Multiple family therapy, the overlooked treatment approach: It's alive and ready for use. *American Journal of Orthopsychiatry* 44:223.

Strelnick, A. H. (1977). Multiple family group therapy: A review of the literature. *Family Process*, 16:307–325.

Thorpe, J. (1956). Addicts in group psychotherapy. In *The Field of Group Psychotherapy*. ed. S.R. Slavson. New York: Wiley and Sons.

EDITORS' DISCUSSION

GROUP COMPOSITION. Adolescent males between the ages of 14 and 27, hospitalized for addiction or multiple drug abuse were selected for this program. The population as diagnosed was composed of individuals manifesting character disorders and borderline conditions. Teenagers with severe ego deficits or psychotic symptoms, not drug induced, were referred elsewhere. The adolescents' parents are first invited to join the group. Mothers and fathers initially interact with each other and after a brief orientation period are joined by their sons. The groups are open-ended with families entering and leaving at various stages of group development. This is presented as a problem that co-therapists handle directly. The author suggests that the MFGT approach encourages participants to act as co-therapists to further openness and communication.

SETTING AND PURPOSE. Treatment took place in a therapeutic community within a hospital. Parents were motivated to attend sessions in part because they received additional visitation rights as part of the process. The major goal was to work out family ambivalences around issues of dependency and separation. Additional goals included consideration of multi-generational conflicts and communication problems when the group required limits to be set. This helped to control acting-out behaviors. The interpretations that were most successful were indirect. Because the therapists were facilitating their patients to improve secondary process, uncovering techniques were not used. The therapists were sensitive to the defensiveness that direct interpretation and confrontation would foster.

LEVEL OF INTERVENTION. The co-therapists, rather than allowing for a transference that may have divided them into "good-parent" or "bad-parent" roles, assumed a stance of "interactor" and "dominator." They soon concurred that this stance and style was confusing for group members, so they stepped back and began to allow members' reactions to occur more spontaneously. They intervened as auxiliary egos.

GROUP PROCESS. This practice vignette is not analyzed in terms of Ego or Self Psychology. Nevertheless, the author is attuned to both the developmental level and the faulty object relations of group members, as well as their narcissistic disturbances. Exchanges between members encouraged learning through analogy (or mirroring) and active sharing of similar problem situations. Empathy thereby developed between members. Peer support was offered by both parents and adolescents. Participants also occasionally took on the role of therapist.

GROUP DYNAMICS. MFGT is described as encouraging less anxiety and defensiveness than does individual family therapy. Indirect interpretations are effective and less likely to provoke confrontations when defenses appear. Too frequently, humiliation and assaultive confrontation have been used with addicts. The group described is mainly at a pregenital level; patients' behaviors suggested movement toward separation and individuation. Interestingly, when termination is described, the therapists recognize the members' lack of ability to mourn. Because group members do not seem to experience termination as loss, it is suspected that object constancy is not fully developed. The threatening issues of separation are avoided.

The most difficult countertransference issue involved the therapists' assumed roles as "dominator" and "reactor." This was surrendered as the genuine fragility and narcissistic vulnerability of the group members were recognized by the leaders. The therapists were able to discuss their reactions and change their own stance as leaders. Recognizing the "less than neurotic" composition of the group, the members' basic ego deficits and propensity for ego disorientation and merger, the leaders responded effectively.

CHAPTER 12

A Therapeutic Group Experience for Fathers

RICHARD R. RAUBOLT, Ph.D.
ARNOLD W. RACHMAN, Ph.D.

EDITORS' NOTES
The importance of the father in male adolescent development is highlighted in this primarily cognitive-educative group experience. Through thinking and remembering their adolescent selves, fathers begin to feel greater self-confidence, more empathy toward their sons, and less father-son conflict. The integration of Ego Psychological principles enhances a deeper understanding of the problems fathers face in raising teenagers. This chapter originally appeared as an article in the International Journal of Group Psychotherapy *and is reprinted here with permission.*

Psychoanalytic theory has traditionally emphasized the position of the mother in child and adolescent development, and viewed the father as a secondary agent. With the exception of the development and resolution of oedipal conflicts and struggles, fathers are rarely mentioned. Yet the important role of the father becomes apparent to any therapist involved in the treatment of adolescent males. There is a need to delineate the role of the father in adolescent development and to develop treatment procedures that recognize, encourage, and support active fathering.

Rachman (1970), recognizing the importance of the father with delinquent adolescent males, noted that fathering provides four crucial functions in fostering ego identity formation: (1) final emotional separation from mother; (2) and full emotional communion with father the prime model for masculine identity; (3) emotional support for judicious role experimentation in the areas of sexuality, assertiveness, authority relations, independence, decision-making, social responsibility; and (4) encouragement to pursue independent behavior in education, career, recreation, and so forth. The significant point here is that the father must be available and involved, a bridge from the family to the outside world. The father's involvement assists the son in developing a firm sense of masculine identity and independence. The father must be willing to engage his son, to share his beliefs, goals, and ideals; in short, to serve as an ego identity role model.

Fathers, however, are often not available to their children because they are involved in their own developmental "mid-life transitions" (Lionells and Mann 1974). In fact, Levi, Stierlin, and Savard (1972) propose an interlocking crisis of integrity and identity between fathers and sons. Describing the father's integrity crisis, they have written:

With increasing awareness of declining physical and sexual power and of the imminence of death, the middle-aged father pauses to evaluate both his work and his personal relationships, especially his marriage. He goes through a normative crisis in which he will likely doubt the value of his work efforts and the meaning of his marriage. If the resolution is successful, he will achieve a state of more solid self-esteem basic to integrity....Where the man fails to grieve his unattained goals or find value in his achievements, he may indeed strike out on a new course, either in work or in marriage. In our observations of the families of troubled adolescents, however, fathers were unable either to grieve successfully or to find a satisfying new course of action....If the father cannot do this, he may envy and disparage his son or, alternatively, overidentify with his son in trying to relive through him what he feels he has missed. (p. 49)

Lesse (1969), approaching the absence of fathering from a different position, has emphasized the effects of our current economic structure.

A large number of adolescents and young adults seen in psycho-therapy today have not had fathers with whom they could develop a strong, positive identification. This appears to be particularly so in families in which fathers work for large organizations, whether it is a large industrial company, the government, or as a member of a large union. This type of father typically comes home and talks in terms of "we" in which he is an integral part of the organization. (p. 381)

Frequently the male child cannot identify with a father whose self-definition evolves out of alliances with his colleagues.

FORMING THE GROUP: GOALS AND STRUCTURE

An opportunity to translate theoretical concepts into clinical practice was presented when one of the authors (Raubolt) became a psychological consultant to an affluent suburban school system. In four adolescent psychotherapy groups, a striking number of father/son conflicts became evident. These conflicts ranged from struggles over academic work, use of drugs and/or alcohol, to use of the family car and evening curfews. The issue of authority and discipline was complicated, however, by the fact that the fathers of these boys were seldom home. They worked long hours and their professional positions required a great deal of travel. For all intents and purposes they were "absent fathers."

It became clear that the most meaningful way to help these youngsters was to actively engage their fathers. It was decided to offer, with the support of the school system, a group for fathers. The concept of an "educational group seminar" was developed to suit the needs of the fathers and encourage maximum participation. The rationale for this format included the following considerations:

1. An educational focus would be perceived as more helpful and less threatening than a therapeutic focus.
2. A time-limited format of ten sessions would relate to their busy schedules and frequent need to be out of town.
3. A seminar designation was a familiar, acceptable training experience for both business and professional men.
4. A group conducted in a school setting for the community seemed appropriately advertised as an educational experience.

A news release was sent to the community to announce the availability of an educational group seminar for fathers who wished to improve relationships with their sons. Written invitations and telephone calls were also employed to secure a population of fathers from which to form the group.

The group was initially structured to conform to the prototype of a seminar that business men and professionals had experienced in their work lives. The setting was the guidance suite at the high school. Members were gathered around a small round table. Coffee was served at each meeting. It was expected that as the group coalesced and special techniques were introduced, this table would be removed and a more traditional group format would be adopted.

GROUP PROCESS AND FOCUS

A group of six fathers was formed as a result of the news release and written invitations. Those who were approached directly by letter were fathers of sons who were seen by the pupil personnel team as having academic problems (defined as truancy or class failures) and social problems (defiant, disruptive behavior or, in one case, social isolation). All six fathers were professional men in their late 40s and early 50s. Each had, in his own way, established financial security as well as a high degree of professional status and power. In fact this group of fathers had far surpassed their own fathers in this regard. Four of these fathers were corporate executives, one was a high-ranking school administrator, and one was a dentist. Five of these six fathers came because they felt frustrated and confused in their interactions with their sons. They stated that their sons appeared to have little respect for parental guidance. These fathers also admitted to having significant trouble in talking with their sons. They felt their sons disregarded their advice and defiantly resisted their rules. One father stated that he had a good relationship with his son but wanted to improve it. Significantly, the son of this father was the previously referred to socially isolated boy, who, though anxious, was not a behavior problem.

The fathers were selected on the basis of interest and availability. Each was contacted by phone and a convenient time was arranged. Initial questions and concerns were answered. They were asked to identify one facet of their relationship with their sons that they wished to improve. Prior to the composition of the group, four fathers were screened out because they could not make a ten-week time commitment, and one because his son was pre-adolescent. An additional one dropped out just before the first session, feeling family therapy was more appropriate. Three of the selected fathers had sons who were being seen in groups. The problems, as defined by the fathers, varied, though there were two common areas of conflict: lack of academic success and poor communication between father and son.

THE INITIAL PHASE

In the first session, after introductions were made and individual expectations articulated, the group's purpose was described in the following manner:

Since I (Raubolt) have been in the position of initiating and organizing this seminar, let me build on our stated goals and share the three basic ways I would like to proceed to realize our goals. I conceive this seminar as (1) information-giving, imparting to you some basic information. I have prepared a packet on adolescent development and common problems between boys and their fathers. (2) A second method will be getting in touch emotionally with the problems of adolescents and the problems of being a father. In order to reach our emotional goal, I will ask you to share, as best you can, feelings about yourself and your adolescent youngster, the kinds of joys and hopes and the kinds of conflicts and angers that you have. The more we share, the more comfortable we are going to feel together in recognizing the typical difficulties of adolescent growth. As a special part I would like you to consider sharing what your adolescence was like with your father. This will serve to give a perspective on how your interaction with your father has influenced your son's perspective of you. (3) Once we have discussed the information and shared the experience of being an adolescent and a father, we will have a unique opportunity here to learn in an experiential way. This can be created by role-playing. We are going to set up role-playing situations with everyone taking a turn being an adolescent and a father in a shared father/son conflict.

We then proceeded over the next few sessions to explore excerpts from Erikson (1968), Josselyn (1952), and Rachman (1970, 1975) on normal adolescent development and the vicissitudes of fathering. As the group began to talk about the concept of identity conflicts in adolescence, the topic of values became more and more prominent. The discussion centered on identity questions: Who am I? What do I believe? Where am I going? The fathers reacted by vacillating between being very dogmatic and being unsure about their own values and beliefs.

Initially, the exploration revealed the fathers' need to have their sons adopt their own strict code of values. This code of hard work, academic success, and "pleasure in moderation"—relaxation, drinking, sports—was initially presented as an unyielding, nonnegotiable set of standards. Any violation of this code by their sons was dealt with harshly. Physical punishment was seen as an often necessary last resort.

In order to highlight this clash in value codes, a role-playing experience was developed. In this way the group was able to examine the specific flavor of father/son interactions. It soon became apparent that the fathers themselves were often unsure of what to believe in because of their own developmental crises. These professional men were all highly successful in their companies/businesses or in the schools they administrated, but, while they maintained the respect of those above and below them in their professions, they had reached the peak of their careers and did not expect to progress much further. It was a time in their lives when they began to realize that most of their financial dreams had been achieved (in some cases, surpassed). They realized they had succeeded. The question was, now what? This life crisis (and it is important to note these feelings were shared by five of six members) was heightened by their sons' disregard for the code the fathers had lived by all of their professional lives. Since they themselves were unsure of what might lie ahead and did not want to force the "limits of their success" (as one father put it), they reacted severely to their sons' desires to take risks.

This became particularly evident in the third session during the following role-play situation: "Your son came home really drunk last night and your wife has been telling you all morning, 'Go talk to him'. When you come down for brunch he is alone in the kitchen. What are you going to say and/or do?" One of the fathers played the son and another the father. The exchange lasted for about twenty minutes, with the father calmly trying to talk to and reason with his son about drinking and the son not giving an inch, answering all questions with a simple no. Finally, the father, in desperation, stated to his 15-year-old son "It's not that I expect you to be a teetotaler, but you have to moderate your drinking." When the role-play ended the other fathers were adamant in their disapproval of this statement. The theme of their responses was, "You were too calm. I would have laid the law down," and "Who is he—the son—to argue with you? It wasn't like that when I grew up. I respected my father. What he said went. There were no two ways about it." In the ensuing discussion, it became evident that the group viewed punishment as necessary to maintain respect and that the trait they could tolerate least from their sons was insolence.

In order to achieve greater clarity and understanding of the issues involved here, we began to focus on Erikson's concepts of "free role experimentation and psychosocial play." The intent of the discussion was to develop an awareness for the fathers of the difference between positive and negative experimentation. Positive examples cited included interest in ecology, civil rights, Eastern thought, and structured risk-taking activities, such as racing and athletics. Negative examples cited included drug abuse, vandalism, and violence. These distinctions became necessary as the fathers, in an attempt to maintain their authority and control, had lost sight of the need for positive guidance. Discipline became synonymous with punishment, rather than as a means of providing guidance and direction.

To provide another experience that might assist them in understanding this conceptualization and also to develop a new level of participation and intensity, a reminiscent experience was suggested. In terms of group process, it had become apparent that the role-playing experience had introduced a more emotional quality to the group that the fathers found helpful. It now became clear that the group format could be restructured along more psychotherapeutic lines. The group interaction was expanded to include a balance between the original cognitive format and shared life experiences.

FATHERS REEXPERIENCE THEIR ADOLESCENCE

Using the technique of "clinical meditation" in groups (Rachman 1976), the following presentation was made:

I would like to suggest a positive associative experience to help you remember your adolescence. I am going to turn off all but three lights over the bookshelves to reduce all outside stimulation so we can concentrate. I would like all of you to close your eyes and get comfortable in your chairs, relax. I would like you to let your imagination go back to the time when you were 15.

Picture in your mind how you looked as a 15-year-old. You are getting dressed to go out and meet your friends on the corner. You are putting on your favorite outfit. What does it look like? What kind of shoes are you wearing? What is your hair style? Now you are fully dressed and on your way to meet the guys.

Picture yourself saying, "Hi." Picture your group of friends. How are they dressed? What do you talk about? After standing on the corner for five or ten minutes, someone says, "Hey, why don't we . . . ." Fill in the blank. It's the kind of crazy notion that excites everyone, and you begin planning. Get in touch with what you do to make this happen. Now fully concentrate for a moment on this "crazy" experience: so that when we finish you can share it in detail. Take a minute.

Okay, now I'd like everyone to open his eyes and keep alive the experience you had as a 15-year-old. Okay, now I'd like to discuss what you have just fantasized. Go around and each person describe to the group how you looked at 15, what your group of friends looked like, what the crazy experience was, and who thought of it."

The results of this experience were dramatic. The group shared in an open, direct manner many of the exciting "risky" pranks of their own adolescence. These included stealing from a local fruit stand, staying out all night playing cards and shooting pool when they were thought to be attending a religious retreat, and trying to "gang bang" a girl known for her sexual activity only to "chicken out" when she really showed up. The tone of the group at this point was active, loud, and excited as the fathers began spontaneously to mention other events of their adolescence.

Before long a significant theme began to emerge. Many of the group members recalled a very distant relationship with their own fathers. They were all sons of immigrants who were trying to establish businesses and better themselves economically. Consequently, there was little father/son interaction. As one of the fathers noted at the time, "We had to learn how to be fathers by ourselves, trial and error. We had to develop a role we had never experienced for ourselves."

THE LOVING FIGHT: LEVELS OF DIALOGUE AND ACCEPTANCE BETWEEN FATHERS AND SONS

When the fathers became aware of the discrepancies between their value code and their sons' and its relationship to their own adolescence, they were freer to explore alternative, less aggressive modes of responding to their sons. We then focused on improving father-son communications skills.

In order to assist the group in developing fathering skills, we developed seven necessary communication skills for fathers. They included:

1. Talking It Out: becoming involved, being present with your son, i.e., "I want to talk with you." "Let's talk this out." "I won't run from you, don't you run from me."
2. Creating an Open Dialogue: allowing your son to say what he feels and thinks; encouraging your son to say anything he wishes, whether you like it or not; being free to say what you feel about him.
3. Developing Emotional Communion: identifying true feelings, owning up to your own feelings, being aware of and taking responsibility for feelings of anger, frustration, fear, inadequacy, failure, as well as tenderness, compassion, vulnerability; being emotionally responsive; allowing yourself to be known to your son.
4. Confrontation: being able to say you don't agree; the art of the loving fight, i.e., "Hey look, you want to do this, but let me tell you how I see it"; giving your son something to bounce off; taking a stand.
5. Sharing: being known to your son, i.e. what you believe in and that you hold true to your beliefs, philosophy of life, your values, your identity.
6. Compromising: being able to give in, i.e., "Well, I really don't agree. I wish you would do it my way, but you have your own life, and I'll just have to sweat it out."
7. Maintaining the Relationship: giving your son room to breathe, staying with him, i.e., "I will be here with you and for you. I will not excommunicate you; I will stand by you as you

go your own way. I will not give up on you. Even though we don't agree, I am still connected with you."

This guide created a great deal of discussion, particularly point seven. The idea of *never* giving up on their sons was a hard notion for them to accept.

In order to provide a structure where they might try out these skills we presented a series of videotapes done by the high school drama class. In these videotapes an adolescent boy spoke directly to the camera and expressed rage, confusion, and sadness. The fathers took turns responding to the filmed vignettes. Interaction was greatly enhanced after each response, and the fathers were actively involved in trying out the new skills.

RESULTS AND EVALUATIONS

Upon termination of the group, the leader noted a number of significant changes occurring in the sons of the fathers involved. There was a dramatic decrease in school absences, with only one unexcused absence coming to the school's attention during the time the group was meeting. There were also fewer reported incidents of disruptive classroom behavior. Teachers noticed an improvement in academic performance; more work was being turned in with fewer failing grades.

To substantiate these clinical impressions, evaluation measures were developed. A 14-point questionnaire was constructed and given to the fathers to elicit their reactions to the group experience. Those questions that measured the father/son relationship before and after the group included:

1. With what problem(s) or concern(s) in your relationship with your son did you want help when you joined the group?

2. Have you changed any of your attitudes, feelings, or behaviors toward your son as a result of this group experience?

3. Did your relationship with your son improve? If so, please cite specific examples of improvement in your relationship with him.

4. Did your son show any changes in his behavior or attitudes, for example with the school, in his relationships with other family members, or with his friends?

5. Did you find yourself reevaluating any of your beliefs, values, feelings, or ideas as a result of this group experience?

A majority of the fathers (five out of six) indicated they had joined the group because of communication problems with their sons and a desire for help in this area. According to the results of the questionnaire, this goal was accomplished as all six indicated improved relationships with their sons, with more activities engaged in together, less fighting, and greater academic success cited as examples. In response to the question on perceived changes in the son's behavior, five of the fathers noted there was a change in their attitudes toward the family, with more consideration and friendliness.

All six fathers mentioned that the group encouraged them to reexamine their values and beliefs. This reexamination centered on "life goals and priorities." Three of the fathers felt that they had shortchanged their families and realized now the importance of their involvement. All the fathers, in one way or another, said they now saw the need for greater communicating, sharing, and understanding between father and son.

For all of us concerned, the personal meaning of this group may perhaps be best summed up by the following letter received two months after the completion of the group: "I am sorry I could not get back to you sooner. I have had a chance to reflect on the impact that the sessions had on me and I feel I ought to let you know. When I started I had basically given up. Matt was on his way toward excommunication. I was at the end of my wits. I can say that I have gained a better perspective, and therefore hope. I think I can do something about the situation because I have learned to be more patient and more tolerant. P.S. Matt naturally did not submit his term paper on time, but he did get it in a week late. I hope and pray the English teacher will accept it."

REFERENCES

Erikson, E. (1968). *Identity, Youth and Crisis*. New York: Norton.

Josselyn, L. (1952). *The Adolescent and His World*. New York: Family Service Association.

Lesse, S. (1969). Adolescence in psychotherapy: A psychological view. *Psychotherapy: Theory; Research and Practice*.23: 381–398.

Levi, S., Stierlin, H., and Savard, R. (1972). Fathers and sons: The interlocking crisis of integrity and identity. *Psychiatry* 35:48–56.

Lionells, M., and Mann, C. (1974). *Patterns of Mid-Life in Transition*. New York: William Alanson White Institute.

Rachman, A. (1970). Role of the father in child development. Paper delivered at Emanuel Midtown YMCA Parents-Teachers Association, New York.

——— (1974). The role of "fathering" in group psychotherapy with adolescent delinquent males. *Journal of Corrective and Social Psychiatry* 20:11–22.

——— (1975). *Identity Group Psychotherapy with Adolescents*. Springfield, Ill.: Charles C. Thomas.

——— (1976). Clinical meditation in groups. Unpublished paper.

EDITORS' DISCUSSION

GROUP COMPOSITION. Fathers of adolescent males compose this group. Fathers were selected through written invitation and phone contact. Those invited were referred by school personnel and consulting psychologists. Referrals were based on the fact that the children were having difficulty in school. Time pressures, motivation, and appropriateness of group treatment were the major criteria for participation. All the fathers were successful businessmen and professionals. Their functioning is best described as falling within the neurotic range of behavior.

SETTING AND PURPOSE. Meetings took place in the guidance office. An informal school atmosphere was emphasized by serving coffee and seating members around a table. The group was presented as an "instructive seminar." The emphasis was on sharing information about adolescence. Educational materials and shared memories of the fathers' adolescence were used as bases for group activity. Again we see how the educative and the therapeutic intertwine. As group participants exchanged past experiences, they developed insight and empathy and began to have a new understanding of themselves and their sons. This is a result of the additional information, self-examination, and their growing acceptance of themselves and their feelings. The group was the facilitator of the fathers' increased capacity for effective parenting.

LEVEL OF INTERVENTION. The therapist guided the sessions carefully. Ten educative sessions were planned. In groups such as these, the level of intervention needs to be appropriately monitored so that uncovering does not create anxiety that cannot be handled within the time restrictions. The techniques of role-playing and focused remembering were employed. Emotional reactions to memories and materials were encouraged. The interesting aspect of this type of group experience is that spontaneous feelings are elicited in a structured framework in response to the therapist's encouragement. The therapist's familiarity with developmental Ego Psychology enabled him to clarify pertinent normative conflicts and dilemmas in the father-son relationship.

GROUP PROCESS. The sessions devoted to an intellectual understanding of adolescence led the members to question their principles and modify their superego reactions. Role-playing stimulated the fathers' feelings and inspired the therapist to try clinical reminiscence. Basically, this technique might be labeled focused free association. The individual relaxes and free associates with particular times and places in mind. These experiences contributed to the group's interactions and ability to empathize. The fathers were able to practice simulated experiences that appear to have carried over to their home life.

GROUP DYNAMICS. Both Ego Psychology and Self Psychology theory seek to comprehend an individual's psychological development and show where such development went awry. The fathers, through their reminiscing, were able to recognize their parents' failures to provide them with idealizing transferences. Goldberg maintains that the "working-through process consists of the ego's repeated reactions to temporary losses of the narcissistically experienced self-object....In order to achieve this Kohut emphasizes equally, the cognitive and affective components of interpretations" (1978, p. 8). The shared group experience seemed to allow individual members to face their early losses with equanimity. The therapist's sensitivity to the fathers' unfulfilled needs was manifested through corrective interventions on cognitive and emotional levels centering around adolescent identity conflicts and father-son interactions.

"For each of the transference configurations one can commonly see typical countertransference phenomena, e.g., the fear of merger on the analyst's part during the merger transference, the resistance to being overstimulated by one's own grandiose exhibitionistic drives during an idealizing transference, and so forth" (p. 7). This group experience quickly engaged the fathers. They seemed ready and willing to mirror the therapist and to idealize him. The large amount of didactic material used may have been partially an attempt to handle countertransference feelings by reducing the closeness experienced by participants. Again we must emphasize, however, that in this short-term therapy a reduction of the transference responses is in order.

The experiences of a father may be different in degree or kind from those of a mother, but fathers as well as mothers find in parenthood a recapitulation of many emotional events from their childhood. Ross says, "like motherhood, fatherhood may make for ... a developmental phase in its own right" (1979, p. 319). Goldstein calls fatherhood a much neglected function and comments that "as contemporary therapists, we need to take an active role in avoiding the omissions that so many of our teachers have made. We need to help ... fathers to make this developmental phase of parenting a more meaningful experience for them" (1977, p. 335).

Goldberg, A., ed. (1978). *The Psychology of the Self: A Casebook*. New York: International Universities Press.

Goldstein, M. A. (1977). Fathering—a neglected activity. *American Journal of Psychoanalysis* 37:325–336.

Ross, J. M. (1979). Fathering: A review of some psychoanalytic contributions on paternity. *International Journal of Psychoanalysis* 60:317–327.

CHAPTER 13

Parent Groups in the Long-Term Treatment of Hospitalized Adolescents

MADY CHALK, A.C.S.W.
MARY LOU COSTANZO, A.C.S.W.

EDITORS' NOTES
This chapter presents a means to significantly improve parent relationships with psychotic adolescents through educative group work in a hospital setting. Additionally, the group serves to enhance parent functioning and parental self-esteem. The authors convey the ego dysfunctioning and narcissistic injury parents present at the time of their children's admission.

In psycho-analytic treatment the intervention of the relatives is a positive danger and, moreover, one which we do not know how to deal with. We are armed against the inner resistances of the patient, which we recognize as necessary, but how can we protect ourselves against these outer resistances? It is impossible to get round the relatives by any sort of explanation, nor can one induce them to hold aloof from the whole affair; one can never take them into one's confidence because then we run the danger of losing the patient's trust in us, for he—quite rightly, of course—demands that the man he confides in should take his part. Anyone who knows anything of the dissensions commonly splitting up family life will not be astonished in his capacity of analyst to find that those nearest to the patient frequently show less interest in his recovery than in keeping him as he is ... the relatives ... should not oppose their hostility to one's professional efforts. But how are you to take up this attitude? You will naturally also conclude that the social atmosphere and degree of cultivation of the patient's immediate surroundings have considerable influence upon the prospects of the treatment.

This is a gloomy outlook for the efficacy of psycho-analysis as a therapy, even if we may explain the overwhelming majority of our failures by taking into account these disturbing external factors! (Freud 1929, pp. 385–86)

Since the early 1950s many attempts have been made to study the interaction between family and individual psychopathology. Some literature has suggested that family communication styles, structure, and boundaries are related to individual symptomatology (Searles 1966; Watzlawick, Beavin, Jackson et al 1967; Wynne, Ryckoff, Day and Hirsch 1958). Few studies have been done regarding the relationship of family involvement in treatment to individual patient outcome (Anderson, C. 1977). Any inpatient, long-term facility that treats severely ill psychiatric patients has had the experience of attempting to treat individuals in the face of family resistance, intrusion, and acting-out. Yet it has been difficult for treatment settings to provide an organized structure that maximizes family involvement in treatment. Hospitalization of a family member has been shown to threaten the homeostatic balance of the family; indeed, a good deal of literature has been devoted to crisis intervention at the point of hospitalization (Parad 1965). However, little attention has been devoted to examining long-term treatment of families during an inpatient hospitalization.

We will consider the function of parent groups for parents, staff, and hospital. A review of the literature on groups for parents of hospitalized adolescents shows that little has been written about the meaning of such groups for parents. Most of the literature emphasizes treatment of the identified patient and discusses how groups for parents can facilitate such treatment (Arnold 1978, Williams 1975). We will focus attention in this chapter on parents' needs during hospitalization of an adolescent child.

HISTORICAL BACKGROUND AND DEVELOPMENT

The Yale Psychiatric Institute (YPI) is an inpatient facility for the long-term treatment of adolescents, young adults, and their families. The current parent group program at YPI was originated in February 1960 by a former chief social worker. The impetus for such a treatment program grew out of the expanding interest in and awareness of the hospital as a small community that had an inevitable impact on the patient. As defined by Edelson, the primary goal of the psychiatric hospital is "to cope with the consequences of emotional illness for the individual patient, for patients as a social group..." (1970, p. 3). If this definition is broadened to include "and for families," involvement of parents (as individuals and as a group) with the hospital organization becomes a priority. A fundamental notion underlying the development of a collaborative program for parents and staff is that "mechanisms of treatment are inherent in the [parents'] participation in the life of the [hospital] community" (p. 3).

Specifically, the parent group was seen as providing a treatment and "therapeutic milieu" analogous to the newly created patient-staff meetings in the hospital. In a sense, the hospital milieu was expanded to incorporate the parent groups. While the parent groups were not in any way designed to replace or duplicate the individual family treatment relationship between the social worker and the family, it was hoped that the parent groups would help to reduce the isolation of parents by providing a small "community" within which problems common to all families could be addressed.

Initially attempts were made to clarify the variables that differentiated parents from each other (e.g., degree and type of individual, or marital and family pathology) in an effort to form homogeneous groups which, it has been thought, would ultimately provide each parent with a more meaningful and appropriate treatment experience. However, for both theoretical and practical reasons the attempt was abandoned; subsequently, group membership became largely heterogeneous.

Since 1960 there has been a gradual expansion and evolution of the parent group program. As a result of a major policy change in 1969 that required all parents who lived within a 120-mile radius of YPI to join a parent group, the program has expanded and now consists of eight groups and a transitional multiple family group. Clinical evidence seems to indicate that participation in a parent group ultimately contributes in a major way to the patient's treatment.

One of the early consequences of participation in parent groups was increased involvement of parents in the hospital as a "community." As a result, parents developed a greater awareness of and concern about general hospital issues and policy. Parents and senior staff now collaborate in bi-monthly open meetings. The meeting provides an open channel of communication between parents and senior medical and nonmedical administrative staff. Agenda for the meeting is established collaboratively by senior staff and parents; minutes of each meeting are sent to all parents. In addition to facilitating open communication among parents, staff, and hospital administration, these meetings have resulted in the use of parent skills and talents in relation to special tasks. As an example, a group of parents became interested in the need for a halfway house and were instrumental in starting such a living facility. Parents are currently helping to develop plans and funding for a supervised apartment program and a group home in the community.

DESCRIPTION OF PROGRAM

The current treatment program for parents and families at the YPI involves individual family treatment, parent groups, and administrative meetings of the senior staff of the hospital with parents. Individual family treatment requires weekly family meetings with a family therapist/social worker and continues throughout the hospitalization of the identified patient and often beyond. Parent groups meet weekly and are composed of a maximum of ten parents. Divorced parents are placed in separate groups. Parent groups meet with two co-leaders, a social worker and a nurse. The seminar provides an opportunity for theoretical and clinical training in group process and is an arena for peer supervision. The third component of the program for families is the bi-monthly senior staff meeting with parents. Issues dealt with in these meetings explore aspects of hospital living and functioning.

GOALS OF THE PARENT GROUP PROGRAM

Parents whose adolescents are hospitalized for long-term psychiatric treatment seem to be socially isolated and either overly involved in or seriously detached from their families. Often it seems that parents' peer relationships have become superficial, owing to their inability to maintain any attachments outside of the nuclear family. Pathological patterns originating in the parents' own families are seen in both family and marital relationships. Parent couples often seem unable to support each other as individuals. Parents of hospitalized adolescents usually manifest their own long-standing difficulties in ego functioning. Often these parents have not received adequate parenting themselves. Hospitalization of an adolescent or young adult child becomes a serious, guilt-inducing event to parents who are already detached and isolated. Insecure about themselves as individuals, they have little sense of their ability to function competently in many areas of their lives. They often feel that they have failed as parents, and that they are responsible for their child's illness.

The admission process in most long-term, inpatient psychiatric units emphasizes historical, developmental and family history, and often exacerbates parents' feelings of blame and guilt (Anderson 1977). During a long-term hospitalization it is not surprising to see parents, influenced by their continuing sense of failure, withdraw passively from their children and the hospital or intrude inappropriately in order to reestablish parental control. Often they retaliate against the hospital system which is held responsible for removing their child and usurping parental roles. Not infrequently, they reject their child out of their despair and lack of understanding.

Hospital staff who, by necessity, are involved and identified with their patients, commonly have little energy for or commitment to identifying or empathizing with parents and families. Families are rarely uninvolved during an inpatient hospitalization. Often their participation in the treatment process remains covert and is mystifyingly acted out against patients, staff, and hospital administration.

A hospital treatment program can be designed to take into account not only the family's immediate reactions to hospitalization but its investment and involvement in the hospital treatment process as well. Making covert processes of institutional transference overt and available for discussion is one of the primary goals of the YPI parent group program. Parent groups allow for surrogate parenting by both members and staff and provide an arena in which parents can learn to modify their own reactions and attitudes. The opportunity to develop mutually satisfying interactions, and satisfy needs for empathy, support, learning, and self-expression is provided by the parent group program.

THEORETICAL FOUNDATIONS

The conceptual base of the parent group program at the YPI incorporates systems theory, social group work theory, role theory, family theory, and psychoanalytic developmental theory. It integrates concepts from these areas that can enhance understanding of the functions and tasks of parent groups during long-term hospitalization.

In interaction with as complex a system as a long-term psychiatric hospital, parents often feel powerless; in fact, power is unequally distributed between institution and family. Both parents and hospital therefore require "a force ... to keep the interaction alive when each party is tempted to dismiss the other as unreachable....The approaches [of each toward the other] may involve conflict, cooperation, confrontation, negotiation ... the demand is not for conciliation, but for a realistic exchange, based on the actual business between them" (Schwartz 1976, p. 183). Within a treatment program that seeks to involve parents in multiple transactions, family treatment, and collaborative work with the administration of the hospital, the parent group introduces the element of "mutual aid."

Initially, parents tend to reveal few emotions. As Schwartz points out, "... beginnings tend to stir up feelings of self-doubt and hesitancy about one's competence ... " (p. 187). In its early phases, each parent group struggles to develop a consensus of what parents need and what staff can offer. Rarely are parents' expectations of each other or staff within the group made explicit; rather they emerge and are elaborated on in the course of their work together. The primary focus of most parent groups is on the relationships between parent and hospital, parent and parent, and parent and child.

Mr. and Mrs. M are parents of a 15-year-old boy admitted to the YPI with acute psychotic symptoms precipitated by excessive drug use. His behavior has been characterized by both drug use and delinquent behavior for several years. Mrs. M is a youthful, energetic woman in her mid-40s; Mr. M is a quiet, reserved man in the teaching profession. When their son was admitted to the hospital, Mrs. M was the focus of her son's rage, which was often nonspecific and uncontrollable.

In the course of family treatment, the M's were able to acknowledge the extent of their son's aggression and the amount of discord in their family as a whole. Entry into the parent group occurred at a time of great stress in the family therapy. The M's quickly became integrated and expressed their despair and confusion about both the outcome of their son's hospitalization and their family discord.

After three months, with the help of the parent group and their therapist, the M's realized that despite some improvement in their relationship with their son, it was doubtful that he could live at home after discharge. In exploring alternatives, the M's were faced with the realization that appropriate resources for adolescents in the community did not exist. They brought their concern about their son's future to the group and discussed this over several sessions. The M's received encouragement and support from their group to approach the hospital with an offer of fund-raising and planning assistance to develop new resources in the community. Although the M's became the spokespersons, this venture was clearly a group project. The effort crystallized the ability of these parents to plan with the hospital. Having a sense of engagement in family treatment, and receiving nurturance and affirmation of their adult capabilities in the group, allowed the M's to utilize their energies for the benefit of their son and to help others as well.

Overcoming a sense of separateness between oneself and others, and among parts of oneself, is an overriding emphasis of parent groups. When emotionally significant friends are absent, and social contacts outside the family are few, parent groups tend to be used as a network in which interpersonal attachments develop.

Mr. and Mrs. A are a couple in their mid-40s. Their 20-year-old schizophrenic daughter was transferred to the YPI from another long-term treatment facility where she had been hospitalized for 1½ years. She came into the hospital in the midst of an acute psychotic episode manifested primarily by severe paranoid delusions about food. As a parent, Mrs. A was intrusive in regard to her daughter's body, peer relationships, eating habits, and treatment management; in addition, she quickly became involved in conflicts with the staff and hospital administration in regard to such issues as cleanliness of the ward and nutrition. Mr. A, though attempting to be the "rational" member of the family, was often drawn into his wife's struggles with the hospital.

Early in their participation in the parent group, Mr. and Mrs. A became a central focus of attention for other members. They viewed the parent group as a place where they could express their intense primitive feelings of depression, rage, impotence, and guilt. Group members responded to these expressions of feeling with interest and concern. They spent a great deal of time and effort helping to differentiate their intense feelings from their daughter's treatment. The group members' outpouring of empathy was experienced by the A's as comforting and as affirmation of their value as adults. Though often irrational, the A's were listened to attentively and cared for by the group members, and they were able to draw on this support as an aid in other hospital contacts.

By providing a safe channel for the parents' intrusive demands, the hospital supported the needs of both the parents and their daughter to have these intense feelings ventilated in an arena where she was not present. The other parents, through their own understanding of the A's need to express primitive feelings, provided validation that staff were not able to supply. Without the group, not only would the A's have been isolated and their guilt needlessly increased, but their daughter's treatment would undoubtedly have been jeopardized by increasing tension between the A's and the staff.

As parents begin to feel secure in the parent group, they are able to seek help and reinforcement from each other; feelings of anger, despair, and guilt which, if unexpressed, are a barrier to effective functioning, are shared. Expressing feelings, in fact, is seen as a group task. Acceptance and recognition of self-disclosure encourages an awareness of a different kind of strength and increases self-esteem. Parents use the group to test the effectiveness of their own behavior. They explore ways of handling the developmental tasks of adulthood, marriage, and parenthood, and increase their ability to judge themselves objectively.

Role theory points out that being a parent, spouse, or worker is emotionally intense and deeply significant to an individual's self-concept (Linton 1945). Roles must be carried out via interaction with others; they must fulfill idiosyncratic needs, expectations, and demands. Parents and spouses invest their roles with hopes, anxieties, and expectations. Some parents involved in the long-term hospitalization of an adolescent naturally wonder about the costs and rewards of parenting. At this time of crisis parents often question every aspect of their role and task performance.

"The sense of self as one who is competent, who is held to be of worth by others derives from the repeated transactions in valued life roles in which there is repeated experience of oneself as able and adequate *plus* repeated experience that this adequacy and ability yields recognition or admiration or affection from valued others" (Perlman 1974, p. 54). This sense of self (and self-esteem) is seriously undermined in parents whose children have been hospitalized. Generally, strain is put on both the parent-child relationship and that of husband-wife. The more difficult the demands placed on a given role, the more taxing it is to maintain a sense of personal identity.

When we function well we are rarely conscious of how strongly role demands and expectations influence our sense of well-being. When we have difficulty meeting our own and others' expectations, a spiraling sense of self-doubt ensues and increases feelings of emptiness. Hospitalization of a child is viewed by most parents as an undifferentiated attack on their ability to function as adults. The parent groups facilitate partialization of roles and tasks within roles. "In brief, focus upon one problematic area of a person's social functioning not only partializes the task so that the ego does not need to run from it or defend against it, but it also provides a repeated exercise of selective attention which is basic to competent coping" (p. 219).

Parents in the group program experience a variety of capacities and roles in which they can function well: as peers, helpers, friends, and workers. When parents are rewarded by others, they experience a sense of competence and pleasure. The strengths derived from satisfying interchanges in the group help parents to face other difficulties. Through the group process some parents "learn role elements they have never known, others to differentiate clearly between role elements that have always been unclear to them, and still others to muster the correct role behavior when it is required" (Cumming and Cumming 1963, p. 166).

Mr. R is an extraordinarily successful and creative corporate executive. His extended family was likewise creative, artistic, and successful. The R's were members of a society that placed value on social graces and competency. However, the price for these attributes was that Mr. R became overly defended, distant, isolated, and detached. Mr. R's 16-year-old son, an only child, was admitted to the YPI with a history of drug abuse, running away, isolation from peers, and one acute psychotic episode. At the time of admission Mr. R had been divorced from his son's mother for one year and was living with another woman.

The history of the nuclear family was impressive, given the rigidity of the roles that had been assigned to all family members. Mr. R, throughout his son's childhood, worked long days, seeing his child and wife rarely. He performed as he was expected, and became successful and powerful; he expected that his son would do the same. He had little energy left to meet the emotional aspects of fathering and the needs of his son, both of which would have required modification of expectations, demands, and aspirations. This was especially difficult for Mr. R, as he lacked a model for flexibility in parenting in his own father. Mr. R entered the parent group as an arrogant, glib, distant, and guilt-ridden man. He entered the group alone and six months later was joined (with the group's agreement) by his spouse to be.

Initially he talked exclusively of his son's achievements and difficulties. Over time Mr. R was able to share with the group the serious extent of his personal isolation and his overwhelming sense of inadequacy as a father. His difficulty with interpersonal adult peer relationships was most evident in his inability to discuss these feelings in any other than the third person. His isolation and fear of intimacy were most evident when he insensitively compared his son's assets with those of the other parents' children. Despite these difficulties, group members took enormous pride in Mr. R's accomplishments, expressing both their respect for his work and their pleasure in his achievements. They were able to talk with Mr. R both about his professional competence and his deficits as a peer and as a father.

Mr. R began to feel less socially isolated as he responded to the supportive, though critical comments, of group members. The group shared in celebrating Mr. R's marriage and, at a later time, in mourning the death of his father. Despite Mr. R's attempts to distance himself from the meaning of the group's interest in him, he was deeply moved by the group members' emotional participation in his life.

Mr. R, in characteristic style, expressed resentment toward the group until the day of his son's discharge, saying he was not "helped in the least" by participation. Yet, he had difficulty separating from the group and refused to attend a final session in which other group members planned a party for him. Mr. R was able to admit, however, to having become increasingly conscious (in the course of his involvement in the parent group) of both his professional competence and his inadequacies as a parent. Allowing himself to think and have feelings about himself in a differentiated manner was a new and significant experience for Mr. R.

Developmental and structural family theory, particularly that aspect of theory developed by Salvador Minuchin (1974), has focused attention on the protective function of boundaries in the differentiation of sub-systems and individuals within the family. Families who come for long-term treatment have often experienced serious breakdowns in boundary functioning. Self/other boundaries are often confused. At times they are overly rigid; at other times, overly fluid. Faced with the stress of hospitalization, families tend to increase the rigidity of their interactions and boundaries and to avoid exploring alternatives.

The parent groups, in collaboration with the family therapist, help make boundaries and clarify boundary problems. Complementarity and mutual accommodation, necessary skills for effective marital and parental functioning, are also central to group function. Mutual interdependence is an explicit issue in parent groups. As in the marital subsystem of the family, the group often serves as a refuge from external stresses. As Minuchin has pointed out, for effective functioning both marital and parental sub-systems "must achieve a boundary that protects them from interference by demands and needs of other systems" (p. 57).

Dr. Q is a 50-year-old psychiatrist whose first-born schizophrenic son was admitted to the YPI. She was divorced from her son's father 15 years ago and has been remarried approximately 10 years. She is bright, a talented musician, and presents a veneer of social adequacy. Dr. Q became a mother during her psychiatric residency. She described her early parenthood and the early years of her marriage as times of total social isolation. She felt competent in her residency, but inadequate as a marital partner and mother. Unable to form an alliance with her husband, who was a physician and socially "hyperactive," Dr. Q virtually lived her entire day either inside a hospital or inside her home. She formed few friendships with peers and developed no attachments. She felt totally dependent on her husband and had few, if any, resources to devote to her son. As her feelings of inadequacy (despite a live-in nurse) emerged, her husband became involved in taking care of his son. His anger at this involvement (it conflicted with his own needs for structure and emotional distance) ultimately caused overt violence between the couple.

Dr. Q's feelings of inadequacy increased; her husband, owing to his own pathology, became not only involved but "fused" with his son, and Dr. Q began to view them as one. She was no longer able to differentiate "the couple"; her anger at her husband and her child became unified into overwhelming rage toward them and guilt about her inadequacy. Her husband joined his rage and violence to his son's in united attacks on Dr. Q which persisted over many years until the couple's divorce. Despite the fact that the divorce increased Dr. Q's self-esteem, she felt unable to differentiate her husband and her son. She completely gave up the parenting of her son when she allowed him to go to live with his father. At the time of her son's admission to the YPI, Dr. Q's guilt and feelings of impotence in regard to the fusion of her husband and son were unabated.

Her entry into the parent group and family treatment was difficult and painful. She was apprehensive about her similarity to other parents, whom she viewed (based on her psychiatric training) as "severely pathological." In contrast to her fears, Dr. Q had strong needs for attachments to people with whom she could share her feelings of guilt, disgust, and hopelessness about her son. Over time, it was the latter set of needs that propelled Dr. Q to become an integrated member of her parent group. She began to share her feelings as a parent and to receive support and nurturance from other members of the group. Another parent in the group (Mr. L) whose relationship with his schizophrenic son recalled Dr. Q's anger at her ex-husband's behavior, helped her express her feelings and eventually recognize the difficulty she was having differentiating her son from his father.

With the group's support, Dr. Q began to confront Mr. L and to feel less powerless. Furthermore, she was able to establish appropriate generational boundaries between herself and her child. Her differentiation of her ex-husband and her son permitted her to view their thoughts, feelings, and behavior separately and to consider realistic relationships with each.

Adolescent patients express significant interest in their parents' newly found identification with other members of the parent groups. Patients often seem to see clearly that their parent's investment in themselves, their own functioning and treatment, is crucial to improved family relationships. The reinforcement of generational boundaries, supported by the parent group program, seems to provide an element of security for adolescent patients that permits them to involve themselves in their own treatment in the hospital. A crucial aspect of a parent's learning process is the development of concern for self, boundaries, and internal needs.

PARENT AND DIRECTOR MEETINGS

The bi-monthly parent meeting with the senior staff and directors of the hospital makes the power structure of the hospital accessible. Parents use these meetings to raise issues about the hospital and to promote change. Access to the leadership of the hospital, both affectively and cognitively, models the parenting process itself. The sharing of power to create change within the hospital system (the kind of sharing so necessary to families with adolescent and/or young adult members) is legitimized. Expression of conflictual feelings in these meetings is viewed as constructive and generally stimulates parents to explore alternatives in their own families. Functionally, parents are included in the long-range planning of the hospital and in the development of a variety of hospital programs. This type of parental involvement is felt to be therapeutic for parents as it utilizes their healthy ego resources; in addition, they can be a significant support to the hospital as well.

The considerable control over their children that parents give up in the course of hospitalization finds new expression. Parents who tend to be overly intrusive with their children, or floor staff, are frequently encouraged to channel their needs into facilitating constructive change in the hospital community. Parents seem more willing and able to maintain their commitment to an arduous, long-term treatment process when they feel incorporated into the hospital community, able to communicate with senior staff directly, and able to effect change in the hospital as a system.

STAFF GROUP

Since the goals and functions of the parent group program are to facilitate interdependent relationships among parents, staff, and the hospital administration, the group of staff working with parent groups requires special attention.

The staff must:

1. consider their own emotional needs
2. study, day-to-day, the details of the parent groups' current functioning—which groups or parts of the total program are in difficulty, why, and what are the possible remedies
3. increase the skill of members through peer consultation and through developing an understanding of group processes
4. develop a framework for thinking about the goals and functions of the parent group program, evaluate the program, and assess the results of any proposed changes, desirable or otherwise
5. promote collaboration and cooperation between the parent group staff and other staff groups related to the program

6. educate fellow staff in the area of parent interaction with the hospital (Edelson 1970)

These tasks require continuous attention to and discussion of staff values, beliefs, feelings, and sentiments. All staff participate in a weekly parent group seminar and supervision that attempts to provide an arena for didactic and experiential learning. The seminar provides a protected environment within which staff can share views of parents' interaction with their children and with the hospital. The strict administrative boundaries provided by the leadership within the seminar allow for open examination of professional issues within the seminar. Through experiential learning in the seminar, staff are able to freely explore the roles of parents as caretakers and as adults. Staff use the seminar to share their frustrations and anxieties. Often the central issue in the seminar is the leaders' frustration with their need "to act," "to cure," to say the "right" words. Leaders learn and re-learn that sharing their thinking, feelings, hopes and despairs, is useful and "curative."

One of the important outcomes of relinquishing the need to find the "right" intervention is an increased awareness of the complexity of human interaction. Staff begin to realize that "the 'truth' comes best in little pieces, slowly but surely, and with the emotions fully engaged in the acquisition" (Foulkes and Anthony 1966, p. 143). Staff learn to tolerate their own lack of knowledge and to "sit on" their wisdom, to assist the parent groups in their learning rather than to become their teachers. A recognition of the complexity of parental roles enhances the staff's affective and cognitive ability to empathize with parents. Finally, through the seminar, staff develop a unified perspective, a vision about parents' feelings and functioning that can be communicated to other staff groups within the hospital.

The aim of supervision is to alert co-leaders to each other's diverse competencies, to assume, as much as possible, equal but not identical roles in the group. Individual supervision of co-leaders fosters intensely collaborative relationships. Most often in supervision, co-leaders and supervisor focus on issues of parental interaction among parent members and with staff, as well as the development of relationships between staff pairs. Although theoretical issues are often carried over from the seminar into supervision, in supervision these issues become more intimately connected with the specific group and thus are made more "real" and potentially manageable for staff. By offering staff the freedom to explore issues in depth, supervision increases the sensitivity of staff to their own interventions. The active search for appropriate interventions, differentially applied in each group, is encouraged by co-leaders' developing skills.

SUMMARY

The family treatment program described represents an expansion of the hospital organization to include parents. The parent group program facilitates transformation of covert parental transferences to the hospital to overt involvement by parents in the treatment process and in the hospital as an organizational whole. Increased participation in the hospital as a "community" seems to permit parents to differentiate and separate more effectively from their adolescent or young adult children.

The parent group in its mediating function supports the growth of feelings of competence and effectiveness necessary to adequate adult functioning and self-esteem. Recognition of oneself as an individual with specific hopes, aspirations, and feelings, facilitated by the parent group, enhances an empathic understanding of others. The development of differentiated capacities permits parents a more realistic appraisal of themselves. With this increased ability to differentiate and partialize their own experience, parents become more able to establish and/or maintain self/other, generational, parental, and marital boundaries. The parent groups themselves, composed as they are of a heterogeneous population (new and old members), provide an opportunity for parents to use empathic and ego-integrative skills to help one another.

The staff leadership of a parent group program requires special attention. Staff seminars and supervision develop skills and encourage an awareness of the differentiated competencies of each leader. The need for staff to share their frustrations, disappointments, and aspirations about each other and the group, a central focus of the seminar, is a model for parent participation in the program.

Parent groups are a major component of the long-term treatment of hospitalized adolescents and young adults. The parent group program attempts to integrate theoretical constructs with the needs of individual parents, and is part of an overall collaborative program between parents, their children, and the hospital during long-term, inpatient psychiatric treatment.

REFERENCES

Anderson, C. (1977). Family intervention with severely disturbed inpatients *Archives of General Psychiatry* Vol. 34:697–702.

Anderson, C., Kressman, D. E., and Joy, F. D. (1974). Family response to the mental illness of a relative: A review of the literature *Schizophrenia Bulletin* 10:34–57.

Arnold, L. E. (1978). *Helping Parents Help Their Children*. New York: Brunner/Mazel.

J. Cumming and E. Cumming (1963). *Ego and Milieu*. New York: Atherton Press.

Edelson, M. (1970). *The Practice of Sociotherapy*. New Haven and London: Yale University Press.

Fleck, S., Cornelison, A. R., and Norton, N. (1957). Interaction between hospital staff and family. *Psychiatry* 20:343–350.

Foulkes, S. H. and Anthony, E. J. (1966). *Group Psychotherapy* Baltimore, Maryland: Penguin, 1957.

Freud, S. (1929). Introductory lectures on psycho-analysis. New York: Norton.

Linton, R. (1945). Concepts of role and status. In *Readings in Social Psychology* eds. T. M. Newcomb and E. L. Hartley, pp. 367–370. New York: Holt, 1958.

Minuchin, S. (1974). *Families and Family Therapy*. Cambridge, MA: Harvard University Press.

Parad, H. (1965). *Crisis Intervention, Selected Readings*. New York: Family Service Association of America.

Perlman, H. H. (1974). *Persona*. Chicago and London: University of Chicago Press.

Schwartz, W. (1976). Between client and system: The mediating function. In *Theories of Social Work with Groups*, eds. R. W. Roberts and H. Northen. New York: Columbia University Press.

Searles, H. (1965). The contributions of family treatment to the psychotherapy of schizophrenia. In *Intensive Family Therapy*, eds. I. Boszormenyi-Nagy and J. Framo. New York: Harper and Row.

Watzlawick, P., Beavin, J., and Jackson, D. (1967). *Pragmatics of Human Communication*. New York: Norton.

Williams, F. (1975). Family therapy: Its role in adolescent psychiatry. In *The Adolescent in Group and Family Treatment*, ed. M. Sugar. New York: Brunner/Mazel.

Wynne, L., Ryckoff, I., Day, J., and Hirsch, S. (1958). Pseudomutuality in the family relations of schizophrenics. *Psychiatry* 32:205–220.

EDITORS' DISCUSSION

This group case again steps outside the realm of typical group psychotherapy. Treating parents requires the ability to incorporate both education and therapy models. Indeed, Edgcumbe states that "there is no border at all between education and therapy as far as the usefulness of a psychoanalytic theory of childhood development is concerned. Both educator and therapist are aided... by the knowledge of normal developmental processes and stages. The border is to be found, rather, in the differing ways of using this understanding" (1975, p. 133). The parent group depicted by Chalk and Costanzo, relies on systems, social work, role, family, and developmental psychoanalytic theory. They are also working within the context of Ego and Self Psychology principles.

In these groups "education is essentially directed toward strengthening and enlarging the ego: by means of external stimulation, guidance, and example, to tame drive behavior; to divert drive energy; to promote adaptive defenses; to aid the growth of independence from primary objects in thinking and behavior; and to establish a wide variety of mature relationships through the enjoyment of interaction and cooperation with peers" (pp. 133–134). The therapists are cognizant as well of the enormity of the narcissistic injury sustained by parents whose children become psychotic. Group treatment focuses on restoring the self to these parents by enhancing their self-esteem. They adopt the tragic view of the world and man, common among Self Psychoanalysis, which holds that individuals need to accept limitations and live with their ambivalence (Messer and Winokur 1980).

GROUP COMPOSITION. Parents of adolescents and young adult inpatients comprise these groups. The mothers and fathers are not formally diagnosed. Their children, who are not group members themselves, have had at least one psychotic episode. Some adolescents are drug abusers. When this group technique first began, over 20 years ago, there was an attempt to match parents homogeneously. Now, except for the division between divorced and married parents, all groups are formed heterogeneously. Although it seems that pragmatic considerations take precedence in this decision, the experience of having a hospitalized child is sufficient to spark group feelings of commonality.

SETTING AND PURPOSE. The Yale Psychiatric Institute houses these groups. Staff members have found over the years that families act more cooperatively and constructively as a result of participation in this program. What started out as voluntary involvement is now mandated by the hospital for all parents within a reasonable traveling distance.

The goals are twofold. For the hospital staff, the parent group meetings result in less undercutting of therapeutic gains made by the inpatient. For parents, the group establishes a support system and provides parents with an outlet for pent-up reactions of disappointment toward their children and offers an avenue for creative planning on behalf of their children. Indirectly, the group attempts to enhance the self-esteem of individuals whose sense of self has been diminished as a result of the belief that they have failed as parents.

LEVEL OF INTERVENTION. Two co-therapists work together in each group. In the past they were social workers, but currently one is a social worker and the other a nurse or psychiatric aide. The stance seems to be primarily educative and parents participate in bi-monthly staff planning meetings. Group leaders are supervised by more senior staff members.

Although educative treatment methods are employed, therapists also conduct psychotherapy within these groups through "surrogate parenting," confrontation, clarification, consideration of parents' emotional needs, analysis of groups' functioning, and facilitation of group interaction. Outside of the group the therapists have the responsibility of interpreting parental behavior to other staff members.

GROUP PROCESS. Interactions between parents form the core of the group experience. Therapists seem to facilitate these interactions and anticipate change as a consequence of mutuality and shared confidences. The feelings of separateness and isolation described as fundamental to these parents are expected to diminish as a result of the group process.

GROUP DYNAMICS. Little is described in terms of resistance or transference. There seems to be an initial reluctance on the part of some to identify with others in the group. Once identification does occur, resolution of problems between parents and children is possible. Relating incidents that occur within the family gives members the chance to reconsider old relationships. Transference is avoided via the educative and problem-solving approach.

Decreasing parents' needs to merge with their children or to see their children as merged with spouses is a significant group goal. Consequently, the adolescents view their parents as less threatening and their own quests for independence are helped by the realization that the parents are building a support system outside of the family. The group encourages the developmental goals of parents and offspring.

Major countertransference issues are highlighted. Primarily, leaders are pressured by their own rescue fantasies. Apparently, the need to take over and ensure parental change is a prevalent problem and one that the authors feel can be conquered by open communication. Since a goal is to restore group members' confidence in their own functioning, therapists require patience and self-restraint in order to refrain from usurping the parents' attempts to gain control and mastery.

Edgcumb, R. (1975). The border between therapy and education. In *Studies in Child Psychoanalysis Pure and Applied*, ed. Staff of Hampstead Child Therapy Clinic, pp. 133–147. New Haven: Yale University Press.

Messer, E. R., and Winokur, M. (1980). Some limitations to the integration of psychoanalysis and behavior therapy. *American Psychologist* 35:818–820.

Our concern is not merely with the contribution of psychoanalysis to the prevention of pathology, but rather to the facilitation of positive growth.

Search of Love and Competence, Rudolf Ekstein

Index

Abstinence, 61
Abstract thinking, 23, 121
Ackerman, N., 214
"Acting-out," 21, 31
Activity group therapy, 145–147
Adelson, J., 179
Adolescence
   and addiction, 207–222
   early, 177–178
   late, 178
   normal, 180
   pathology in, 179
   reexperience of, 229–230
   therapy, 31
Adolescent(s)
   and parents in group therapy, 177–182
   psychotic, 237–255
Adolescent turmoil, 178–180
Adoption, 54
Agency function, 26–27
Aggression, parental, 181
Aichhorn, A., 57
Als, H., 143
American Society for Psycho-Prophylaxis in Obstetrics (ASPO), 66
Anaclitic depression, 54
Anderson, C., 238, 241
Anthony, E.J., 4–5, 35, 53, 68, 78, 100, 129, 177, 252
Aries, P., 97
Arnold, L.E., 238
Assessment, *see* developmental assessment
Auerswald, E., 187, 188

Autonomy, 5
Axline, V.M., 25

Baby blues, 65
Bales, R., 200
Balikov, H., 180–181
Balint, M., 58n
Balint, A., 58n
Beavin, J., 238
Behavioral disorders, 39
Bellak, L., 20, 198
Bender, M.B., 120
Benedek, T., 51, 52, 59, 78, 100
Berger, M., 39
Bergman, A., 78, 93, 116, 129, 154
Berkovitz, I.H., 5, 66, 116
Bibring, E., 187
Blanck, G., 20, 29–31, 33, 35–36, 38, 40, 41, 43, 96, 109, 142, 154, 204
Blanck, R., 20, 29–31, 33, 35–36, 38, 40, 41, 43, 96, 109, 142, 154, 204
Blos, P., 177
Borderline condition, 9, 34–35
Borgotta, E., 200
Bowen, M., 210
Brazelton, T.B., 143
Buchholz, E.S., 141
Buxbaum, E., 14

Chadwick, O., 180
Chess, S., 115
Child development, 85–87
Child guidance movement, 82

Child, other, 160–161, 163
Children
  competitiveness of, 88
  differing from adults, 92
  egocentricity of, 84–85, 92
  ego impoverished, 145–152
    selection of, 146–148
  fatherless, 95–107
  foster, *see* foster children
  fragile, 117
  "good," 115
  group therapy with, 4–5
  increase in psychopathology of, 52
  intervention with latency age, 115–117
  neurophysiologically handicapped, 120–121
    treatment of, 126–127
  pre-school, 81–93
  primitively fixated, 157–174
  sexual misperceptions of, 90
  therapeutic alliance with, 36
  time sense of, 91
Cobbs, P., 187
Coffey, H., 157
Cohen, A., 197
Cohen, R., 180–181
Confidentiality, 103
Confrontation, 30–31
Corrective emotional experience, 214
Co-therapists, 42–43
Countertransference, 40–41
  with adolescent drug addicts, 222
  with ego impoverished children, 154–155
  in groups, 41–44
  in parent groups, 255
Cumming, E., 245
Cumming, J., 245

Davies, I.J., 209
Day, J., 238

Defenses, 7
  assessment of, 22–23
  building of, 195
  and cognitive changes, 115
  denial, 7
  identification as, 33
  in parent group setting, 60
  sublimation, 7
Dependency, 5
Depression
  anaclitic, 54
  of girls in foster care, 185–205
  postpartum, 70, 79
Development assessment, 13–14, 19, 35–36
Developmental Ego Psychology, 4–6 (*defined*)
  applied to group therapy, 3–15
  ego support, 29–30
  ego teaching, 149–152
  and group process, 32–35
DeWald, P.A., 40
Dinkmeyer, D.C., 25, 34, 67, 70, 140
Discipline and punishment, 87–88
Dominators, 214
Douvan, E., 179
Drive modulation, 21
Duval, E., 117

Edelson, M., 239, 250
Edgcumbe, R., 253
Ego, 6–7 (*defined*)
  observing, 24, 30
  protection of, 149
Ego-alien, 7
Ego blindness, 148
Ego functions, 7
  assessment of, 20–24
  autonomous, 21–22
  synthetic, 24
Ego ideals, 99–100
Ego identity, 223–224
Ego impoverishment, 145–155

INDEX

Ekstein, R., 102–103, 257
Ellison, G., 209
Empathy, 9, 12, 52, 192
Erikson, E., 20, 32–33, 51, 115, 177, 185, 227, 229
Erotic pair, 101
Eubanks, E.E., 3
Exhibitionism, 91
Externalization, 60

Family
　of adolescent drug addicts, 207–222
　function of, 96–97
　and individual psychopathology, 238
　introspection in, 212
　pathological interaction and development in, 211
Family ego mass, 210
Fantasy, merger, 44, 255
Father(s)
　absence of, 97–99
　authoritarian, 212
　groups for, 223–236
Fatherhood, development of, 236
Fearful pair, 101–102
Ferenczi, S., 58
Focused free association, 235
Foster children
　depression of, 186–188
　groups with, 185–205
Foulkes, S.H., 32, 250
Fraiberg, S., 90
Frank, M.G., 142
Freedom, 88
Freud, A., 5–6, 20, 37, 38, 92, 94, 100, 106n, 115, 158, 178–179, 188, 195
Freud, S., 57, 100, 115, 160, 187, 197
　on group psychology, 3, 14, 68, 138
　on outer resistances, 237–238
　on physiological base of psychology, 121
　on transference, 37
Fried, H., 32, 34, 67–70, 72
Fries, M., 57
Frosch, W.A., 211
Furman, E., 57, 177

Ganter, G., 157
Gardner, H., 115
Garland, J., 190
Gediman, H., 20
Gedo, J., 181
Germain, C., 188
Ginott, H., 13–14, 20, 21, 25, 28, 132–134, 139, 157
Gitterman, A., 188
Glasser, N., 210
Glass, S., 19, 25, 66–67, 70, 132
Goldberg, A., 44, 110, 235
Goldstein, J., 188
Goldstein, M.A., 236
Graham, P., 180
Grandiose self, 10, 159 (*defined*)
Greenacre, P., 38
Greenson, R., 36–37, 39
Grier, W., 187
Grotjahn, M., 42, 204
Group(s)
　with adolescent drug addicts and their parents, 207–222
　　community involvement phase of, 218–219
　　differentiation phase of, 218
　　power and control phase of, 217
　　transference in, 214
　composition of, 13–14, 19
　　academic underachievers, 226
　　adolescence, 178–180
　　adolescent drug addicts, 220
　　anxiety, 21, 69
　　borderline patients, 39, 158, 168

Group(s) (*continued*)
  ego impoverished children, 152
  girls in foster care, 203
  learning disabled, 121
  mother guidance, 93
  narcissistic personality, 168
  neurotic features, 111
  new mothers, 77
  optimal, 25
  parent, 63, 253–254
  preoedipal disturbances, 167
  primitively fixated
    children, 172
  psychotic disorders, 39, 158,
    170–171
  single mothers, 108
  in special education setting,
    132–133, 141
  withdrawal symptoms, 10, 13
  with ego impoverished children,
    145–152
    formation of, 148–149
    setting and purpose of,
      152–153
    therapy as progenitor,
      146–148
  evolution of, 32
  for fathers, 223–236
    composition of, 234
    dialogue and acceptance,
      231–232
    formation of, 225–226
    initial phase of, 227–229
    reexperience of adolescence
      in, 229–230
    results and evaluation of,
      232–233
  formation of, 24–26
  with girls in foster care, 185–205
    beginning phase of, 189–191
    endings and transitions of,
      199–200
    formation of, 188–189
    mutual aid in, 197–199
    work phase of, 191–197
  with latency age children,
    115–174
  length of sessions of, 28–29
  milieu of, 27–28
  "Mother-," 161–162
  mother guidance, 81–93
    duration of, 92
  of new mothers, 65–79
    introductory phase of, 67–68
    leader's role in, 66–67
    organization of, 65–66
    power phase of, 68–70
    productive phase of, 70–71
    termination of, 71–72
  "Noah's Ark" principle of, 25
  and objectal development,
    160–162
  open, 25–26
  parental, 57–64
  for parents of hospitalized
    adolescents, 237–255
    background and development
      of, 239–240
    goals of, 240–244
    parent and director meetings,
      248–249
    staff working with, 249–251
  with primitively fixated children,
    157–174
    composition of, 172
    frequency and duration of
      sessions, 169
    patient selection, 167–168
    physical arrangements and
      selection, 168–169
    structure of sessions, 169–170
  setting and purpose of, 26–29
  with single mothers, 95–107
  in special education setting,
    131–143
    composition of, 132–133, 141
    development of, 131–132
    goals of, 135–136

membership of, 133–134
physical setting of, 134–135, 141–142
process and dynamics of, 136–141
transference and countertransference in, 41–44
as transitional object, 161–162
Group dynamics, 35–45
with adolescent drug addicts, 221–222
with ego impoverished children, 154
of fathers' group, 235–236
in foster care group, 204–205
in mother guidance groups, 94
in new mothers' group, 78–79
in parental groups, 63, 254–255
with primitively fixated children, 170, 173–174
in single mother groups, 111
in special education setting, 136–141, 143
Group members, withdrawn, 20
Group process, 32
with adolescent drug addicts, 221
with ego impoverished children, 153–154
Ego Psychology applied to, 32–35
in fathers' groups, 226–227, 235
with foster care group, 204
in mother guidance group, 94
in new mothers' group, 78
in parent group setting, 60, 63, 254
with primitively fixated children, 173
in single mothers' groups, 110–111
in special education setting, 136–143
Group psychoanalysis, 4
Group psychology, 3

Group therapy
Ego and Self Psychology applied to, 3–15, 151–155, 172–174, 203–204, 253–255
indications and contraindications for, 13–14
principles of intervention with parents and children, 4–5
Group transference, 41
Guttman, D., 61

Hamburg, B.A., 177
Handlon, J.H., 209
Hare, P., 200
Hartmann, H., v, 20, 21, 94
Heacock, D.R., 13
Hendricks, L., 212
Hersko, M., 195, 200
Hirsch, S., 238
Hoffer, W., 159
Hospital, psychiatric, 237–255
Hostile pair, 101
Hurn, H.T., 40
Hurvich, M., 20

Idealization, 44
Identification, 33
mutual ego, 197
selective, 33, 204
in special education group, 138–139
Infancy, 85
Interpretation
of countertransference, 41
indirect, 213–214
Intervention
early, 51–54
educative, 52–53, 65–79, 93
insight oriented, 57–64
with latency age children, 115–117
levels of, 29–31
in adolescent drug addict groups, 221

Intervention (*continued*)
   with ego impoverished group, 153
   empathic, 12, 21, 110
   with fathers' group, 234–235
   in foster care group, 203–204
   in mother guidance group, 93–94
   in new mothers' group, 77–78
   in parental groups, 63, 254
   with primitively fixated children, 173
   with single mothers, 102–104, 109–110
   in special education setting, 142
  preventative, 51–54
  rationale, 102–104
  supportive, 81–94
Isaacs, S., 97

Jackson, D., 238
Jacobs, L., 57
Jacobson, E., 11, 33, 36, 154, 178, 187
Jones, H., 190
Josselyn, I.M., 12, 227

Kaplan, H., 4
Katan, A., 30
Kauff, P., 161
Keith, C.R., 36–37, 110, 154
Kennedy, H., 39
Kephart, N.C., 120
Kernberg, O., 9–11, 20, 22, 110
Kestenberg, J.S., 100
Kimbro, E., 210
Kliman, G., 53, 54
Kohut, H., v, 8–11, 15, 38, 43, 53, 159–160, 235
  on adolescence, 181–182
Kolodny, R., 190
Kris, K., 60

La Leche League, 65
Lamaze teachers, 65–66
Lane, B., 36
Lansing, C., 157
Laquer, P., 208
Lasch, C., 95, 97, 104
Latency, 115–174
  and learning disabilities, 119–130
Laufer, M.W., 128, 177
Leader
  as expert, 105–106
  as idealized parent, 105
  as link with past, 106
  in new mothers' group, 66–67
  as new object, 105
  in single mothers' group, 105–107
Learning disabilities, 119–130
Lecker, S., 212
LeFrancis, G.R., 115
Lesse, S., 224–225
Levi, S., 224
Levy, C.S., 11
Lewis, J.C., 210
Libido, 11
Lifton, 157
Limit setting, 149
  and non-abandonment, 181
Linton, R., 244
Lionells, M., 224
Loewald, H.W., 97
Lubin, A.W., 117
Lubin, B., 117

MacLennan, B., 210
Magical thinking, 90–92
Mahler, M., 11, 20, 53, 58n, 78, 93, 116, 129, 143, 154, 158, 159, 171
Mann, C., 224
Marcus, D., 177, 179
Masterson, J., 179, 186
Maternity center, 65

Maturity, 6
McDougall, W., 68
Medical model, 5
Meissner, W.W., 36
Merger fantasies, 44
Messer, E.R., 253
MFGT (multiple family group therapy), 207–222
  dominators and interactors in, 214
  open-ended structure of, 214–215, 218
  setting of, 210–212
  theory of, 208–210
Michaels, C., 106n
Mid-life transitions, 224
Minuchin, S., 246
Mirroring, 8, 44, 143
Mother(s)
  "good," "bad," 159
  guilty feelings of, 85–86
  in mother guidance group, 83
  new, 65–79
    advantage of group setting for, 66
  overprotective, 212
  pairing with child, 101–102
  reciprocity with child, 97–99
  single working, 95–96
  special task during oedipal development, 99–102
Mother-group, 161–162
Mother guidance group, *see* groups, mother guidance
Multiple family group therapy, *see* MFGT
Muro, J.J., 25, 34, 140
Mutual aid, 197–199

Nagera, H., 51–52, 116
Narcissism
  normal, 9, 54
  pathological, 9–11, 22
Narcissistic development, 159–160

Narcissistic personality, 11, 13
  countertransference to, 41
Neubauer, P.B., 96, 97
Nevin, D., 208
Newman, R.G., 68–69
Northern, H., 27
Novick, J., 36

Object(s)
  archaic, 10
  leader as new, 105
  lost love, 187
  "real," 43
Object choice, 99
Object constancy, 37, 159
Object development, 10, 158–159
Object love, 43
Object relations, 20–21
Observing ego, 24, *see also* therapeutic alliance
  confrontation and, 30
Oedipal phase, 89
  and addicts, 211–212
  single mother's task during, 99–102
Offer, D., 177, 179, 180
Oldham, D., 180

Parad, H., 238
Parallel stories, 91–92
Parent(s)
  of adolescent drug addicts, 207–222
  of adolescents in group therapy, 177–182
  early intervention with, 51–54
  group therapy with, 4
  narcissistic injury to, 253
Parental aggression, 181
Parental guilt, 63
Parent education, 57–64
Parenthood, development of, 59, 78
Parenting, "good," 152
Parloff, M.B., 209

Part-object, 8
Pathological narcissism, 9–11
Patient
    impulsive narcissistic, 40–41
    Self Psychologist's description of, 9
    supposedly untreatable, 11–12
Perception, 120
Perlman, H.H., 244
Peterson, J., 186
Piaget, J., 23
Pine, F., 78, 93, 116, 129, 154
Polansky, N., 158
Postpartum depression, 70
Postpartum period, 65
Prevention, 5, 51–54
Privacy, 89–90
Proctor, J.T., 40–42, 154
Propinquity, forced, 28
Protection, 149
Pseudo-alliance, 37, 110
Psychoanalysis, group, 4
Psychoanalytic method, modification of, 57–58
The Psychological Birth of the Human Infant (Mahler, Pine, and Bergman), 93
Psychology
    ego, *see* Ego Psychology
    physiological base of, 121
    self, *see* Self Psychology
Punishment
    discipline and, 87–88
    and protection, 149

Rage, 34
Reality testing, 22
"Real object," 43
Reddy, W.B., 117
Redl, F., 19, 197, 200
Regression, 29
Rehabilitation, 26
Resistance, 35–36
    in parent group setting, 60
    outer, 237–238
    stage of, 69

Ritvo, S., 39
Role playing, 150–151, 228, 234
Role theory, 244
Ross, J.M., 236
Rothstein, A., 11
Ruben, M., 57
Rutter, M., 97, 180
Ryckoff, I., 238

Sabshin, M., 177, 179
Sadock, B., 4
Sado-masochism, 20
Sander, L.W., 24
Sarnoff, C., 116
Savard, R., 224
Scapegoating, 12, 70, 193
Schafer, R., 181
Scheidlinger, S., 29, 32–33, 42, 161, 197, 200
Scherz, F., 177
Schiffer, M., 21, 134, 138, 157
Schizophrenia, 34
Schizophrenia, and family group therapy, 208–209
Schwartz, E., 4
Schwartz, W., 26, 186, 188–190, 200, 242
Searles, H., 238
Self
    archaic, 10
    constancy, 53
    grandiose, 44, 159
    objects, 10, 43
Self Psychology, 8–9 (*defined*)
    applied to group therapy, 3–15
    and parent role, 12
    self-soothing mechanisms, 110
Separation-individuation, 116
Sessions, length of, 28–29
Setting limits, 149
Setting and purpose, 26–29
    of adolescent drug addict groups, 221
    of ego impoverished groups, 152–153
    of fathers' groups, 234

of foster care groups, 203
of mother guidance groups, 93
of new mothers' groups, 77
of parental groups, 63, 254
of primitively fixated children's groups, 172–173
of single mothers' groups, 108–109
of special education group, 141–142
Sex education, 89–91
Sexual differentiation, 99
Shange, N., 187
Shapiro, B., 158
Shelty, T., 128
Silver, L., 128–129
Silverman, L.H., 35
Slavson, S.R., 4, 21, 53, 57, 105, 134, 138, 145, 157
Smally, R., 26
Smolen, E., 157
Solnit, A., 188
Somatopsychic problems, 121
Speers, R., 157
Spitz, R.A., 54, 58n, 94, 158
Splitting, 22–23
  in groups of schizophrenics, 34
Stierlin, H., 41, 154–155, 224
Stolerow, R.D., 31
Stone, W.N., 12, 43–44, 111, 155
Strauss, A.A., 120
Stuart, R., 29
Sturgies, C., 186
Sublimation, 7
Superego
  formation of, 99
  group, 197
Symbiosis, 158, 161
Symptoms
  formations of, 38–39
  see also group composition
Synthetic functions, 24
Systems theory, 5–6

Taschman, H., 210
Taylor, A., 117

Terman, D., 181
Termination phase, 39–40, 139, 199–200
  of new mothers' groups, 71–72
Tests, diagnostic, 20
Therapeutic alliance, 36–37, 143
  pseudo-alliance, 110
Therapist
  roles in multiple family group therapy, 212–219
  as teacher of ego capacities, 149–152
Therapeutic stance, 63, 77, 93, 109, 142, 154
Therapist team, 42–43, 161
Thomas, A., 115
Thought processes, 23–24
Toilet training, 86–87
Tolpin, M., 24, 38–39, 111, 204
Transference, 37–40 (*defined*)
  in adolescent drug addict groups, 214
  in groups, 41–44
  with "less than neurotic," 43
  mirror, 44
  in new mothers' group, 69, 79
  in parent education, 59–60
  self-object, 8
Transitional object, group as, 161–162
Transmuting internalizations, 160
Turanski, J., 212

"Understanding fallacy," 84

Vailliant, G.E., 115
Van der Waals, J.G., 9, 11
Verbalization, 30

Watzlawick, P., 238
Weiner, L., 157
Whitman, R.M., 12, 43, 44, 111, 155
Williams, F., 238
Winnicott, D.W., 58n, 103, 162
Winokur, M., 253
Withdrawal, 10, 13

Wolf, A., 4
Wolf, E., 181
Wylie, H., 210
Wynne, L., 238

Yeakel, M., 157
Young, R., 209
Yule, W., 180

Zalba, S.R., 26
Zetzel, E., 36, 39, 154